Middle East Today

Series Editors
Fawaz A. Gerges
Department of International Relations
London School of Economics
London, UK

Nader Hashemi
Center for Middle East Studies
University of Denver
Highlands Ranch, CO, USA

The Iranian Revolution of 1979, the Iran-Iraq War, the Gulf War, and the US invasion and occupation of Iraq have dramatically altered the geopolitical landscape of the contemporary Middle East. The Arab Spring uprisings have complicated this picture. This series puts forward a critical body of first-rate scholarship that reflects the current political and social realities of the region, focusing on original research about contentious politics and social movements; political institutions; the role played by non-governmental organizations such as Hamas, Hezbollah, and the Muslim Brotherhood; and the Israeli-Palestine conflict. Other themes of interest include Iran and Turkey as emerging pre-eminent powers in the region, the former an 'Islamic Republic' and the latter an emerging democracy currently governed by a party with Islamic roots; the Gulf monarchies, their petrol economies and regional ambitions; potential problems of nuclear proliferation in the region; and the challenges confronting the United States, Europe, and the United Nations in the greater Middle East. The focus of the series is on general topics such as social turmoil, war and revolution, international relations, occupation, radicalism, democracy, human rights, and Islam as a political force in the context of the modern Middle East.

More information about this series at
http://www.palgrave.com/gp/series/14803

Alaa Tartir · Timothy Seidel
Editors

Palestine and Rule of Power

Local Dissent vs. International Governance

Editors
Alaa Tartir
The Graduate Institute of
International and Development
Studies (IHEID)
Geneva, Switzerland

Timothy Seidel
Department of Applied Social
Sciences and Center for Justice and
Peacebuilding
Eastern Mennonite University
Harrisonburg, VA, USA

Middle East Today
ISBN 978-3-030-05948-4   ISBN 978-3-030-05949-1 (eBook)
https://doi.org/10.1007/978-3-030-05949-1

Library of Congress Control Number: 2018964577

© The Editor(s) (if applicable) and The Author(s) 2019
This work is subject to copyright. All rights are solely and exclusively licensed by the Publisher, whether the whole or part of the material is concerned, specifically the rights of translation, reprinting, reuse of illustrations, recitation, broadcasting, reproduction on microfilms or in any other physical way, and transmission or information storage and retrieval, electronic adaptation, computer software, or by similar or dissimilar methodology now known or hereafter developed.
The use of general descriptive names, registered names, trademarks, service marks, etc. in this publication does not imply, even in the absence of a specific statement, that such names are exempt from the relevant protective laws and regulations and therefore free for general use.
The publisher, the authors, and the editors are safe to assume that the advice and information in this book are believed to be true and accurate at the date of publication. Neither the publisher nor the authors or the editors give a warranty, express or implied, with respect to the material contained herein or for any errors or omissions that may have been made. The publisher remains neutral with regard to jurisdictional claims in published maps and institutional affiliations.

Cover illustration: Victor Shupletsov/EyeEm

This Palgrave Macmillan imprint is published by the registered company Springer Nature Switzerland AG
The registered company address is: Gewerbestrasse 11, 6330 Cham, Switzerland

Foreword

From any informed realist perspective, Palestinian prospects for achieving a just peace seemed, after more than a century of struggle, to have reached a dead end as a result of a series of setbacks. Not only has Israel managed over the course of recent decades to establish an internal situation in which Zionist goals of gaining effective control over the whole of "the promised land" of biblical Israel seem within reach, but it has also managed to coopt and corrupt formal Palestinian leadership in ways that weaken resistance, dim hopes, and seek to shift the focus from politics to economics. The diplomatic project launched in Oslo in the early 1990s with great fanfare as the gateway to peace for Palestinians and Israelis turned into a major vehicle for Israeli expansionism, primarily via the settlement process, the separation wall, and ethnic engineering in Jerusalem—each of these Israeli steps taken at the expense of legitimate Palestinian expectations that its fundamental rights would finally be realized as a result of this diplomatic breakthrough.

While this process unfolded Israel demonstrated to itself and the world that it could defy international law without suffering any adverse consequences. In this regard, the geopolitical leverage exerted by the United States actively, and Europe mostly passively, crucially enabled Israel to do whatever it wanted with respect to the Palestinian people, while the world looked on, expressing sympathy for the Palestinian plight from time to time, especially when Israel resorted to excessive force in forms too visible to ignore, most often cruelly directed at an oppressed civilian population. Such token acknowledgements of Israel's flagrant violations of international law did nothing more than underscore the lack of minimum political will in international society needed to insulate Palestinians from acute suffering, much less the necessary motivation, capabilities, and resolve to implement and impose legal constraints. After the establishment of Israel in 1948, it became clearer to close observers that Israel was, in effect, continuing to dispossess Palestinians, physically (through conditions that make residence intolerable or no longer tolerated) and normatively (through deprivations of rights). In effect, Palestinians were being gradually made into strangers in their own land, alienated from their native society, and variously victimized by a perverse political order that had innovated a distinctive form of apartheid being applied to the Palestinian people as a whole (that is, whether their residence was the West Bank, Jerusalem, Gaza, refugee camps in neighboring countries, or involuntary exile).

And if this were not enough of a burden to dim Palestinian spirits further discouraging developments have clouded the Palestinian skies over the course of the last decade. The regional turmoil in the Middle East has turned the governing elites (but significantly, not the peoples) in the Arab world away from their earlier ardent posture of solidarity with the Palestinian struggle. Saudi Arabia has actually aligned with Israel, and the United States, in confronting Iran, and recently, with a supreme expression of arrogance and moral obtuseness, told the Palestinians to accept whatever Washington tidbits the Trump presidency was prepared to offer.

The government of post-Nasser Egypt, while never really supportive of the Palestinian struggle, in recent years after the counterrevolutionary Sisi coup of 2013, has gone further even than complicit Sadat, joining with Israel in trying to destroy Hamas, which the new military rulers regard as a menacing offshoot of the Muslim Brotherhood, the archfoe of both Cairo and Riyadh. In effect, regional developments in the Middle East have hurt the Palestinians in two major ways: creating an agenda for the leading Arab countries that puts the ongoing Palestinian struggle on a back burner of indifference amounting to abandonment; engaging in partnership with Israel in several sites of struggle that have also led the world to worry about Iraq, Syria, ISIS, Yemen, Libya, Iran, refugees, and all but forget Palestine in the process, a damaging development accentuated by the fact that the mainstream media in the West is, as usual, tagging along.

If this were not already more than enough, it is impossible to ignore the adverse impact of the rise of Trump and Trumpism. Trump's America has lifted its longstanding one-sided pro-Israeli policies to almost unimaginable heights, placing diplomatic responsibility in the hands of ultra-Zionists such as Jared Kushner and David Friedman, unapologetic supporters of maximalist forms of the settler movement together with the inflammatory treatment of all forms of Palestinian resistance, even if nonviolent, as terrorism. Such officials have already shown themselves ready to cast off even the earlier nominal pretense of impartiality maintained by prior Washington administrations, and manage to find ways to blame the Palestinians for every major act of Israeli wrongdoing. Moving the American embassy to Jerusalem, in defiance of overwhelming opposition at the UN, and ignoring the massacres associated with the killing and wounding of thousands at the Gaza fence in the Great March of Return, are provocative indicators of this green light shining so brightly these days in the predatory eyes of the Netanyahu leadership. Israel has been given unprecedented discretion to do what it wishes, regardless of its legal and moral status, and without concern about damaging human consequences.

In this atmosphere it hardly surprising that one of the leading Zionist ideologues in the United States, Daniel Pipes, has launched what he calls a "Victory Caucus" designed to bring the conflict to an end, not by diplomacy or negotiation, but by inducing the Palestinians to accept defeat, and acknowledge and abide by an Israeli victory in their basic struggle to establish a Jewish state in a non-Jewish society. Pipes has been energetic in promoting this "Prussian Solution," enlisting bipartisan support in the American Congress and enthusiasm in the Israeli Knesset. Nothing more unmistakably brands a political project as "settler colonialism" (an instance of "the rule of power" than does such an initiative). Such an ahistorical outrage has now been given the imprimatur of a new basic law of Israel recently adopted by the Knesset declaring "Basic Law—Israel as The Nation State of the Jewish People," psychopolitically disenfranchising Palestinians and other non-Jews no matter how strong their indigenous credentials. In one sense the adoption of such a law both expresses the true nature of Zionist aspirations and the degree to which Israelis feel that the geopolitical wind at their back allows them to be open about their repudiation of peace diplomacy and any responsibility for respecting the rights of the Palestinian people.

And yet! This book consisting of a group of exceptionally fine analytical contributions gives convincing and fascinating content to the assertion "and yet." My intention by highlighting these two words is to convey the startling realization that despite all these frustrations and obstacles, the Palestinian struggle continues, with creativity, extraordinary resilience, and despite the daunting array of challenges should be perceived as gaining momentum rather than being written off as a lost cause.

A familiar folk saying imparts a bit of political wisdom relevant here: "it is not where you look, but what you see, that matters." For too long we have looked at what governments do or at the body counts associated with armed struggle, and fail to notice that most of the dramatic advances of history, are overwhelmingly associated with what people do and don't do. The mainstream media and the propaganda of governments help make this realization almost inaccessible in current arenas of public awareness. We are taught over and over again that history is made by international diplomacy or armed struggle, which helps makes us overlook the transformational potential of a mobilized, resourceful, and resilient people. It is these qualities that the Palestinians as a people have brought to their national struggle over the course of the last century, making their share of mistakes along the way, but never losing sight of their fundamental entitlements to self-determination and other human rights, in a sense, "the power of rights" as over time, and through struggle, prevailing over "the rule of power."

Without any resort to preaching, *Palestine and the Rule of Power* is an extraordinary confirmation of the vitality and resilience of the Palestinian people. It brings to readers an admirably documented understanding of the inner dynamics of the ongoing Palestinian national movement as waged by people in the spaces of maneuver that remain to a people subject to the kind of apartheid matrix of control that Israel continually reinforces. What this talented group of authors see and depict, making sophisticated use of social science empirical methodologies, is an archipelago of resistance tactics and strategies brilliantly adapted to the changing specifics of the oppressive structures of occupation. Such tactics not only maintain the morale of a struggle by an oppressed and fragmented people (seen inclusively as including refugees, the non-Jewish minority in Israel, and the millions of involuntary exiles), but search for *transformational* tactics that alone can establish a non-sentimental foundation for affirming an eventually hopeful future for the Palestinian people.

This stimulating volume also contains several illuminating chapters of critique that explain why the possibly well-meaning liberal approaches to an improved Palestinian experience are at best naïve, being based on an economistic train of thought: IMF logic, neoliberal ideology dovetailing disastrously with influential international donor NGOs, having as a principal effect the partial cooptation of the Palestinian Authority, with the startling result of making the supposed leadership of the Palestinian struggle play the role of dependent accomplice of Israel in the maintenance of Israeli security, which above all is understood to mean upholding the *political* status quo as defined by Tel Aviv. In ways difficult for outsiders even to comprehend the PA has become a principal adversary with respect to Palestinian resistance, imprisoning and even torturing activists.

It is this kind of neoliberal approach to "peace" that has set the stage for years to propose "the deal of the century," the essence of which is the substitution of an economistic agenda of promises that when applied to the structural realities of Palestine end up hardening security and softening resistance without changing the abusive and corrupting victimization of the Palestinian people, likely worsening its burdens by disguising the nature of the integral patterns of victimization.

What then, do the authors of this excellently edited volume, see when they do the looking? They see first of all the failed paths of a UN decreed partition, also of a prolonged diplomatic charade within the Oslo framework, and of Palestinian empowerment by way of suicide bombing and armed struggle waged outside the frame of international legality, and of all approaches that purport to substitute "economic peace" for elemental political and civil rights under international law, and of support from Arab neighbors, and of Zionist good faith with respect to finding a political compromise sensitive to the self-determination claims of both peoples. Against this background of critique is the awareness that resistance is nevertheless possible, and offers benefits associated with respect to political will and a message to the world that Palestinian claims remain the great unresolved moral scandal of our time, a settler colonial state established in the face of an anti-colonial historical tidal wave, which for this very reason, requires ever more oppressive and unrestrained severity to contain the situation. But this severity is what also gives strength to the Palestinian will to resist and adds weight to the global solidarity movement.

In these respects it is helpful to recall the anti-apartheid struggle in South Africa that also when looked at through a conventional realist lens seemed hopeless until all of a sudden the regime cracked wide open and an utterly unexpected dismantling of apartheid occurred, enabling a peaceful transition to constitutional democracy to take place. Of course, history does not repeat itself, and there are crucial differences between the situation of Africans in South Africa and of the Palestinians, nevertheless, the comparison seems instructive for several central reasons. South Africa, as with Palestine, flaunted global norms, gave rise over time to a committed and militant solidarity movement, and eventually created a political climate in which even strategic partners of the government in Pretoria were forced by a surge of grassroots pressure into supporting sanctions imposed on apartheid South Africa. Losing the legitimacy war for the heights of legal and moral authority has in recent history almost invariably meant neutralizing the advantages of military domination, and hence has led the stronger side militarily to a loss of control over the outcome of a political struggle. This happened over and over again in the context of the anti-colonial wars of the last half of the twentieth century, and as these authors collectively demonstrate it could happen here to bring an end to the long ordeal of the Palestinian people.

One aspect of the geopolitical outreach of Israel is to enlist the Trump presidency in a completely misleading attack on the United Nations as an anti-Israeli, even anti-Semitic institution, that obsesses about Israel's wrongdoing while turning a blind eye to far worse happenings elsewhere. What such a criticism ignores is that the UN had accepted responsibility after World War II for ensuring a peaceful and just future for Palestine after the United Kingdom gave up its role as the administrator of the territory as the Mandatory Authority acting on behalf of the League of Nations. It is the Palestinians who are entitled to be disillusioned by the failure of the UN to discharge successfully this responsibility that they accepted, and mishandled from the outset. Not only did the UN embrace a partition solution in 1947 without consulting the wishes of the majority population of Palestine, their many resolutions affirming Palestinian rights under international law with respect to refugees, settlements, Jerusalem, use of force, and collective punishment were utterly ignored by Israel, which led to more resolutions but nothing tangible or effective. The UN has failed the people of Palestine with tragic consequences, and its rhetorical effort to compensate for this failure by periodic disapproval of Israeli policies and practices can be best understood as rather pathetic efforts to live up to their of institutional responsibility with respect to the Palestinian people.

Although this volume doesn't deal directly with this failure of the UN and the international community, its focus on the achievements of and potentialities of ongoing resistance, as well as its critique of the effects of relying on a neoliberal reconstruction of a people living under oppression provide readers with a clear understanding of what is happening in Palestine and what needs to be done if peace with justice is ever to be the destiny of Palestinians and Jews alike. What is more, it conveys this understanding by relying on the highest quality of scholarship, including making innovative use of the best methodologies that contemporary social science offers.

Yalikavak, Turkey Professor Richard Falk
July 2018

Richard Falk is Albert G. Milbank Professor Emeritus of international law at Princeton University, and a research fellow in global studies at the University of California at Santa Barbara. He is the author of over thirty books, most recently *Palestine's Horizon: Toward a Just Peace*, and a specialist on the role of international law in global politics. The United Nations Human Rights Council appointed Falk as the United Nations special rapporteur on the situation of human rights in Palestine from 2008 to 2014.

Acknowledgements

First and foremost, we would like to thank the contributing authors to this edited volume, not only for their inspiring commitment and their intellectually stimulating chapters but also for making this book project a joyful and delightful experience. This edited volume is not merely a collection of chapters, but has been a joint project and a collaborative scholarly effort over the past few years. It is the collective intellectual scholarship and ownership of this book that led us throughout the different phases of producing this book and guided us in our reviews, debates, and discussions.

Special and sincere thanks go to Professor Richard Falk who continues to inspire us with his generosity, kindness, and sharp and comprehensive knowledge and wisdom. We are honored and grateful for all his support and endless encouragement, and for being a role model and compass to be led by.

We also would like to thank our publisher, Palgrave Macmillan, and in particular the editorial team, Alina Yurova and John Stegner, for all their support, patience, and guidance throughout the process of producing this book. We also would like to thank our colleagues at the *Journal of Palestine Studies* and *Journal of Middle East Critique* for their support to our book project. Many of the chapters in this book were presented at the 2018 annual meeting of the International Studies Association, April 4 to 7 in San Francisco, CA, on two panels sponsored by the Global Development Studies and Peace Studies Sections. We are grateful to all those who participated in the robust conversations at those panel sessions. We also would like to extend our warm thanks and appreciation to all scholars who accompanied us in the journey of producing this book. Without their critical engagement, constructive feedback, and rigorous reviews and thoughtful feedback, we would not be where we are now.

Last but not least, we thank our families for all their support and patience, and for all the sacrifices they made for us in order to finish this book project. We owe you many free-of-work weekends and holidays, and we are in debt for all your kindness, generosity, patience, support, and love.

We have heard it said that if you want to go fast, go alone, but if you want to go far, go together. We have chosen the latter route, and we hope that we, together through an engaged scholarship, are contributing to the process of going far through advancing the scholarly knowledge on Palestine and beyond.

Finally, we dedicate this book to the future generations of Palestine, not only to learn from past mistakes, but also to imagine new ways of being and draw new paths that bring them closer to freedom.

PRAISE FOR *PALESTINE AND RULE OF POWER*

"*Palestine and Rule of Power*, with its exceptionally fine analytical contributions relying on the highest quality of scholarship, is an extraordinary confirmation of the vitality and resilience of the Palestinian people. It brings to readers an admirably documented understanding of the inner dynamics of the ongoing Palestinian national movement."
—Richard Falk, Professor Emeritus of International Law, *Princeton University*

"Bringing together an impressive list of scholarly and intellectual talents, *Palestine and* Rule of Power makes an important and distinctive contribution to that growing body of literature examining features of local dissent and resistance and international governance in occupied Palestine. The edited volume offers a rich menu of food for thought."
—Fawaz A. Gerges, *Professor of International Relations, London School of Economics and Political Science (LSE)*

"This rich, timely, and rigorous volume enriches and expands our understanding of the Palestinian question. Thoughtful, historically-contextualized and yet forward looking, the work deftly draws on penetrating conceptual insights to offer remarkably fresh policy perspectives."
—Mohammad-Mahmoud Ould Mohamedou, *Professor of International History, The Graduate Institute of International and Development Studies (IHEID), Geneva*

"*Palestine and Rule of Power* makes a significant contribution by assembling a collection of cutting-edge essays that illuminate the present range of scholarship while providing a welcome breath of fresh air. Through rigorous and bold new theorizing, contributors to this book not only describe the changing frameworks for international ethics and action on this grueling conflict but refine and expand on relevant theory to cast new light on its essential political character and potential futures. This volume has a place in any core library on theory of this conflict."
—Virginia Tilley, *Professor of Political Science, Southern Illinois University Carbondale*

"In *The Wretched of the Earth*, Franz Fanon stated: 'The business of obscuring language is a mask behind which stands the much greater business of plunder.' *Palestine and Rule of Power* rips off the mask of the obscure language that surrounds Palestine and the Palestinian people by analysing the intersection of Israeli settler colonialism and neoliberal forms of rule as a system of oppression. At a time when justice and rights are being cast aside in favour of a victor's peace, incisive analyses of the cruel and unjust context that Palestinians face in their struggle for survival and self-determination are necessary and urgent. This book is an important contribution to our knowledge about this context, as well as Palestinians' determination to resist and insist on their right to a life free of oppression."
—Mandy Turner, *Director of the Kenyon Institute (Council for British Research in the Levant)*

"So much analysis of the Israeli–Palestinian conflict limits itself to descriptions of Israeli strength and Palestinian weakness, leaving the reader to conclude that the only probable outcome is further Palestinian losses and Israeli gains. *Palestine and Rule of Power* offers something entirely new: a deep and unconventional analysis by cutting edge scholars of the means by which Palestinians can accumulate achievements despite the gross imbalance of power and the complicity of Europe, the US, and the donor community in upholding a status quo that denies them freedom. Every student of Palestinian politics should read it."
—Nathan Thrall, *author* The Only Language They Understand: Forcing Compromise in Israel and Palestine

"In *Palestine and Rule of Power*, editors Alaa Tartir and Timothy Seidel wrestle with a daunting task: Understanding how each of the pernicious forces of settler colonialism and neoliberalism apply power, and how these forces are intertwined to control and rule Palestine today. But they do not stop there. They have invited seven other scholars noted for their thoughtful analysis and insights to join them in examining not just the force of power, but also the power of resistance. Together with an introduction by the formidable Richard Falk, these essays draw on the literature and on lived experience to dissect the past and present of Palestine, offering a solid foundation to build for the future."
—Nadia Hijab, *President, Board of Directors, Al-Shabaka: The Palestinian Policy Network*

"With all the depressing news coming from Palestine there is a danger that Palestinians and their supporters would fall into despair and defeatism. This brilliant volume shows that the struggle against settler colonialism in Palestine is far from over and that the resistance continues on a daily basis. If readers are seeking an honest depiction of how the oppressive power operates on the ground in Palestine and more importantly how it is resisted, you cannot ask for a better guide than this valuable and informative volume. Recording the resistance to evil power is by itself an act of resistance."
—Ilan Pappe, *Director of the European Center of Palestine Studies, University of Exeter*

Contents

1   The Rule of Power in Palestine: Settler Colonialism, Neoliberal Governance, and Resistance   1
Timothy Seidel and Alaa Tartir

Part I   Resistance and Mobilization Against Apartheid, Settler Colonialism, and Repression

2   The Settler Colonial Present: Palestinian State-Building Under Apartheid   23
Ben White

3   Sovereign Bodies, Sovereign States: Settler Colonial Violence and the Visibility of Resistance in Palestine   47
Timothy Seidel

4   Active and Transformative *Sumud* Among Palestinian Activists in Israel   71
Nijmeh Ali

5   Who Protests in Palestine? Mobilization Across Class Under the Palestinian Authority   105
Dana El Kurd

Part II External Intervention and International Aid

6 More Important Than Other Conflicts: The Uniqueness of the Israeli–Palestinian Conflict in EC/EU Discourse   131
Anders Persson

7 Neoliberalism as Aid for the Settler Colonization of the Occupied Palestinian Territories After Oslo   153
Jeremy Wildeman

8 Solidarity Donors and Popular Education in the West Bank   175
Melanie Meinzer

Part III Security Sector Reform, Resistance, and Authoritarianism

9 Criminalizing Resistance: Security Sector Reform and Palestinian Authoritarianism   205
Alaa Tartir

10 Securitizing Peace: The EU's Aiding and Abetting Authoritarianism   227
Alaa Tartir

Index   249

NOTES ON CONTRIBUTORS

Nijmeh Ali is a political and academic activist with an educational background in Political Sciences and Sociology. This includes B.A. from Haifa University and M.A. from the Hebrew University in Jerusalem. Between 2014 and 2018, Nijmeh was a researcher in the National Centre for Peace and Conflict Studies at the University of Otago in New Zealand where she earned her Ph.D. Her research focuses on the power of resistance theory in exposing the "power of powerless" and the capacities of oppressed groups in creating genuine social change, particularly among the Palestinians in Israel.

Dana El Kurd received her Ph.D. in Government from The University of Texas at Austin in June 2017. She specializes in Comparative Politics and International Relations. Dana works as a researcher at the Arab Center for Research and Policy Studies at the Doha Institute. Theoretically, Dana is interested in the conflicts between states and their societies and the contentious politics they produce. She examines how authoritarian regimes try to implement their policies, and how external intervention may affect their success. Dana is currently working on a book manuscript entitled *Legacies of International Involvement: Authoritarianism and Polarization in the Palestinian Territories*.

Melanie Meinzer is a postdoctoral researcher at Denison University. She conducts research in the West Bank and Jordan on how social movements use foreign aid and education to subvert state-sanctioned forms of knowledge, identity, and political activism.

Anders Persson is a postdoctoral researcher at the Centre for European Politics at University of Copenhagen/Lund University—where he is conducting a research project funded by the Swedish Research Council on the EU's normative power in the Israeli–Palestinian conflict. He has written three books about the Israeli–Palestinian conflict of which the latest is *The EU and the Israeli-Palestinian conflict 1971–2013: In Pursuit of a Just Peace* (Lanham, Lexington Books: 2015). He has also published peer-reviewed articles in journals such as *Journal of Common Market Studies*, *Mediterranean Politics*, *Journal of European Integration*, *Journal of Conflict Transformation and Security* and *New Middle Eastern Studies*. He is an expert commentator on Swedish TV/radio/press on Israel–Palestine and also writes a blog for *Huffington Post* and contributes regularly to *Haaretz*, *Politico EU* and *EU Observer*.

Timothy Seidel is an Assistant Professor in the Department of Applied Social Sciences and the Center for Justice and Peacebuilding at Eastern Mennonite University in Harrisonburg, VA, where he also serves as director for the Center for Interfaith Engagement. He holds a Ph.D. from the School of International Service at American University in Washington, DC.

Alaa Tartir is a research associate at the Centre on Conflict, Development and Peacebuilding (CCDP), and a visiting fellow at the Department of Anthropology and Sociology, at the Graduate Institute of International and Development Studies (IHEID) in Geneva, Switzerland. He is also a policy and program advisor at Al-Shabaka: The Palestinian Policy Network, and a Visiting Professor at Paris School of International Affairs (PSIA), Sciences Po. Among other positions, Tartir was a postdoctoral fellow at The Geneva Centre for Security Policy (GCSP), a visiting scholar and lecturer at Utrecht University, and a researcher in international development studies at the London School of Economics and Political Science (LSE), where he earned his Ph.D. Tartir can be followed on Twitter @alaatartir and his publications can be accessed at www.alaatartir.com.

Ben White is a journalist, analyst, and author. He has had hundreds of articles published by a variety of media outlets, including *The Guardian*, *The Independent*, *Al Jazeera*, and *Newsweek Middle East*. He has appeared as a guest expert on television and radio and spoken at dozens of events and conferences on university campuses in Europe and North

America. Ben is the author of four books, the latest of which—*Cracks in the Wall: Beyond Apartheid in Palestine/Israel*—was published in May 2018 by Pluto Press. Ben is a contributor for Al-Shabaka: the Palestinian Policy Network.

Jeremy Wildeman is a research associate at the University of Bath Department for Social and Policy Sciences, where he carries out analysis in international relations, foreign aid and the role of donors and aid in the occupied Palestinian territories. Prior he worked for many years as an aid provider in the region.

Abbreviations

AHLC	Ad Hoc Liaison Committee
BDS	Boycott, Divestment, and Sanctions Movement
CSDP	Common Security and Defence Policy
DCAF	Geneva Centre for the Democratic Control of Armed Forces
DFID	Department for International Development, UK
DoP	Declaration of Principles, Israel-PLO
EU	European Union
EUPOL COPPS	European Union Coordinating Office for Palestinian Police Support
HRW	Human Rights Watch
ICC	International Criminal Court
ICG	International Crisis Group
ICJ	International Court of Justice
IDF	Israeli Defense Forces
IFI	International Financial Institution
IHL	International Humanitarian Law
IMF	International Monetary Fund
INGO	International Nongovernmental Organization
IR	International Relations
MBO	Membership-Based Organization
NGO	Nongovernmental Organization
NSF	National Security Forces
OECD	Organization for Economic Cooperation and Development
oPt	occupied Palestinian territory
PA	Palestinian Authority
PASF	Palestinian Authority Security Forces

PCBS	Palestinian Central Bureau of Statistics
PCP	Palestinian Civil Police
PFU	Palestinian Farmers Union
PLO	Palestinian Liberation Organization
SSR	Security Sector Reform
UN	United Nations
UN OCHA	United Nations Office for the Coordination of Humanitarian Affairs
UNCTAD	United Nations Conference on Trade and Development
UNRWA	United Nations Relief and Works Agency for Palestine Refugees in the Near East
USAID	U.S. Agency for International Development
USD	United States Dollar
USSC	United States Security Coordinator
VAT	Value-Added Tax

List of Figures

Fig. 1.1	Map of the occupied West Bank (*Source* PLO-NAD)	7
Fig. 2.1	Areas A, B, and C in the occupied West Bank (*Source* United Nations OCHA oPt)	28
Fig. 5.1	Number of protests by area	113
Fig. 5.2	Mobilizations in camp vs. non-camp areas	114
Fig. 5.3	Average number of Israeli incursions compared with average number of protests by area	115
Fig. 5.4	Map of East Jerusalem (*Source* PLO-NAD)	121

List of Tables

Table 5.1	Oneway ANOVA test results	113
Table 5.2	*T*-test of mobilization in camp vs. non-camp areas	114
Table 6.1	*Bulletin of the European Communities* and *Bulletin of the European Union* coding schedule	147

CHAPTER 1

The Rule of Power in Palestine: Settler Colonialism, Neoliberal Governance, and Resistance

Timothy Seidel and Alaa Tartir

Introduction

A professor of ours once told the story of an instructor who, on the first day of a course on international politics, began by quoting Thucydides, from his *History of the Peloponnesian War*, that the strong do what they will and the weak suffer what they must. The instructor declared that this is international politics, then walked out of the room to signal there was no further conversation to be had on the topic. We begin with this anecdote because, in a way, this volume reinforces that notion, of the rule of power in late modernity. However, as the chapters in this volume will

T. Seidel (✉)
Department of Applied Social Sciences and Center for Justice and Peacebuilding, Eastern Mennonite University, Harrisonburg, VA, USA
e-mail: timothy.seidel@emu.edu

A. Tartir
The Graduate Institute of International and Development Studies (IHEID), Geneva, Switzerland
e-mail: alaa.tartir@graduateinstitute.ch

describe, power expresses itself in many different ways: settler colonialism, neoliberal governance, liberal peacebuilding, institution-building, foreign aid and its inflections of power in terms of security and political economy. But in another way, this book challenges this sort of Thucydidean power politics inasmuch as it recognizes that the "weak" do not simply "suffer what they must" but act—as social and political agents—in terms that we refer to as the resistance that co-constitute power. This volume explores some of those ways in particular in Palestine today.

Some observe that the rule of power in late modernity relates critically to the power and politics of life and death. Achille Mbembe (2003) calls this "necropolitics"—the subjugation of life to the power of death. This has unique effects on the colonized indigenous because in the era of necropower, as Mbembe describes, weapons are deployed "in the interest of maximum destruction of persons and the creating of death-worlds, new and unique forms of social existence in which vast populations are subjected to conditions of life conferring upon them the status of living dead" (40). Mbembe identifies this as a key element of late-modern colonial occupation, and argues that the "most accomplished form of necropower is the contemporary colonial occupation of Palestine" (27). And he describes three major characteristics in relation to the working of the specific terror formation he calls necropower: territorial fragmentation, vertical sovereignty, and splintering occupation.[1] This rule of power and the local dissent discussed below takes Mbembe's description as a critical point of departure.

Expressions of Power in Palestine: International Governance

The logic and effects of international governance is one critical way to observe and understand the rule of power in Palestine. This volume considers expressions of the rule of power in two particular ways: settler colonialism and neoliberalism. First is settler colonialism. Power is expressed through the ongoing settler colonial present in Palestine (Salamanca et al. 2012). In this volume, we understand settler colonialism as a global, transnational phenomenon that is as much a thing of the present as a thing of the past (Veracini 2015), distinct from other forms of colonialism in several ways. One critical feature is that, unlike colonial agents such as traders, soldiers, or governors, settler colonizers "come to stay" (Wolfe 1999) with the intention to permanently occupy. Settlers are founders of political orders who carry with them a distinct sovereign capacity, asserting sovereignty over indigenous lands (Veracini 2010). In this way, settler colonialism is not just an event but a structure "that persists in the ongoing elimination of indigenous populations and extension of state sovereignty and juridical control over their lands" (Barker and Lowman, n.d.).

Wolfe (2006) underscores another key feature of settler colonialism, that it is inherently eliminatory (387). And while settler colonialism has typically employed the organizing grammar of race, Wolfe argues that, regardless of what settlers may say, the primary motive for elimination is access to territory. "Territoriality is settler colonialism's specific, irreducible element" (388). This logic of elimination animates both the negative goal of the dissolution of native societies and the positive goal of constructing a new colonial society on expropriated land. As Wolfe puts it:

> settler colonizers come to stay: invasion is a structure not an event. In its positive aspect, elimination is an organizing principal of settler-colonial society rather than a one-off (and superseded) occurrence. The positive outcomes of the logic of elimination can include officially encouraged miscegenation, the breaking-down of native title into alienable individual freeholds, native citizenship, child abduction, religious conversion, resocialization in total institutions such as missions or boarding schools, and a whole range of cognate biocultural assimilations. All these strategies, including frontier homicide, are characteristic of settler colonialism. (388)

As Veracini (2010) observes, this marks a critical distinction between settler colonialism and other forms of colonialism, in that settlers want indigenous people to vanish (while making use of their labor before they are made to disappear). The "peaceful settler hides behind the ethnic cleanser" who enters a "new, empty land to start a new life." Indigenous people "naturally and inevitably 'vanish'; it is not settlers that displace them." In this way, "settler colonialism obscures the conditions of its own production" (14).

The "natural" and "inevitable" vanishing of the indigenous population points to what Wolfe (1999) emphasizes, not the indispensability but the dispensability of the indigenous person in a settler colonial context:

> The primary object of settler-colonization is the land itself rather than the surplus value to be derived from mixing native labour with it. Though, in practice, Indigenous labour was indispensable to Europeans, settler-colonization is at base a winner-take-all project whose dominant feature is not exploitation but replacement. The logic of this project, a sustained

institutional tendency to eliminate the Indigenous population, informs a range of historical practices that might otherwise appear distinct – invasion is a structure not an event. (163)

The role of land is central in settler colonial struggles. In Palestine, the legacy of settler colonialism is that it has destroyed in order to replace and has renamed in order to erase.[2] And yet not simply to replace but a process of replacement that "maintains the refractory imprint of the native counter-claim" (Wolfe 2006, 389). Settler colonialism endeavors to recast indigeneity onto the settler, requiring the elimination and erasure of the native population. This is another key feature: settler colonialism seeks its own end in that it trends toward the ending of colonial difference in the form of a supreme and unchallenged settler state and people. However, as Barker and Lowman (n.d.) point out, "this is not a drive to decolonize but to eliminate the challenges posed to settler sovereignty by indigenous peoples' claims to land by eliminating indigenous peoples themselves and asserting false narratives and structures of settler belonging."

The second expression of power this volume considers is the neoliberal political and economic order defining appropriate behavior in late modernity, seen most clearly in Palestine in the state-building project.[3] Over the last twenty-five years, since the Oslo Accords and the establishment of the Palestinian Authority (PA), the rule of power has been displayed through institution-building agendas and commitments, expressing itself in terms of humanitarianism, foreign aid, and dependency, as well as political economic and security sector terms. A critical feature of this volume is how the chapters consider the ways settler colonialism and neoliberalism interact with each other to express a very specific kind of power that rules in Palestine today.

There has been a robust conversation in recent years identifying the role of neoliberalism and the liberal peace thesis in contemporary state-building, peacebuilding, and development. In his essay "International Peacebuilding and the 'Mission Civilisatrice,'" Paris (2002) notes the liberal bias in peacebuilding with its resemblance to old imperial modes of global governance: "One way of thinking about the actions of peacebuilders is to conceive of liberal market democracy as an internationally-sanctioned model of 'legitimate' domestic governance…as the prevailing 'standard of civilization' that states must accept in order to gain full rights and recognition in the international community" (650).

One feature of the liberal peace project in particular explored by Vivienne Jabri (2010) is its characteristic as interventionist, cosmopolitan, and largely in the hands of Europeans and North Americans. She argues it contains a disciplinary, governmentalizing effect that results in a dispossession not simply of material resources but of political agency and "the capacity to determine what constitutes political identity" (42).

Jabri understands the liberal peace project as a project of war that "has the element of 'humanity' as its organizing principle," the purpose of which is "the management of populations" (42). Drawing on Foucault's analytics of power, she argues that the liberal peace governmentalizes postcolonial societies while depoliticizing social conflict. Far from being an emancipatory project, the liberal peace project reinforces "a hierarchical conception of subjectivities premised on the primarily European liberal self as against others whose modes of articulation remain 'other'" (43).

Jabri underscores the implications for political subjectivity when she discusses resistance in terms of the claim to politics, a particularly salient point in the context of what she sees as the liberal peace project's characteristic of dispossession, in that it "seeks to depoliticize the temporal and spatial articulation of selfhood in place of a globally affirmed, institutionalized discourse that seeks conformity to a liberal international political economy" (48). As a project of dispossession and governmentalization, Jabri sees the liberal peace's complicity in the banishment of politics and political agency, so that

> societies targeted for liberal intervention come to be reduced…to a division between culprits and victims, where the former come to be defined as the enemy while the latter constitute the biopolitical mass to be protected or rescued…There is in this scheme of things not so much a right to politics, which assumes agency and distinct subjectivity framed in the contingencies of social and political life, but a life lived as mass, simply one element in a category inscribed elsewhere and by others. (55)

Political subjectivity and resistance in terms of the "claim to politics" or the "right to politics," argues Jabri, is not conferred from the outside, but is framed in struggle and contestation. In her attempt to articulate a decolonial agenda, Meera Sabaratnam (2013) reveals ways in which the intellectual Eurocentrism underpinning the liberal peace is reproduced even in the critique of the liberal peace. One aspect of a decolonial approach is "an engagement with how those targeted by an intervention experience and interpret the material effects of that intervention" (273). The second aspect is an analysis

> that politicizes the various forms of entitlement, dispossession and accumulation that characterize the rationales for intervention and its distributive effects. This must avoid entangling itself in the language of "development" – already widely recognized as a fundamentally colonial and depoliticizing approach to poverty and economic policy…and begin to challenge the historical terms on which this dysfunctional political economy is made thinkable. (274)

The conclusion critical to Sabaratnam for a decolonial agenda are efforts not simply to dismiss the "old crude versions" of Eurocentrism, but to be vigilantly attentive to new manifestations in which "it quietly re-presents itself." She suggests, "this is best achieved through taking seriously questions of subjects' presence, positionality and the materiality of experience as the starting points for critical understandings of intervention" (274).[4]

How does this relate to Palestine? What purchase does that critique have for our particular conversation? One way it matters to our discussion is that neoliberalism and liberal institutionalism with its (technical) problem-solving approach to governance depoliticizes in a manner similar to how Ferguson (1994) described the effects of (neo)liberal peacebuilding and development as an "anti-politics machine" in Lesotho (see Turner 2012, 2015).

The attention to postcolonial/decolonial conversations makes clear the ways that (neo)liberal peace has always been made possible because of the violence and dispossession of colonialism. Neoliberalism depoliticizes the situation in Palestine in a way that obscures the settler colonialism that has been and continues to happen (as well as the resistance to it), allowing it to continue, in a way, as if it is not really there because it has been depoliticized. This is the neoliberal logic—that politics doesn't matter, that this is not a political issue (or at least politics follows economics).[5] Following Ferguson, Jabri, and Sabaratnam, we understand this depoliticization as a kind of erasure that takes a contested social, political, or economic issue and renders it invisible and inaccessible to debate. There is no need to debate these institutions and agendas because "common sense"[6] says it is not up for debate because it is not really "there." So what we observe in Palestine is a neoliberal logic,

1 THE RULE OF POWER IN PALESTINE   7

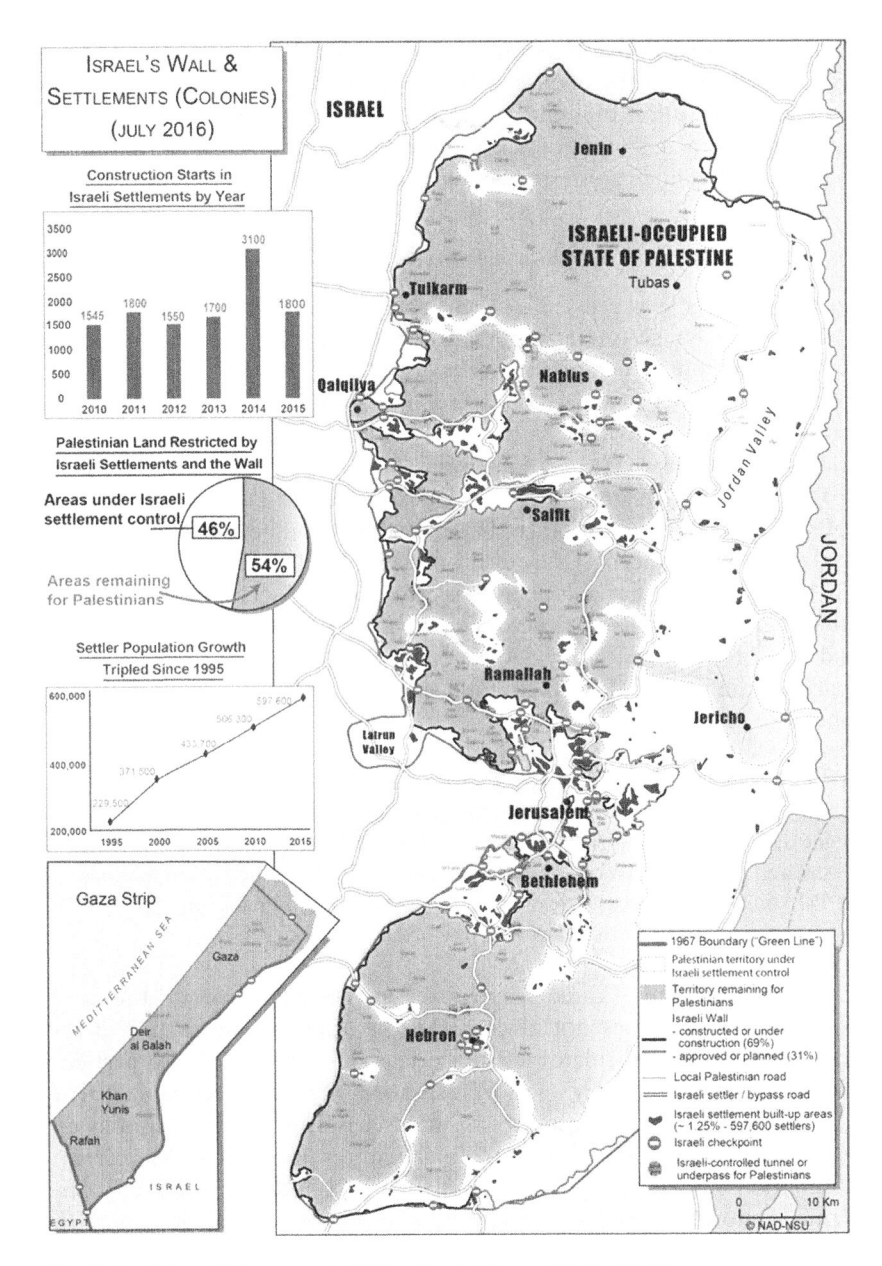

Fig. 1.1 Map of the occupied West Bank (*Source* PLO-NAD)

agenda, and order with depoliticizing effects, and varieties of resistance and local dissent with repoliticizing effects. By excavating the claims of neoliberal institution-building and settler colonialism, the chapters in this book engage in acts of repoliticization, revealing these agendas and institutions as very much contested issues subject to debate (Fig. 1.1).

Expressions of Resistance in Palestine: Local Dissent

So while power is expressed in these particular ways in Palestine today, power is always accompanied by resistance. Another major contribution of this volume is an exploration of resistance and local dissent in Palestine today, particularly in response to—or even co-constituted with—the rule of power seen through the logics and regimes of neoliberal governance and settler colonialism.

Critical to understanding the context of occupied Palestinian territory (oPt) is this everyday resistance that accompanies and even co-constitutes settler colonial projects. Drawing from Wolfe (2006), Dana and Jarbawi (2017) describe settler colonialism as "fundamentally based on the operative logic of 'eliminating the native' and failing to utterly marginalize and 'minoritize' him" (197). And yet, as they point out, this project is foiled by the non-erasure, the refusal to be erased, of Palestinians on the land.

> The vibrant Palestinian presence in the land, the everyday resistance to the colonial order, and the robust Palestinian adherence to their rights all stand as structural obstacles to the ultimate realization of the "Zionist dream." Despite Israel's relentless colonial power and domination, Palestinian steadfastness means that this project will remain impeded and incomplete, a matter that may lead to its future demise. (197)

A critical feature of these chapters is that they signal toward this kind of resistance that does not always take the shape of nonviolent direct action but instead articulates resistance as popular struggle, with particular attention to "everyday" acts of resistance. This focus recognizes that to confine resistance to instances of direct action not only overlooks an entire layer of activity in settler colonial context but also belies certain assumptions about what "civil" resistance is. It produces limited conceptualizations that not only overlook other forms of resistance, but also risk imposing our own notions of what "counts" as struggle. In contrast, by broadening our understanding, we can better understand the many acts of resistance and local dissent undertaken on a daily basis—"everyday" acts of resistance and popular struggle accessible to and embodied by Palestinian communities (see Scott 1985; Zaru 2008; Meari 2014; Johansson and Vinthagen 2015; Pogodda and Richmond 2015; Tartir 2015). In other words, we begin to hear and see a much larger and more powerful landscape of resistance in Palestine.[7]

This problematization begs the question: If we do not have the language, categories, or frameworks to identify or talk about something—such as resistance—does that mean it is not there? Addressing this challenge is central to discussions on "everyday" acts of resistance, where local, place-based experiences are privileged, alternative forms of everyday life are respected, and critical agency is expressed in unanticipated forms of resistance. Dipesh Chakrabarty (2000) describes the challenge as a "struggling, or even groping, for nonstatist forms of democracy that we cannot not yet either understand or envisage completely" because, instead of erasing difference, "we stay with heterogeneities without seeking to reduce them to any overarching principle that speaks for an already given whole" (107).

By destabilizing hierarchical binaries,[8] we follow the lead of scholars such as Chakrabarty who points out that these binaries, as well as their political implications, have emerged from a "historicizing" modernist discourse that consigns "rude" nations (like Palestinians, Indians, or Africans) to an imaginary waiting room of history—waiting until they move out of their anachronistic "prepolitical" stage to the stage of the "modern citizen" (2000, 8). These instabilities can be ignored in an effort to totalize our categories of resistance, thus locating populations who do not conform to those categories in a certain stage along the historicist continuum of appropriate modern behavior. This discussion leads us toward an interrogation of international governance, liberal peacebuilding and development, the claim to politics, and the category of resistance that will have an impact on our observations of the kind of local dissent that is occurring in Palestine.

Structure of the Book

The book starts with a foreword by Professor Richard Falk who reflects on the key arguments and thematic focuses of the book's chapters, and on the interaction between Palestine and rule of power. Professor Falk argues that despite Israel's flagrant violations of international law and the stark failure of the formal Palestinian leadership to address the aspirations of the Palestinian people, the transformational potential of a mobilized, resourceful, and resilient people should not be overlooked. It is the vitality and resilience of the Palestinian people, as argued by Professor Falk, that allowed them not to lose sight of their fundamental entitlements to self-determination and other human rights, in a sense, "the power of rights" as over time, and through struggle, prevailing over "the rule of power."

The book is divided into three parts. Part I "Resistance and Mobilization Against Apartheid, Settler Colonialism, and Repression," discusses and illustrates how the settler colonial present, the framework and structures of apartheid, as well as the failure of the Palestinian state-building project, are all resisted and confronted. The Foucauldian assertion "where there is power, there is resistance" is examined through multiple inward–outward relations to illustrate how repressive rules and the expressions of power are manifested and also challenged by the Palestinian people.

Chapter 2, written by Ben White, sets the settler colonial context and contextualizes the state-building project of the PA within a de facto condition of apartheid imposed by Israel. White shows that the de facto status quo of a single state in all of Mandate Palestine—which is being increasingly identified as matching the definition of apartheid in international treaties and conventions—is unlikely to change soon, as none of the Israeli political parties who either currently hold power, or who could conceivably form an alternative government, recognize the Palestinian people's right to self-determination or sovereignty. Given these realities, White argues that the PA leadership especially in the occupied West Bank and Palestinian political factions more broadly, are facing difficult and significant questions, including whether a focus on "state-building" under occupation has, in fact, laid the foundations for a Bantustan.

Illustrating how sovereignty and its rules can be challenged through the everyday practices of colonized people and through steadfastness and resistance is the focus of Chapter 3 written by Timothy Seidel. In his chapter, Seidel demonstrates that despite the significant constraints imposed by the fragmented political and economic geography of Palestine, the story of many Palestinian communities is not one of resignation but of steadfastness and resistance. In particular, the chapter explores ways in which this resistance is rendered visible or invisible by interrogating the violence of Israel's settler colonial occupation with the concepts of sovereignty, and claims that a focus on bodies helps us visibilize, helps us see the violence and the resistance as embodied subjectivity. In conclusion, Seidel argues that attention to embodied subjectivities not only challenge the centrality of the state in our political and geographic imaginations but also takes the embodied experiences of Palestinians as a starting point for talking about political claims and resistance.

The concept and practice of steadfastness (*Sumud*) is further explored in Chapter 4 written by Nijmeh Ali through focusing the analysis on the actions and perceptions of the third generation of Palestinian activists in Israel. In her chapter, Ali reveals an alternative approach to understand *Sumud* that moves away from the dominant passive and cultural understandings of *Sumud* toward a forward-looking approach that adopts active and transformative *Sumud* to alter social and power relations in Israel. The chapter presents four patterns that characterize that transformative *Sumud*: practical, personal, cultural, and active. It argues that challenging the monopoly of *Sumud* as cultural resistance and demand moving to active *Sumud* as political, allows the Palestinians in Israel to fulfill their potential away from romanticizing their physical remaining in their homeland. The ultimate aim of the chapter is to offer new openings as they relate to the debate about resistance, its terminology, its nature, and its potential, through the perspectives of third-generation Palestinian activists in Israel.

The thematic focus on resistance continues in Chapter 5 written by Dana El Kurd. "Who Protests in Palestine?" is the main question tackled by El Kurd, and addressed through a class and social strata lens. The chapter utilizes an original dataset on daily mobilizations in the West Bank, from 2007 to 2015, to assess the pattern of mobilization quantitatively, and illustrates that mobilizations occur overwhelmingly in rural areas and refugee camps. The chapter argues that the middle class does not mobilize precisely because its interest is tied to the status quo; mainly, the retrenchment of the PA and, unwittingly, the occupation. And therefore, the relation of individuals in society to the status quo regimes determines mobilization, hence why mobilization is concentrated in areas that are more rural with less organizational capacity and with members that do not necessarily have more education or information. The chapter concludes that future research on this matter would benefit from bringing class "back in" to the analysis, as well as looking at a class in novel ways and considering new resources.

Part II of the book, "External Intervention and International Aid," examines the uniqueness of the Palestinian–Israeli conflict in European Union (EU) discourse, and discusses the impacts of international aid regimes driven by neoliberal logics as well as the expressions of solidarity in the international donor community that seeks to accompany popular education in the occupied West Bank.

In Chapter 6, Anders Persson reviews 820 EC/EU statements published in the *Bulletin of the European Communities and Bulletin of the European Union* between 1967 and 2009 and asks: why has the Palestinian–Israeli conflict dominated European foreign policy discourse for over five decades now? And what were the major policy departures that induced the shifts in the views and positions of the European Union over the decades? The chapter argues that while the EU proved to forward-thinking in promoting Palestinian claims as legitimate demands, however the Israeli accusation that the EU is inherently anti-Israeli has little merit. The chapter ends with an open question that remains to be answered: with an EU in relative decline and disunity, and with the rise of various right wings, nationalist or populist governments and parties in Europe in recent years, would the EU continue to be a "normative power" in the Palestinian–Israeli conflict?

External intervention takes different shapes and forms, however since the Oslo Accords international aid comprises a major tool that has been used and abused by multiple local and foreign authorities and actors at stake. In Chapter 7, Jeremy Wildeman describes how Western donors have used their power to radically refashion Palestinian institutions and the economy while building a state based on neoliberal Western values. However, this approach was flawed from the onset because it adopted an ahistorical and decontextualized neoliberal approach to Palestinian development that specifically ignored Israel's aggressive behavior as a settler colonial entity. So rather than nurture economic growth and peace, donors have ended up feeding into a process of de-development, dispossession and violence. In other words, this chapter describes how neoliberal development aid has contributed to the settler colonization of Palestine. The case of Palestine, this chapter argues, is far from being without precedent as Western liberalism has had a long history of acting in tandem to, and often been the handmaiden of, colonialism.

Chapter 8, written by Melanie Meinzer, examines other dimensions in the Palestinian aid industry to illustrate how popular education can be used to counteract the depoliticizing and demobilizing tendencies of the donor liberal development paradigm. While some argue that the dependence of Palestinian nongovernmental organizations (NGOs) on donor funds diminishes their ability to challenge the Israeli occupation, Meinzer explains in her chapter how aid recipients can resist depoliticization by collaborating with "solidarity" donors on popular education programs. In particular, Palestinian educational NGOs and membership-based organizations in the West Bank work in the informal spaces around the donor-funded official Palestinian curriculum to reinsert Palestinian historical narratives into education. In other words, this chapter demonstrates how these actors' shared visions of education and development as long-term, grassroots processes of sociopolitical change challenge the depoliticizing and demobilizing tendencies of the donor-driven development paradigm. Consequently, the chapter contributes to new theorizing on popular education as a means of cultivating the values and knowledge that support political resistance and ensure cultural survival.

Part III of the book, "Security Sector Reform, Resistance, and Authoritarianism," examines and problematizes the trajectories of security sector reform and the accompanying emergence of, and resistance to, authoritarianism in Palestine, by focusing on donor-driven security reform and its ramifications on criminalization of resistance and the professionalization of authoritarianism. While international aid had failed to bring a lasting peace to Palestine–Israel, it is argued in this part of the book that aid has been successful in setting the rules for a securitized version of peace as well as for securitized processes of state-building and political reforms. In fact, cementing Palestinian authoritarianism is a direct result of the shifts in powers and rules dictated by donors' conditionality and the status of aid dependency.

Chapter 9, written by Alaa Tartir, argues that security sector reform under the PA's post-2007 state-building agenda did not only aim to enhance the PA security forces functionality and effectiveness and to ensure stability and security for Israel, but it also sought to tame resistance to Israel's occupation and colonial domination by criminalizing militancy and stripping it of its basic infrastructure. In particular, the chapter tackles the consequences of the post-2007 PA's security campaigns in Balata and Jenin refugee camps in the West Bank from the people's perspective through a bottom-up ethnographic methodological approach to illustrate how and why resistance against Israel has been criminalized. The chapter concludes by arguing that conducting security reform to ensure stability within the context of colonial occupation and without addressing the imbalances of power can only ever have two outcomes: "better" collaboration with the occupying power and a violation of Palestinians' security and national rights by their own security forces.

The thematic focus on the consequences of security sector reform on the sustainability of the status quo and the denial of Palestinian democracy extends to Chapter 10, written by Alaa Tartir. As the PA's state-building process has atrophied, Tartir argues, securitization has found a renewed impetus, being elevated at the expense of initiatives that seek to promote democratization. In particular, Security Sector Reform (SSR), far from being a neural process, has strengthened the foundations of Palestinian authoritarianism. In focusing upon the development of the EU's police mission in the West Bank (EUPOL COPPS), this chapter argues that EU-sponsored "reform" has directly contributed to the "professionalization" of Palestinian authoritarianism. The chapter therefore suggests that the EU has consistently failed to acknowledge the political implications that extend from its technical mandate and interventions. The EU has become, to the extent that its interventions extend Israel's colonial project, part of the problem, the chapter concludes.

Stuart Hall once said, "The only interest in history is that it is not yet finally wrapped up. Another history is always possible. Another turning is waiting to happen" (Page 2017). We hope that through the collective scholarly and intellectual effort presented in this volume we are contributing to both, to another history and to another turning.

Notes

1. Mbembe describes territorial fragmentation as "the sealing off and expansion of settlements" meant both "to render any movement impossible and to implement separation along the model of the apartheid state. The occupied territories are therefore divided into a web of intricate internal borders and various isolated cells" (2003, 28). Mbembe draws from Eyal Weizman's "Politics of Verticality" in describing a regime of "vertical sovereignty," in which "colonial occupation operates through schemes of over- and underpasses, a separation of the airspace from the ground…Says Weizman: 'Settlements could be seen as urban optical devices for surveillance and the exercise of power'" (28). This relates to the third feature of late-modern colonial occupation, a splintering form of occupation "characterized by a network of fast bypass roads, bridges, and tunnels that weave over and under one another in an attempt at maintaining the Fanonian

'principle of reciprocal exclusivity.' According to Weizman, 'the bypass roads attempt to separate Israeli traffic networks from Palestinian ones, preferably without allowing them ever to cross. They therefore emphasize the overlapping of two separate geographies that inhabit the same landscape'" (28–29). For more discussion on Mbembe, see Seidel's Chapter 3 in this volume titled "Sovereign Bodies, Sovereign States: Settler Colonial Violence and the Visibility of Resistance in Palestine."
2. Wolfe reminds us of Theodor Herzl, founding father of Zionism, who "observed in his allegorical manifesto/novel, 'If I wish to substitute a new building for an old one, I must demolish before I construct'" (388). Half a century later, former deputy-mayor of West Jerusalem Meron Benvenisti recalled, "As a member of a pioneering youth movement, I myself 'made the desert bloom' by uprooting the ancient olive trees of al-Bassa to clear the ground for a banana grove, as required by the planned farming' principles of my kibbutz, Rosh Haniqra." Central to this replacement is a kind of erasure possible through remapping and renaming: "Renaming is central to the cadastral effacement/replacement of the Palestinian Arab presence that Benvenisti poignantly recounts" (388). To illustrate this, Wolfe points to Walid Khalidi and his team who memorialized the "obsessively erased Arab past" in *All That Remains: The Palestinian Villages Occupied and Depopulated by Israel in 1948* (1992).
3. For an overview of the history and development of neoliberalism see Harvey (2005), Rodrik (2006), Mitchell (2002), and Haddad (2016). While its usage is wide and varied, we explore neoliberalism in both its political and economic effects as a logic and an order that advances an understanding of social and political freedom that can only be realized in free market terms. The market itself is cast as a natural phenomenon where, as George Monbiot (2016) describes it, competition is the defining characteristic of human relations. "It redefines citizens as consumers, whose democratic choices are best exercised by buying and selling, a process that rewards merit and punishes inefficiency." Monbiot also points out that this logic sees attempts to limit competition as inimical to liberty because it is the market that reveals a natural hierarchy of winners and losers. Monbiot says, "inequality is recast as virtuous…Efforts to create a more equal society are both counterproductive and morally corrosive. The market ensures that everyone gets what they deserve." On a point particularly salient in this "post Oslo" era in occupied Palestine, Monbiot underscores Naomi Klein's conclusions that "neoliberal theorists advocated the use of crises to impose unpopular policies while people were distracted: for example, in the aftermath of Pinochet's coup, the Iraq war and Hurricane Katrina, which Friedman described as 'an opportunity to radically reform the educational system' in New Orleans."

4. Sabaratnam argues that a more radical critique of the liberal peace requires "a more radical disruption of its Eurocentric epistemic underpinnings as well as a repoliticization of that sensibility of Western distinctiveness that is taken as an ontological given" (2013, 270). She acknowledges that this is no easy task, both in terms of research and "the personal and psychological disorientation that this kind of research may involve." "Moreover," she points out, "one may never be able to fully erase the sedimentations of Eurocentric knowledge, which in some ways goes to the very heart of the practice of professional scholarship" (274). This acknowledgment resonates with the epistemological precarities and problems of representation—what Spivak referred to as the "'epistemic violence' that is always at play in the retrieval of the subject, so that she, and perhaps we, must always acknowledge that, as she puts it, 'the subaltern cannot speak,' for 'representation has not withered away'" (Jabri 2012, 78). Wainwright (2008) talks about this as well in terms of skepticism toward practices that represent subaltern voices: "The skepticism is not so much scientific or empirical as it is political and ethical. The challenge is to become open to subaltern histories and geographies without *speaking for* or contributing otherwise to epistemic violence" (16).
5. George Monbiot (2016) identifies a key feature of neoliberalism in which "democracy is reduced to theatre" as neoliberal policies are "imposed internationally." Wider effects become clearer as we consider the impact of neoliberalism not only in terms of the economic crises it has caused, but the political crises. "As the domain of the state is reduced, our ability to change the course of our lives through voting also contracts. Instead, neoliberal theory asserts, people can exercise choice through spending. But some have more to spend than others: in the great consumer or shareholder democracy, votes are not equally distributed. The result is a disempowerment of the poor and middle. As parties of the right and former left adopt similar neoliberal policies, disempowerment turns to disenfranchisement. Large numbers of people have been shed from politics."
6. Antonio Gramsci described the need to problematize this "common sense" and historicize one's conception of the world—to develop "a consciousness of its historicity and of the fact that it contradicts other conceptions or elements of other conceptions." This was critical for Gramsci because "one's conception of the world is a response to certain specific problem posed by reality" (1971, 324).
7. For more on this discussion of nonviolence and civil resistance in occupied Palestine, see Seidel (2017). A portion of this section is taken from that essay.

8. The destabilizing effects of postcolonial inquiry—such as Chakrabarty's and Edward Said's—underscores these ontological implications. Indeed, an important argument for Said in *Orientalism* (1978) was that categories such as the Orient or the West have no ontological stability but are the result of human efforts to read and write "worlds."

References

Barker, Adam, and Emma Battell Lowman. n.d. "Settler Colonialism." *Global Social Theory*. https://globalsocialtheory.org/concepts/settler-colonialism/.

Chakrabarty, Dipesh. 2000. *Provincializing Europe: Postcolonial Thought and Historical Difference*. Princeton: Princeton University Press.

Dana, Tariq, and Ali Jarbawi. 2017. "A Century of Settler Colonialism in Palestine: Zionism's Entangled Project." *Brown Journal of World Affairs* 24 (1): 197–219.

Fanon, Frantz. 1963. *The Wretched of the Earth*. Translated by C. Farrington. New York: Grove.

Ferguson, James. 1994. *The Anti-politics Machine: "Development," Depoliticization and Bureaucratic State Power in Lesotho*. Minneapolis: University of Minnesota.

Foucault, Michel. 1980. *Power/Knowledge: Selected Interviews & Other Writings, 1972–1977*. Edited by C. Gordon. New York: Pantheon Books.

Gramsci, Antonio. 1971. *Selections from the Prison Notebooks*. Edited and Translated by Q. Hoare and G. N. Smith. London: Lawrence and Wishart.

Haddad, Toufic. 2016. *Palestine Ltd: Neoliberalism and Nationalism in the Occupied Territory*. London: I.B. Tauris.

Harvey, David. 2005. *A Brief History of Neoliberalism*. Oxford: Oxford University Press.

Jabri, Vivienne. 2010. "War, Government, Politics: A Critical Response to the Hegemony of the Liberal Peace." In *Palgrave Advances in Peacebuilding: Critical Developments and Approaches*, edited by O. P. Richmond, 41–57. New York: Palgrave Macmillan.

Jabri, Vivienne. 2012. *The Postcolonial Subject: Claiming Politics/Governing Others in Late Modernity*. London: Routledge.

Johansson, Anna, and Stellan Vinthagen. 2015. "Dimensions of Everyday Resistance: The Palestinians *Sumud*." *Journal of Political Power* 8 (1): 109–139.

Khalidi, Walid. 1992. *All That Remains: The Palestinian Villages Occupied and Depopulated by Israel in 1948*. Washington, DC: Institute for Palestine Studies.

Mbembe, Achille. 2003. "Necropolitics." *Public Culture* 15 (1): 11–40.

Meari, Lena. 2014. "Sumud: A Palestinian Philosophy of Confrontation in Colonial Prisons." *South Atlantic Quarterly* 113 (3): 547–578.

Mitchell, Timothy. 2002. *Rule of Experts: Egypt, Techno-Politics, Modernity*. Berkeley: University of California Press.

Monbiot, George. 2016. "Neoliberalism—The Ideology at the Root of All Our Problems." *The Guardian*, April 15. https://www.theguardian.com/books/2016/apr/15/neoliberalism-ideology-problem-george-monbiot.

Page, Ra, ed. 2017. *Protest: Stories of Resistance*. Manchester: Comma Press.

Paris, Roland. 2002. "International Peacebuilding and the 'Mission Civilisatrice'." *Review of International Studies* 28 (4): 637–656.

Pogodda, Sandra, and Oliver P. Richmond. 2015. "Palestinian Unity and Everyday State Formation: Subaltern 'Ungovernmentality' Versus Elite Interests." *Third World Quarterly* 36 (5): 890–907.

Rodrik, Dani. 2006. "Goodbye Washington Consensus, Hello Washington Confusion? A Review of the World Bank's Economic Growth in the 1990s." *Journal of Economic Literature* 44 (4): 973–987.

Sabaratnam, Meera. 2013. "Avatars of Eurocentrism in the Critique of the Liberal Peace." *Security Dialogue* 44 (3): 259–278.

Said, Edward W. 1978. *Orientalism*. New York: Vintage Books.

Salamanca, Omar Jabary, Mezna Qato, Kareem Rabie, and Sobhi Samour. 2012. "Past Is Present: Settler Colonialism in Palestine." *Settler Colonial Studies* 2 (1): 1–8.

Scott, James C. 1985. *Weapons of the Weak: Everyday Forms of Peasant Resistance*. New Haven: Yale University.

Seidel, Timothy. 2017. "'We Refuse to Be Enemies': Political Geographies of Violence and Resistance in Palestine." *Journal of Peacebuilding and Development* 12 (3): 25–38.

Tartir, Alaa. 2015. "Contentious Economics in Occupied Palestine." In *Contentious Politics in the Middle East: Popular Resistance and Marginalized Activism Beyond the Arab Uprisings*, edited by F. Gerges, 469–499. New York: Palgrave Macmillan.

Turner, Mandy. 2012. "Completing the Circle: Peacebuilding as Colonial Practice in the Occupied Palestinian Territory." *International Peacekeeping* 19 (5): 492–507.

Turner, Mandy. 2015. "Peacebuilding as Counterinsurgency in the Occupied Palestinian Territory." *Review of International Studies* 41 (1): 73–98.

Veracini, Lorenzo. 2010. *Settler Colonialism: A Theoretical Overview*. London: Palgrave Macmillan.

Veracini, Lorenzo. 2015. *The Settler Colonial Present*. London: Palgrave Macmillan.

Wainwright, Joel. 2008. *Decolonizing Development: Colonial Power and the Maya*. Malden, MA: Blackwell.

Wolfe, Patrick. 1999. *Settler Colonialism and the Transformation of Anthropology: The Politics and Poetics of an Ethnographic Event.* London: Cassell.
Wolfe, Patrick. 2006. "Settler Colonialism and the Elimination of the Native." *Journal of Genocide Research* 8 (4): 387–409.
Zaru, Jean. 2008. *Occupied with Nonviolence: A Palestinian Woman Speaks.* Minneapolis: Fortress Press.

PART I

Resistance and Mobilization Against Apartheid, Settler Colonialism, and Repression

CHAPTER 2

The Settler Colonial Present: Palestinian State-Building Under Apartheid

Ben White

INTRODUCTION

For Israel and the Palestinians, the last two years have seen a glut of significant anniversaries. June 2017 marked fifty years of Israeli military occupation of the West Bank, including East Jerusalem, and the Gaza Strip, the centenary of the Balfour Declaration was mourned—and celebrated—in November 2017, while the following month was the 30th anniversary of the First Intifada. November 2017 also saw the 70th anniversary of the adoption by the United Nations General Assembly of the Partition Plan for Palestine, followed in May 2018, by the 70th anniversary of the Palestinian *Nakba* and establishment of the State of Israel. These dates were important opportunities for historical retrospectives, but their political charge was inextricably linked to their contemporary resonance. For these anniversaries have also represented an opportune moment to take stock of the current situation on the ground in Israel and the occupied Palestinian territory (oPt), and, in particular, to acknowledge how, since 1967, successive Israeli governments have forged a de facto, single state across these territories—that is to say, in all of Mandate Palestine.

B. White (✉)
Cambridge, UK

© The Author(s) 2019
A. Tartir and T. Seidel (eds.),
Palestine and Rule of Power, Middle East Today,
https://doi.org/10.1007/978-3-030-05949-1_2

The longevity of Israel's military rule of the West Bank and Gaza Strip has prompted questions from both activists and academics as to whether or not the occupation paradigm is sufficient to account for what has taken place there over the past half century, and the extent to which International Humanitarian Law (IHL) is inadequate as a means of analyzing—and challenging—Israeli state policies (du Plessis et al. 2009; Tilley 2012; Gross 2017). A growing body of scholarly work asserts the importance of understanding the history and contemporary reality in Palestine/Israel as a form of settler colonialism. "In the absence of a cohesive framework," an essay in *Settler Colonial Studies* put it in 2012, "scholarship often appears to catalogue Zionist practices and offences against Palestinians as a series of distinct – yet related – events" (Salamanca et al. 2012, 2). However, "viewed through the lens of settler colonialism, the Nakba in 1948…is not a singular event but is manifested today in the continuing subjection of Palestinians by Israelis" (2). This chapter, then, assumes the existence of a "settler-colonial present," not purely in terms of specific policies or legislation, but also as an underlying structure.

This chapter will begin by examining the status quo on the ground in Israel and the oPt, and how just under half of the global Palestinian population are residents of this de facto, single state, subjected to various forms of discrimination and exclusion.[1] After assessing this status quo, the chapter will assess the prospects of it changing any time soon, with a particular focus on the visions put forward by both the current Israeli coalition government, as well as those who might conceivably form an alternative government (which, by the time you read this, could already have come to pass). Building on the first two parts of the chapter—the status quo on the ground and the Israeli impasse with respect to what is on offer for the Palestinians—the final part of this chapter will examine the implications of this situation for the Palestinian Authority (PA) leadership in Ramallah, and for Palestinian political factions in general. In particular, the PA is left facing some significant questions, including whether, in focusing on "state-building" under occupation, they may have in fact laid the foundations for a Bantustan.[2]

THE STATUS QUO: A DE FACTO, SINGLE STATE

Israel has established a de facto single state in the territory of former Mandate Palestine, in large part due to the establishment of civilian settlements in East Jerusalem and the West Bank, held by Israel under military occupation since 1967. There are now more than 200 Israeli settlements in the oPt, 137 of which are official, state-authorized settlements, in addition to some 100 so-called "outposts"—smaller settlements which were established without official approval, albeit often with assistance from various governmental agencies (B'Tselem 2017b). The population of these settlements has risen to more than 400,000 in the West Bank, and more than 200,000 in East Jerusalem—territory that Israel unilaterally annexed, a move never recognized by the international community (AFP 2017). While the built-up area of settlements constitutes 2% of the total West Bank, 39% comes under the jurisdiction of settlements' local authorities, land which Israel has "consistently refused to allocate…for Palestinian use," according to UN OCHA; the municipal area of Ariel settlement, for example, "is around four times larger than the built-up area" (UN OCHA 2009; Human Rights Watch 2016).

In addition, the settlement enterprise, and de facto annexation of the West Bank, has also entailed a significant investment in and expansion of related infrastructure, such as transportation links and telecommunications. Indeed, all main economic sectors and industries are involved in the settlement enterprise: banking, tourism, construction, technology, real estate, telecommunications, agriculture, transportation, and manufacturing. In March 2017, Israeli journalist Uri Misgav wrote a piece in *Haaretz* on how the West Bank has been both physically, and "culturally," annexed over the past half century, noting how Supreme Court justices, cabinet ministers, other Knesset members, "as well as a host of government officials" all live in the West Bank.

> The Electric Corporation provides electricity, the Mekorot national water company supplies water, the National Roads Company looks after roads and the National Lottery erects and manages public buildings. Factories, businesses and services operate there without limits, including schools and a university that are under the Ministry of Education's supervision. State-funded cultural institutions are compelled to perform in every settlement. (Misgav 2017)

This de facto annexation of the oPt has proceeded over the past half century at varying speeds, and through different mechanisms. To date, the only explicit act of annexation that has taken place with respect to the territory conquered in 1967—excluding the Occupied Syrian Golan Heights—was the area that became known as East Jerusalem.

In total, Israel annexed 70 square kilometers to the municipal boundaries of Jerusalem, the vast majority of which was land that "belonged to 28 villages in the West Bank" as well as "to the municipalities of Bethlehem and Beit Jala" (B'Tselem 2017a). By late 1970, Israeli authorities had expropriated more than 14 square kilometers of land in the newly expanded municipal boundaries of East Jerusalem, mainly from Palestinian owners, in order to establish the settlements of Ramot, Gilo, and East Talpiot—settlements which Israel considers to be "neighborhoods" of a "united" Jerusalem (Cheshin et al. 2001).

In the West Bank, meanwhile, the establishment of civilian colonies began slowly, with the first handful of settlements established by the Labor Party-led government in the "Gush Etzion" area of the West Bank south of Jerusalem, in Hebron, and in the Jordan Valley (Sheizaf 2017). When Menachem Begin's Likud party came to power for the first time in 1977, there were thus already some two dozen settlements in the West Bank (excluding East Jerusalem), home to around 4500 residents (Weizman 2007, 92). In 1981, however, by the end of Likud's first term in office, the number of settlements had more than doubled to 68, and the number of settlers had quadrupled to 16,200 (92). A road network was constructed to link these settlements to Israeli communities inside Israel's pre-1967 territory, and the Likud government expanded "the number of legal and administrative services which Israeli settlers in the territories could enjoy" (Lustick 1985).

Over the years, some have warned that this process of incremental, de facto annexation was creating a fait accompli that could prove irreversible. In April 1982, former Arab affairs advisor to the Israeli PM, Shmuel Toledano, predicted that "within a few years, if anyone were to suggest giving up any part of the [occupied Palestinian] territories, the suggestion would be regarded as no different than that of giving up part of the Negev or the Galilee" (Lustick 1985). In December 1987, not long after the First Intifada had erupted, Thomas Friedman observed in *The New York Times* how, "for the past 20 years many Israelis have insisted on referring to the West Bank by its Biblical names 'Judea and Samaria' and on viewing these occupied territories as integral parts of a Greater Israel. The Green Line, many Israelis said, did not exist for them anymore" (Friedman 1987). This process, therefore, was already well advanced after two decades of Israeli military rule, and the trend only went in one direction. A few examples will demonstrate what today's status quo means in practical terms.

Inside the pre-1967 lines, Palestinian citizens of Israel face "institutional and societal discrimination" (the words of the US State Department) that affects them in areas of life as diverse as land ownership and housing, through to education budgets, family life, and political expression (US State Department, n.d.). To focus, however, specifically, on land and housing, and a picture comes into view of decades-long, structural discrimination, not just as a result of legislation, but as a result of a strategic decision by successive Israeli governments to restrict the ability of Palestinian communities to naturally grow, their lands seen as fair game for the expansion of Jewish communities. Take Umm al-Hiran, a Bedouin Palestinian village in the Negev that, at the time of writing, Israeli authorities are intending to destroy in order to implement a long-standing plan to expel its residents and replace the village with a Jewish community. Umm al-Hiran's residents, remember, are Israeli citizens—and yet they find themselves dispossessed in what Israeli legal advocacy organization Adalah has called "a clear case of dispossession and displacement for strictly racial reasons" (Adalah 2016).

Not far from Umm al-Hiran—about a dozen or so kilometers north-west—is another Palestinian village threatened with destruction, but this time in the southern Hebron hills area of the West Bank. All of Susya's homes have been deemed to have been built "illegally," thanks to its location in "Area C" of the West Bank, where Palestinians find it almost impossible to obtain the required permit from the Israeli occupation bureaucrats (Berger and Ravid 2016). In other words, as Human Rights Watch has described, "in both the Negev and the West Bank, Israel authorities apply zoning laws in a discriminatory manner that frequently restricts the ability of Arabs to build lawfully" (Human Rights Watch 2015). So, while there are indeed important differences between the plight of Umm al-Hiran and Susya, they are part of the one, same story: namely, an Israeli government policy that "comes at the expense of the people who live in those spaces, their homes destroyed in order to make room for the expansion of Jewish-only communities" (Penina 2016) (Fig. 2.1).

Those restrictions faced by Palestinians in Area C of the West Bank are a key part of the story; in July 2016, European Union diplomat Lars Faaborg-Andersen told the Israeli parliament that out of 2000 permit applications by Palestinians from 2009 to 2013, only 34 were granted—less than 2% (Lieber 2016). During the first six months of 2016, according to Israeli data cited by the United Nations, "during

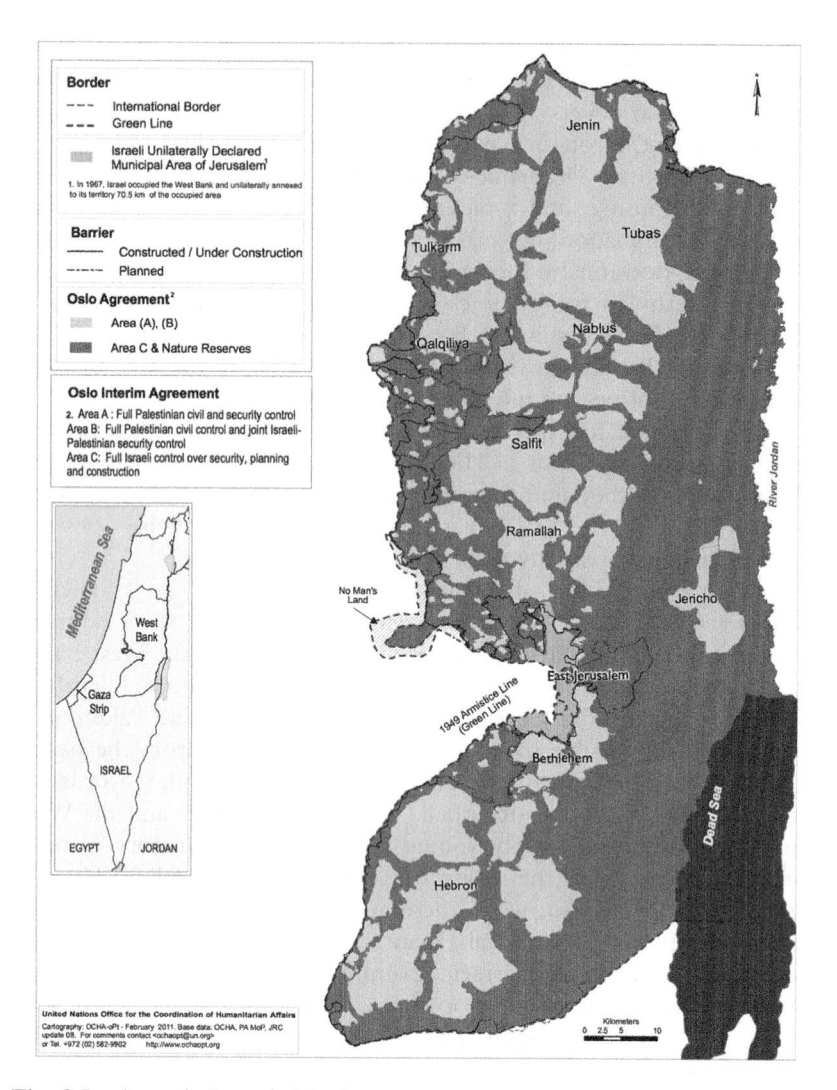

Fig. 2.1 Areas A, B, and C in the occupied West Bank (*Source* United Nations OCHA oPt)

the first half of 2016 there were 428 applications for building permits in Palestinian communities in Area C, of which 391 (91%) were rejected" (UN OCHA 2017). Meanwhile, the Office of the UN Special

Coordinator for the Middle East Peace Process (UNSCO) reported in May 2017, out of 94 submitted outline plans for Palestinian communities in Area C, only five have been approved by Israeli authorities. The "cumulative area" covered by Israeli-approved plans—where Palestinians can "legally" build—is thus less than 1% of Area C (UNSCO 2017).

In East Jerusalem, meanwhile, annexed by Israel but viewed as occupied by the international community, Palestinians—almost all of whom have residency status rather than Israeli citizenship—are subject to home demolitions and Israeli settler takeovers, as well as discrimination in municipal services. In Silwan, for example, a Palestinian neighborhood of East Jerusalem, eviction cases have been filed against 67 households (as of November 2016), threatening more than 300 with displacement (UN OCHA 2016). In parallel to these disturbing developments, settler groups, with the backing of various government bodies, are expanding their presence in the area through "tourism" and "archaeology" projects, in addition to fortified housing.

In the Gaza Strip, meanwhile, almost 2 million Palestinians are fenced-off and blockaded, cut off from Palestinians in the West Bank, after years of deliberate de-development and bloody assaults. The conditions in the Gaza Strip are, of course, unique, but it is a mistake to consider the enclave outside of the framework of the de facto, single state created by Israel over the past half century. Indeed, its isolation goes back some three decades, when, in 1989, "Israel introduced a system whereby only Palestinians vetted by the Shin Bet security service and in possession of magnetic cards were permitted to travel to the West Bank via Israel" (B'Tselem and HaMoked 2005). By the mid-1990s, under then-Prime Minister Yitzhak Rabin, a perimeter fence had been built around the Gaza Strip. Since Israel's unilateral removal of settlers and troop redeployment in 2005, the status of the Gaza Strip is that it has remained under Israeli military occupation, a position affirmed by the UN Security Council, UN General Assembly, and Office of the Prosecutor of the International Criminal Court (United Nations 2009, 2011; International Criminal Court 2014). In political terms, it has become a way for Israel to fence-off some 2 million Palestinians: "I would like Gaza to sink into the sea," Yitzhak Rabin once said, and Israel has settled for the next best thing, fencing in its residents with state-of-the-art technology and weaponry (Beinin 1993).

It is important to note that roughly half of the Palestinian population is not found within the territory of this de facto, single state—the territory of former-Mandate Palestine—but in regional refugee camps and the wider diaspora. According to end of 2015 statistics prepared by the Palestinian Central Bureau of Statistics, 38.4% of all Palestinians live in the oPt, 11.9% are citizens of Israel, while 49.7% live in the Arab world or elsewhere (PCBS, n.d.). These Palestinians, while not present within the de facto, apartheid state, are nevertheless profoundly impacted by the ethnocratic regime established by Israeli authorities, in that they are prevented from returning to their homeland (and in many cases, denied the possibility of even visiting).

The Prospects of Progress: The Maximum Israel Has to Offer

This de facto, single state reality is well documented by many Palestinians, Israelis, international observers—including diplomats and human rights activists—albeit often in terms of discrete, practical manifestations, as opposed to an overarching analysis or framework for understanding Israeli control of the territory between the Jordan River and the Mediterranean Sea. This process of incremental colonization has, in other words, proceeded in plain view. In 2009, Israeli political geographer Oren Yiftachel wrote how "persisting colonial and oppressive practices are working to further Judaise contested space and deny Palestinians – on both sides of the Green Line – their legitimate rights" (Yiftachel 2009). Yiftachel called this process "creeping apartheid," which he defined as "an undeclared yet structural process through which new, oppressive sets of political geographic relations are being institutionalised for Jews and Palestinians living under the Israeli regime between Jordan and the [Mediterranean] sea." This process has, he said, led to "the merging of the colonised West Bank, the besieged Gaza Strip and Israel proper into one system, ultimately controlled by the Jewish state."

However, the fact that this "one system" remains, for the time being, a melange of legal systems, of internationally recognized Israeli sovereign territory, de jure (albeit internationally condemned) annexation, and de facto annexation, has brought significant benefits for Israel. Indeed, it is no accident, but rather a "deliberate ambiguity" that is based on "creating a framework of temporary military occupation that falls in line with international law (and as such is considered a legitimate occupation), but which de facto promotes permanent control and annexation" (Association for Civil Rights in Israel, n.d.). International law scholar Valentina Azarova, for example, has described the situation in the oPt as one of "an unlawfully prolonged occupation," which "arises when an occupying state seeks to permanently transform the international status, government or demographic character of a foreign territory, including through de jure or de facto annexation" (Azarova 2017).

That, until now, the West Bank remains de facto, rather than de jure, annexed, is also one of the reasons why Israel has been able to advance its colonization project so effectively. As Israeli international law expert, Aeyal Gross wrote in his recent book, *The Writing on the Wall*, "Israel acts in the OPT as a sovereign insofar as it settles its citizens there and extends to them its laws on a personal and on a mixed personal/territorial basis" (Gross 2017, 176).

> Yet, insofar as the territory has not been formally annexed and insofar as this exercise of sovereignty falls short of giving the Palestinian residents citizenship rights, Israel is not acting as a sovereign. In the OPT, then, Israel enjoys both the powers of an occupant and the powers of a sovereign, while Palestinians enjoy neither the rights of an occupied people nor the rights of citizenship. The implication is a matrix of control whereby Israel acts as both occupier and non-occupier, and as both sovereign and non-sovereign, one of the ways wherein *legal indeterminacy itself serves as a form of control*. (Gross 2017, 176–177)

A situation where "a state, although empirically sovereign in a territory, deliberately abjured a claim to be the juridical sovereign precisely in order to avoid the international obligations that would pertain if it were" is unusual, perhaps unique (Tilley 2015). But over the last half century, Israel has exploited the "difference between empirical and juridical sovereignty" for its own "strategic advantage."

Perhaps paradoxically, Israel has also been aided in this decades-long process of incremental colonization by an internationally supervised peace process which—dating it from the Madrid Conference and Oslo Accords of the early 1990s—has existed in various forms for a quarter century; half the entire duration of the military occupation of the oPt. As Israeli journalist Chemi Shalev wrote in 2014, "with the benefit of hindsight it hard to counter the argument that the perennial search for a two state[sic] solution has served as a cover for a de facto annexation of the West Bank that absolves Israel's of the need to grant the Palestinians full civil rights. Without the dangled promise of eventual peace, it would be much harder for Israel to look in the mirror and rebuff the claims of apartheid" (Shalev 2014). In 2014, then-US Secretary of State John Kerry described the two-state solution as the only viable option: "Because a unitary state winds up either being an apartheid state with second-class citizens – or it ends up being a state that destroys the capacity of Israel to be a Jewish state" (Rogin 2014). Even former Israeli premier Ehud Barak, speaking in Herzliya in 2010, had said much the same: "as long as in this territory west of the Jordan river there is only one political entity called Israel it is going to be either non-Jewish, or non-democratic," adding: "If this bloc of millions of Palestinians cannot vote, that will be an apartheid state" (McCarthy 2010).

Except the picture painted of a single political entity in which millions of Palestinians cannot vote actually describes the status quo (of some time now), not a *future* scenario. And one of the key ways in which this artificial distinction between status quo and future is maintained, a crucial part of how the illusion of impermanence with respect to Israel's hold on the oPt is preserved, is the politics of the peace process.[3] Even though Kerry, and Barak are describing a situation that—regardless of the lack of Israel's *formal* annexation of the oPt—corresponds to the reality on the ground, it is the prospect of a "two-state solution," the idea that Israel's presence and control over the oPt still have to be determined or are, in some way, temporary or negotiable, which keeps the same international diplomats from denouncing Israeli apartheid as it exists *today*.

In recent years, the Israeli government has pursued a number of strategies intended to expand and consolidate the settlement enterprise. These have included the retroactive legalization of outposts, as well as the establishment of an entirely new settlement, Amichai, deep in the West Bank. Perhaps more significantly, Israeli authorities—driven, often, by the political agendas of hard-right and extreme nationalist coalition government members—have also advanced legislative initiatives whose critics describe as "creeping annexation." Whereas, for the first few decades of Israel's military occupation of the oPt, Israel ruled the territory in question primarily through military orders (albeit with some exceptions, and, notwithstanding the fact that Israeli settlers were, as individuals, subject to civil law), the last few years have seen a gradual increase in the number of times that the Knesset legislates for matters pertaining to the occupied West Bank. For example, in early 2018, a law was passed that saw Ariel University, located in a West Bank settlement of the same name, come under the authority of the Council for Higher Education—rather than the Israeli military (Zur 2018). This is a complicated picture, but it has emerged as a reflection of a simple fact: Israel has forged a de facto, single state in all of former Mandate Palestine, binding the oPt to the pre-1967 territory through a combination of territorial colonization, and shaped by a broad, cross-party consensus that the land captured in 1967 is Israel's by *right*.

At the time of writing, Israeli Prime Minister Benjamin Netanyahu has been in power since 2009, in addition to the three years he served during his first term as premier 1996–1999. His approach to the Palestinian issue has thus had a significant impact on the trajectory of Israel's apartheid regime over the past decade, and even earlier. Netanyahu clearly opposes a sovereign Palestinian state in the oPt; his approach is best summarized as a desire to maintain the status quo. In the final days of campaigning before the March 2015 election, for example, Netanyahu declared: "We won't divide Jerusalem, we won't make concessions, we won't withdraw from land" (Morag 2015). The next day, Netanyahu told an interviewer that a Palestinian state will not be established with him as PM (Lubell 2015). Netanyahu made an arguably more instructive comment in early 2017, when he told colleagues that what he was "willing to give to the Palestinians is not exactly a state with full authority, but rather a state-minus, which is why the Palestinians don't agree [to it]" (Klein 2017). Netanyahu has insisted that "Israel must retain the overriding security control over the entire area west of the Jordan River" *forever* (White House 2017). Netanyahu has also made clear that he sees Israel retaining all of Jerusalem as its "undivided capital," in addition to so-called "settlement blocs" in the southern, central and northern West Bank.

While Netanyahu is happy with the apartheid status quo, some of his ministerial colleagues, as well as influential movements both inside and outside of the Knesset, advocate the formal Israeli annexation of some, or even all, of the West Bank. In both cases, an important role is envisaged for Jordan, whether in terms of some kind of confederation with the West Bank cantons of Palestinian "autonomy," or even with respect to some proposals for Palestinians in the West Bank to actually vote in Jordanian elections. Another important point to note about the pro-annexation camp is that the Gaza Strip is left out of the equation entirely, thus "solving," so the thinking goes, one of the main challenges presented by annexation of all or part of the West Bank: demographics. Absorbing hundreds of thousands of Palestinians in the West Bank—with or without offering them Israeli citizenship—is one matter; but the annexationists do not even consider taking into account the two million Palestinian residents of the Gaza Strip.

Supporters of annexation can be found among Netanyahu's ministers—including from his own Likud party. In early 2017, Intelligence and Atomic Energy Minister Yisrael Katz urged the annexation of "dozens of settlements in the Jerusalem area," including Ma'ale Adumim (Ravid 2017). A few weeks later, Likud minister Ayoub Kara declared that "Israel shouldn't apologize for intending to annex Judea and Samaria [the West Bank]. We should be determined to implement our right to these historic areas of our homeland" (Domb 2017). Perhaps one of the most vocal, pro-annexation voices within Likud is deputy foreign minister Tzipi Hotovely, who, in November 2016, urged the annexation of 60% (Area C) of the West Bank (Lazaroff 2016). A few months later, she advocated a more comprehensive approach: "We need to go to a million settlers in Judea and Samaria - with a US embassy in Jerusalem. We need to think of new ways of thinking that will include Judea & Samaria under Israeli sovereignty forever," she told a receptive audience in Washington, DC (Arutz Sheva 2017). In December 2017, the Likud Central Committee voted to support the annexation of settlements in the West Bank, a move which generated headlines, but had no immediate impact on government policy (Amichay 2017).

One of the most high-profile, and consistent, supporters of annexation is Jewish Home leader Naftali Bennett, whose party platform ahead of the 2015 elections backed the annexation of Area C of the West Bank. Bennett had attracted international attention as early as 2013, for his pro-annexation positions, and view that "Palestinians living in Area C could either take Israeli citizenship or relocate to the Palestinian-governed 40% of the West Bank" (Sherwood 2013). His understanding of "self-government" is, in his own words, "autonomy on steroids" (i24NEWS 2016). In 2014, Bennett explained how the unilateral annexation of Palestinian land could be enacted in stages: first the Gush Etzion so-called "bloc" south of Jerusalem, "and then to Ariel and Ma'ale Adumim and the Jordan Valley"—and finally "all the Jewish communities in Judea and Samaria" (Benari and Ben Porat 2014). Bennett's colleagues in Jewish Home, like ministers Uri Ariel and Ayelet Shaked have also explicitly rejected Palestinian statehood, with the latter telling a D.C. conference in October 2015: "There is not and never will be a Palestinian state" (i24NEWS 2015).

Unilateral annexation—even of portions of the West Bank—would constitute a measure that the Western sponsors of the peace process could not ignore, and its likely diplomatic impact means that—for now, at least—an Israeli government headed by a status quo proponent like Netanyahu is unlikely to formally implement such a step. However, even if the annexationist camp's vision is not being implemented in full, their very existence and relative strength, both inside and outside the Likud party, is enough to hamper the willingness or ability of someone like Netanyahu to establish even a canton-style Palestinian "state-minus" (and note that, as of June 2016, only four ministers in the Israeli cabinet were on the record in support of a Palestinian "state" in any shape or form) (Haaretz Staff 2016). That is to say, putting aside Netanyahu's own views, he is aware of how much he owes politically to the pro-annexation constituency.

Against Netanyahu's policy of maintaining the status quo, and the pro-annexation positions of members of Likud, Jewish Home, and non-parliamentary activists, is an Israeli opposition that unites behind one, main call: separation from the Palestinians. Take Israel's Labor party, for example, which in the 2015 election ran under the banner of the Zionist Camp (sometimes translated as the less militaristic-sounding "Zionist Union"), together with Tzipi Livni's small Hatnuah party. While railing against Netanyahu's approach to the Palestinians, the Zionist Camp's manifesto was, in reality, a blueprint for a Palestinian Bantustan that would be a "state" in name only (White 2015). According to the Zionist Camp, under any "final status agreement," the future Palestinian "state" would be demilitarized, "the settlement blocs in Judea and Samaria [the West Bank]" would be "under Israeli sovereignty," and Jerusalem would remain "the eternal capital of the State of Israel" (Hoffman 2015b). On the campaign trail, the then-leader of Labor and the Zionist Camp, Isaac Herzog, declared that the Jordan River—i.e. the West Bank's entire eastern flank—would be Israel's "security border" (Hoffman 2015a). He also singled out Gush Etzion, Ma'ale Adumim, and Ariel—located in the south, center, and north of the West Bank, respectively—as so-called "settlement blocs" that Israel would keep in perpetuity, noting: "in the ideal world, I would like to keep it all."

A year later, and Labor officially kicked the "two-state solution" into the long grass, adopting a platform at its party conference which urged

Israel to pursue unilateral withdrawal from areas of the oPt in order to "separate" more effectively from the Palestinians (and yes, it is not simply a coincidence that the term "apartheid" in Afrikaans means "separation") (Lis 2016). In embracing Herzog's plan, Labor was endorsing his belief that "a full peace agreement unfortunately isn't around the corner and at this stage; it's not possible to realize the two-state vision," adding: "We must work by every means possible to preserve the two-state vision while separating from the Palestinians until it is realized." According to Labor's platform, Israel would complete the Separation Wall, hold on to the "settlement blocs," and reassign portions of Area C to full Palestinian Authority "control." In February 2017, a few months before he was removed as Labor leader, Herzog laid out a "road map" for Israel's relations with the Palestinians, which had, as its primary framework, a period of ten years during which Israel would de facto annex the "settlement blocs," and the Israeli army "would continue acting throughout the West Bank up to the Jordan River" (Herzog 2017). Only after this period would "direct negotiations" begin—*if* the decade "passed without violence" (as defined by Israel).

Labor—and its temporary alliance, the Zionist Camp—is not the only political party advocating for "separation" from the Palestinians. This is also the approach of self-styled "centrist" Yair Lapid, and his Yesh Atid party, who told Israeli television in 2016: "We need to remove the Palestinians from our lives – we need to do this by building a high wall and making them disappear" (Vile 2016). In its platform, Yesh Atid spells out what this means in more detail; the party supports "two states for two people as part of which the major settlement blocs (Ariel, Gush Etzion, Maale Adumim[sic]) will remain as part of Israel" (Yesh Atid, n.d.). As Israeli political scientist Neve Gordon noted in 2013, it was "telling that Yesh Atid launched its election campaign in Ariel, a settlement located in the heart of the occupied West Bank. Ariel was thus constituted as an eastern suburb of Tel-Aviv, part of normal Israel, rather than an illegal settlement" (Gordon 2013). For Yesh Atid, a permanent deal will also "guarantee Israel's right to act to defend itself and against any terrorist threat without limitations, as well as the demilitarization of the Palestinian state" (Yesh Atid, n.d.). Lapid also remains within the consensus that includes Netanyahu and Herzog when he insists that "Jerusalem will not be divided and will remain the capital of Israel" (Ramallah will be the Palestinian "capital") (Ain 2016; Edelman 2017).

State-Building Under Occupation: Recipe for a Bantustan

In November 2017, an Amnesty International spokesperson revealed that the global human rights organization intended to consider the question of whether Israeli policies toward the Palestinians constituted a form of apartheid (White 2017). "Looking ahead," the spokesperson said, "in any further research into institutional racial discrimination, we'll consider whether the situation in Israel and the occupied Palestinian Territories meets the international definition of apartheid," a process that "will require thorough research and a rigorous legal review of the evidence." These remarks are instructive, an illustration of the extent to which talk of Israeli "apartheid" has moved from being the preserve of a small number of academics and activists (Palestinian, Israeli and others) to being a far more widely accepted mode of analysis or language.

While "apartheid" remains an effective and powerful reference point for Palestinians and their solidarity campaigners—an observation made both positively and pejoratively—it is not merely a rhetorical device or slogan. Apartheid has both a political context—as a form of settler colonialism—as well as a definition within international law.[4] There are also serious critiques of the use of "apartheid" as a means of understanding Israeli policies, past and present, toward the Palestinians. Some focus on the differences between South Africa and Palestine, while for others, "the Palestinian experience has so many different facets that it is impossible to subsume them all under a single term like Apartheid" (Zreik 2004). Increasingly, however, regardless of the conflict's historical or even ideological origins, the situation on the ground as it stands today is being seen as conforming to the definition of apartheid that has developed over the last few decades as part of international conventions.

The existence of this de facto, apartheid single state, with the maximum being offered by the Israeli political class not even close to the minimum Palestinians can accept, has serious implications for the Ramallah-based leadership of the PA and Palestine Liberation Organisation (PLO). For the best part of three decades, the Palestinian leadership—first in exile, then from within the oPt—has sought an independent state in 22% of historic Palestine and, in pursuit of this goal, has taken decisions based on two key assumptions: first, that by establishing the institutions of a state, even while under occupation, Israel and the international community will have no excuse not to move forward from the "autonomy" of the Oslo era to full statehood; and second, that proximity to and good relations with the United States will facilitate pressure from the latter on Israel, to make the concessions necessary to bring about a genuine two-state solution.

These assumptions have shaped Palestinian policy-making (with some exceptions during the first few years of the Second Intifada) even as evidence mounted that this was this a misguided strategy. "State-building" under occupation has alleviated the burden of occupation for Israel but not brought genuine statehood any closer. Israel, currently, gets to have its cake and eat it: the majority of the Palestinian population of the oPt have their day-to-day affairs managed by the PA (education, health, sanitation, refuse collection, etc.), while Israeli authorities—as discussed earlier in this chapter—treat Area C of the West Bank as a land reserve for settlement expansion and the exploitation of natural resources (Keating et al. 2005). The United States, meanwhile, has shown no inclination to apply meaningful pressure on Israeli leaders; US President Barack Obama, who, more than other recent presidents, was both knowledgeable of the Palestinian experience and frequently clashed with Benjamin Netanyahu, was also the president who signed the largest ever military aid package for Israel (Spetalnick 2016). Such results can seem all the more sobering given that there have been high prices associated with key PA/PLO policies, whose only mitigating factors have been the alleged long-term benefit claimed for them. The "security coordination" policy between PA security services and the Israeli military, for example, is unsurprisingly unpopular, given its role in the mass incarceration of Palestinians by Israeli occupation authorities (and has even been tied to the extrajudicial executions of Palestinians by Israeli forces) (Tartir 2015). A donor-shaped economic agenda, meanwhile, has arguably contributed to a growing inequality among Palestinians in the West Bank (Tartir and Wildeman 2013).

High-level discussion of an alternative has, thus far, remained superficial; when Palestinian negotiators declare that the lack of progress toward a two-state solution is forcing the Palestinian leadership to consider a one-state framework, this has been more of a bluff, than an indication of a serious shift in strategy or long-term vision. But might this proposal move from the margins to the political center? Even today, some kind of one-state solution enjoys support among a significant portion of Palestinians in oPt, a majority of Palestinian citizens, and, one can assume, would enjoy popularity among refugees in the diaspora (albeit with the important caveat that assessing the views and goals of this latter, geographically fragmented, constituency is a difficult and sensitive task). For a genuine alternative to the two-state framework to emerge, it would, realistically, require the support of one or more political party or faction. For it to become the clear goal of the Palestinian national movement, it would likely require a rejuvenated and overhauled PLO, not to mention a reconstituted—or entirely dismantled—PA (al-Masri et al. 2016). There is also the question of how a Palestinian leadership that has claimed to represent Palestinians in the oPt and diaspora could relate to the political and communal leadership of Palestinians with Israeli citizenship (and vice versa). Ultimately, as Mahmood Mamdani has written, "the Palestinian challenge is to persuade the Jewish population of Israel and the world that the long-term security of a Jewish homeland in historic Palestine requires the dismantling of the Jewish state" (Mamdani 2015).

Answers to such questions will be slow to emerge and materialize, but their urgency and relevancy are undeniable, as Israeli authorities consolidate their own vision of a permanently temporary occupation, or even move toward unilateral annexation (White 2018). "Recent Palestinian political history has been a long march away from a liberation agenda and towards a piecemeal approach to the establishment of some kind of sovereignty under the structure of the Israeli settler colonial regime," wrote Salamanca et al. (2012). "The historic response to settler colonialism has been the struggle for decolonization," they continued: "in the absence of a settler colonial analysis, Palestinian strategies have tended to target or accommodate settler colonial outcomes rather than aiming to decolonize the structure itself." Without addressing that "structure," and as Israeli and US officials pursue their own priorities, the Palestinian leadership thus confronts the unpleasant, but undeniable, reality that the focus on state-building under occupation has, instead, established the foundations of a Bantustan.

Notes

1. This chapter is partly based on work that appears in my 2018 book *Cracks in the Wall: Beyond Apartheid in Palestine/Israel*, published by Pluto Press.
2. Bantustans ("homelands") were areas established by the Apartheid South African government as a means of excluding the black population from the country's political system; given a semblance of autonomy, the Bantustans were also areas to which the black population was expelled from major

urban centers. For the Apartheid government, the Bantustans were intended to thwart demands for equality in a unitary state.
3. This point is not new. Edward Said, for example, wrote critiques of the peace process long before such perspectives began entering more mainstream spaces (for example, see Said 1998).
4. See the International Convention on the Elimination of All Forms of Racial Discrimination of 1969; the International Convention on the Suppression and Punishment of the Crime of Apartheid, adopted by the UN General Assembly on November 30, 1973; the 1977 Additional Protocol I of the Geneva Conventions of 1949; Article 7 of the Rome Statute of the International Criminal Court.

References

Adalah. 2016. "State Opposes Final Appeal Against Demolition of Umm al-Hiran; Bulldozers Set to Move on Bedouin Village Tomorrow." *Adalah.org*, November 21. http://www.adalah.org/en/content/view/8956.

AFP. 2017. "NGO: Israeli Settlers in West Bank Top 421,000." *Qantara.de*, February 10. http://en.qantara.de/content/ngo-israeli-settlers-in-west-bank-top-421000.

Ain, Stewart. 2016. "'Cut a Deal with the World' on Settlements." *New York Jewish Week*, October 11. http://jewishweek.timesofisrael.com/cut-adeal-with-the-world-on-settlements.

al-Masri, Hani, Noura Erakat, Jamil Hilal, Sam Bahour, Jaber Suleiman, Diana Buttu, Wajjeh Abu Zarifa, and Alaa Tartir. 2016. "Palestine After Abbas: Potential Scenarios and Coping Strategies." *Al-Shabaka*, November 22. https://al-shabaka.org/roundtables/palestine-after-abbas-potential-scenarios-and-coping-strategies.

Amichay, Rami. 2017. "Likud Party Calls for De-Facto Annexation of Israeli Settlements." *Reuters*, December 31. https://www.reuters.com/article/us-israel-palestinians-likud/likud-party-calls-for-de-facto-annexation-of-israeli-settlements-idUSKBN1EP0M2.

Arutz Sheva Staff. 2017. "Celebrating 50 Years Since Liberation of Judea and Samaria." *Arutz Sheva*, March 28. www.israelnationalnews.com/News/News.aspx/227418.

Association for Civil Rights in Israel. n.d. "50 Years—A State Without Borders." www.acri.org.il/campaigns/50yearsen/.

Azarova. Valentina. 2017. "Israel's Unlawfully Prolonged Occupation: Consequences Under an Integrated Legal Framework." European Council on Foreign Relations, June 2. www.ecfr.eu/publications/summary/israels_unlawfully_prolonged_occupation_7294.

Beinin, Joel. 1993. "Money, Media and Policy Consensus: The Washington Institute for Near East Policy." *Middle East Report*, January/February. www.merip.org/mer/mer180/money-media-policy-consensus.

Benari, Elad, and Ido Ben Porat. 2014. "Bennett: First Gush Etzion, Then All of Judea and Samaria." *Arutz Sheva*, May 30. www.israelnationalnews.com/News/News.aspx/181200#.U4gX7fldXs8.

Berger, Yotam, and Barak Ravid. 2016. "U.S: Israeli Demolition of Palestinian Village Sussia Would Be 'Very Troubling.'" *Haaretz*, August 10.

B'Tselem. 2017a. "East Jerusalem." *B'Tselem.org*, November 11. https://www.btselem.org/jerusalem.

B'Tselem. 2017b. "Statistics on Settlements and Settler Population." *B'Tselem.org*, May 11. https://www.btselem.org/settlements/statistics.

B'Tselem and HaMoked. 2005. "One Big Prison: Freedom of Movement to and from the Gaza Strip on the Eve of the Disengagement Plan." Joint B'Tselem and HaMoked Report, March. http://www.btselem.org/download/200503_gaza_prison_english.pdf.

Cheshin, Amir S., Bill Hutman, and Avi Melamed. 2001. *Separate and Unequal: The Inside Story of Israeli Rule in East Jerusalem*. Cambridge: Harvard University Press.

Domb, Yoel. 2017. "Elkin: Declaring Sovereignty Now Would Be a Mistake." *Arutz Sheva*, March 7. www.israelnationalnews.com/News/News.aspx/226254.

du Plessis, Max, Fatmeh El-Ajou, Victor Kattan, Michael Kearney, John Reynolds, Rina Rosenberg, Iain Scobbie, and Virginia Tilley. 2009. *Occupation, Colonialism, Apartheid? A Re-assessment of Israel's Practices in the Occupied Palestinian Territories Under International Law*. Cape Town: Human Sciences Research Council.

Edelman, Ofra. 2017. "Lapid Drops Demand for Palestinian State." *Haaretz*, March 26. www.haaretz.com/israel-news/.premium-1.779437.

Friedman, Thomas. 1987. "How Long Can Israel Deny Its Civil War?" *New York Times*, December 27.

Gordon, Neve. 2013. "Yair Lapid: The Southern Man and His Cosmopolitan Ghetto." *Al Jazeera*, February 12. www.aljazeera.com/indepth/opinion/2013/02/2013211112856254494.html.

Gross, Aeyal. 2017. *The Writing on the Wall: Rethinking the International Law of Occupation*. Cambridge: Cambridge University Press.

Haaretz Staff. 2016. "Only Four of 20 Israeli Ministers Openly Declare Support of Two-State Solution." *Haaretz*, June 27. www.haaretz.com/israelnews/1.727431.

Herzog, Isaac. 2017. "Isaac Herzog Details His 10-Point Plan for Israeli-Palestinian Peace." *Haaretz*, February 23. www.haaretz.com/israel-news/.premium-1.773312.

Hoffman, Gil Stern. 2015a. "Isaac Herzog: I Don't Say the Word 'Peace' so I Don't Raise Expectations." *The Jerusalem Post*, March 1. www.jpost.com/Israel-Elections/Herzog-I-dont-say-the-word-peace-so-I-dont-raise-expectations-392623.

Hoffman, Gil Stern. 2015b. "Zionist Union Platform Aims to Set Israel's Final Borders." *The Jerusalem Post*, March 8. https://www.jpost.com/Israel-Elections/Zionist-Union-platform-aims-to-set-Israels-final-borders-393308.

Human Rights Watch. 2015. "Israel: Court Permits Discriminatory Evictions." *HRW.org*, May 19. https://www.hrw.org/news/2015/05/19/israel-court-permits-discriminatory-evictions.

Human Rights Watch. 2016. "Occupation, Inc.: How Settlement Businesses Contribute to Israel's Violations of Palestinian Rights." *HRW.org*, January 19. https://www.hrw.org/report/2016/01/19/occupation-inc/how-settlement-businesses-contribute-israels-violations-palestinian.

i24NEWS Staff. 2015. "Netanyahu Slams French Proposal for Foreign Observers in Jerusalem." *I24NEWS*, October 18. https://www.i24news.tv/en/news/israel/diplomacy-defense/89389-151018-israel-s-us-envoy-refutes-claim-that-settlements-linked-to-current-violence.

i24NEWS Staff. 2016. "Give Palestinians Autonomy but Not State, Bennett Says." *i24NEWS*, June 5. www.i24news.tv/en/news/israel/diplomacyde-fense/115655-160605-give-palestinians-autonomy-but-not-statebennett-says.

International Criminal Court. 2014. "Situation on Registered Vessels of Comoros, Greece and Cambodia." Article 53(1) Report, November 6. https://www.icc-cpi.int/iccdocs/otp/OTP-COM-Article_53(1)-Report-06Nov2014Eng.pdf.

Keating, Michael, Anne Le More, and Robert Lowe, eds. 2005. *Aid, Diplomacy and Facts on the Ground: The Case of Palestine*. London: Chatham House.

Klein, Menachem. 2017. "Trump Is Just What Netanyahu Needs to Annex the West Bank." *+972 Magazine*, February 10. https://972mag.com/trump-is-justwhat-netanyahu-needs-to-annex-the-west-bank/125141/.

Lazaroff, Tovah. 2016. "Netanyahu Was Right, Transferring Jews Is Ethnic Cleansing." *The Jerusalem Post*, November 23. https://www.jpost.com/Arab-Israeli-Conflict/Netanyahu-was-right-transferring-Jews-is-ethnic-cleansing-473425.

Lieber, Dov. 2016. "UN: Israel 'Systematically' Emptying Area C of Palestinians." *The Times of Israel*, July 28. www.timesofisrael.com/un-israel-systematicallyempting-area-c-of-palestinians.

Lis, Jonathan. 2016. "Labor Adopts Herzog's Plan for Separation from Palestinians as Party Platform." *Haaretz*, February 8. www.haaretz.com/israelnews/.premium-1.702002.

Lubell, Maayan. 2015. "Netanyahu Says No Palestinian State as Long as He's Prime Minister." *Reuters*, March 16. www.reuters.com/article/us-israel-electionidUSKBN0MC1I820150316.

Lustick, Ian. 1985. *The 'Irreversibility' of Israel's Annexation of the West Bank and Gaza Strip: A Critical Evaluation*. US Defense Intelligence Agency.

Mamdani, Mahmoud. 2015. "The South African Moment." *Journal of Palestine Studies* 45 (1): 63–68.

McCarthy, Rory. 2010. "Barak: Make Peace with Palestinians or Face Apartheid." *The Guardian*, February 3. https://www.theguardian.com/world/2010/feb/03/barak-apartheid-palestine-peace.

Misgav, Uri. 2017. "Israeli Lawmaker Miki Zohar Wants to Annex the West Bank, What on Earth Is People's Problem with Him?" *Haaretz*, March 9. https://www.haaretz.com/opinion/.premium-what-on-earth-is-people-s-problem-with-miki-zohar-1.5446450.

Morag, Gilad. 2015. "Netanyahu: Left Knows If Likud Is in Power, No Concessions Will Be Made." *Ynetnews*, March 15. www.ynetnews.com/articles/0,7340,L-4637305,00.html.

PCBS. n.d. "Estimated Number of Palestinians in the World by Country of Residence End Year 2015." Palestinian Central Bureau of Statistics. http://www.pcbs.gov.ps/Portals/_Rainbow/Documents/Population%20e%20s.htm.

Penina, Eilberg-Schwartz. 2016. "There Is No Green Line When It Comes to Home Demolitions." *+972 Magazine*, August 17. https://972mag.com/there-is-no-greenline-when-it-comes-to-home-demolitions/121206.

Ravid, Barak. 2017. "Israeli Minister to Present Cabinet with Proposal to Annex Dozens of Jerusalem-Area Settlements." *Haaretz*, January 22. www.haaretz.com/israel-news/.premium-1.766618.

Rogin, Josh. 2014. "Exclusive: Kerry Warns Israel Could Become 'An Apartheid State.'" *The Daily Beast*, April 27. https://www.thedailybeast.com/exclusive-kerry-warns-israel-could-become-an-apartheid-state.

Said, Edward. 1998. "A Real State Means Real Work." *Al-Ahram Weekly*, October 1–7. http://weekly.ahram.org.eg/Archive/1998/397/op1.htm.

Salamanca, Omar Jabary, Mezna Qato, Kareem Rabie, and Sobhi Samour. 2012. "Past Is Present: Settler Colonialism in Palestine." *Settler Colonial Studies* 2 (1): 1–8.

Shalev, Chemi. 2014. "Should Abbas' Peace Talks Deadline Be the Last Chance for a Two-State Solution?" *Haaretz*, September 3.

Sheizaf, Noam. 2017. "The Settlers' Goal Is Not the Settlements." *+972 Magazine*, June 8. https://972mag.com/the-settlers-goal-is-not-the-settlements/127948/.

Sherwood, Harriet. 2013. "Naftali Bennett Interview: 'There Won't Be a Palestinian State Within Israel.'" *The Guardian*, January 7. www.theguardian.com/world/2013/jan/07/naftali-bennett-interview-jewish-home.

Spetalnick, Matt. 2016. "U.S., Israel Sign $38 Billion Military Aid Package." *Reuters*, September 14. https://www.reuters.com/article/us-usa-israel-statement/u-s-israel-sign-38-billion-military-aid-package-idUSKCN11K2CI.

Tartir, Alaa. 2015. "The Evolution and Reform of Palestinian Security Forces 1993–2013." *Stability: International Journal of Security and Development* 4 (1): Art. 46.

Tartir, Alaa, and Jeremy Wildeman. 2013. "Can Oslo's Failed Aid Model Be Laid to Rest?" *Al-Shabaka*, September 18. https://al-shabaka.org/briefs/can-oslos-failed-aid-model-be-laid-rest/.

Tilley, Virginia, ed. 2012. *Beyond Occupation: Apartheid, Colonialism and International Law in the Occupied Palestinian Territories*. London: Pluto Press.

Tilley, Virginia. 2015. "After Oslo, a Paradigm Shift? Redefining Sovereignty, Responsibility and Self-Determination in Israel-Palestine." *Conflict, Security and Development* 15 (5): 425–453.

United Nations. 2009. "Security Council Calls for Immediate, Durable, Fully Respected Ceasefire in Gaza Leading to Full Withdrawal of Israeli Forces." *UN Press Release*, January 8. https://www.un.org/press/en/2009/sc9567.doc.htm.

United Nations. 2011. "Resolution Adopted by the General Assembly [on the Report of the Second Committee (A/65/443)]: Permanent Sovereignty of the Palestinian People in the Occupied Palestinian Territory, Including East Jerusalem, and of the Arab Population in the Occupied Syrian Golan Over Their Natural Resources." A/RES/65/179, March 22. https://unispal.un.org/DPA/DPR/unispal.nsf/5ba47a5c6cef541b802563e000493b-8c/3f8f382bf9874a50852578770064392b?OpenDocument.

UN OCHA. 2009. "Restricting Space: The Planning Regime Applied by Israel in Area C of the West Bank." *UN OCHA Special Focus*, December. https://www.ochaopt.org/sites/default/files/special_focus_area_c_demolitions_december_2009.pdf.

UN OCHA. 2016. "East Jerusalem: Palestinians at Risk of Eviction." *OCHAOPT.org*, November 3. https://www.ochaopt.org/content/east-jerusalem-palestinians-risk-eviction.

UN OCHA. 2017. "Record Number of Demolitions and Displacements in the West Bank During 2016." *OCHAOPT.org*, February 10. https://www.ochaopt.org/content/record-number-demolitions-and-displacements-west-bank-during-2016.

UNSCO. 2017. "Report to the Ad Hoc Liaison Committee, Office of the UN Special Coordinator for the Middle East Peace Process." Report to the Ad Hoc Liaison Committee, Brussels, May. https://unsco.unmissions.org/sites/default/files/unsco_report_to_ahlc_-_1_may_2017.pdf.

US State Department. n.d. "Country Reports on Human Rights Practices for 2016: Israel and the Occupied Territories." www.state.gov/j/drl/rls/hrrpt/humanrightsreport/index.htm?year=2016&dlid=265500#wrapper.

Vile, Shlomo. 2016. "Lapid: 'I'm the Only Alternative to Netanyahu.'" *Arutz Sheva*, December 11. www.israelnationalnews.com/News/News.aspx/221538.

Weizman, Eyal. 2007. *Hollow Land: Israel's Architecture of Occupation*. London: Verso.

White, Ben. 2015. "The Zionist Union's Plan for a Palestinian Bantustan." *Middle East Monitor*, March 10. www.middleeastmonitor.com/20150310-the-zionist-unions-plan-for-a-palestinian-bantustan.

White, Ben. 2017. "Exclusive: Amnesty Pledges to Consider If Israel Is Committing Apartheid." *Middle East Monitor*, November 21. https://www.middleeastmonitor.com/20171121-exclusive-amnesty-pledges-to-consider-if-israel-is-committing-apartheid.

White, Ben. 2018. *Cracks in the Wall: Beyond Apartheid in Palestine/Israel*. London: Pluto Press.

White House. 2017. "Remarks by President Trump and Prime Minister Netanyahu of Israel in Joint Press Conference." *WhiteHouse.gov*, February 15. https://www.whitehouse.gov/briefings-statements/remarks-president-trump-prime-minister-netanyahu-israel-joint-press-conference/.

Yesh Atid. n.d. "Security and Foreign Relations Platform." *YeshAtid.org*. www.yeshatid.org.il/defense?languagecode=en.

Yiftachel, Oren. 2009. "'Creeping Apartheid' in Israel/Palestine." *Middle East Report*, Winter. www.merip.org/mer/mer253/creeping-apartheidisrael-palestine.

Zreik, Raef. 2004. "Palestine, Apartheid and the Rights Discourse." *Journal of Palestine Studies* 34 (1): 68–80.

Zur, Yarden. 2018. "Israel's Creeping Annexation: Knesset Votes to Extend Israeli Law to Academic Institutions in the West Bank." *Haaretz*, February 12. https://www.haaretz.com/israel-news/israel-votes-to-expand-israeli-law-to-academic-institutions-in-w-bank-1.5810994.

CHAPTER 3

Sovereign Bodies, Sovereign States: Settler Colonial Violence and the Visibility of Resistance in Palestine

Timothy Seidel

Introduction

Signed in 1993, the Oslo Accords is the overarching political framework defining relations between Israel and the Palestinian Authority (PA). It was intended as an interim agreement toward a final settlement based on UN Resolution 242, leading to the creation of a Palestinian State alongside Israel. This "two-state solution" has not been realized and Israel continues its military, settler colonial occupation (Salamanca et al. 2012).[1] In 1995, the Oslo Accords II officially divided the West Bank into Areas A, B, and C (see Fig. 2.1). Area A is made up of the West Bank's major Palestinian population centers, and falls under the Palestinian Authority's civil and security control. In Area B, Palestinians have control over civil affairs, while Israel maintains security control. Area C falls under full Israeli control. Making up roughly 62% of the occupied West Bank,

---

T. Seidel (✉)
Department of Applied Social Sciences and Center for Justice and Peacebuilding, Eastern Mennonite University, Harrisonburg, VA, USA
e-mail: timothy.seidel@emu.edu

© The Author(s) 2019
A. Tartir and T. Seidel (eds.),
Palestine and Rule of Power, Middle East Today,
https://doi.org/10.1007/978-3-030-05949-1_3

Area C is the only contiguous territory in the West Bank, containing the majority of Palestinian agricultural and grazing land as well as land reserves that could be used for future economic development. However, Palestinians cannot create permanent structures in Area C without a permit from the Israeli Civil Administration (MA'AN 2012; Tartir and Challand 2017).

Economic relations between Israel and the Palestinian Authority were outlined in the Paris Protocols, an interim agreement signed in 1994 as part of Oslo (B'Tselem 2012; Arafeh 2018). Like the larger Oslo framework, the Paris Protocols were meant to be an interim agreement. Over twenty years on, the Palestinian economy is still dependent on Israel's economy, with Israel maintaining full control over Palestinian exports and imports, including international aid money.[2] As the MA'AN Development Center points out, the Paris Protocols,

> as part of the Oslo Accords, further punctuate the problematic nature of the state-building model and the terms of international development in the oPt. Without the ability to prioritize Palestinian economic self-sufficiency, as well as social and political rights and control over local development, the State of Israel remains the ultimate decision-maker over every facet of Palestinian life. (2012, 6)

For many, this signaled another stage in Israel's "de-development" of Palestine (Roy 1995; Turner and Shweiki 2014; Farsakh 2016). Sara Roy's seminal work on the Gaza Strip is known for its articulation of this political and economic concept. As she defines it, de-development is the "systematic de-construction of an indigenous economy by a dominant power," with the aim of dispossessing them from the means to "create an economic base to support an independent and indigenous existence" (1995, 4). Key for Roy's analysis is the existence of two distinct political national entities, not simply two economies, within the same geographic space, in which the Israeli part is dispossessing the Palestinian part, arguing that Israel seeks "to dispossess Palestinians of their resources and of their land, as part of its ideological goal of building a strong and exclusive Jewish state" (124).

The physical fragmentation of the West Bank—and of the West Bank from Gaza—along with Israel's settlement expansion and its complete control over the Palestinian economy, has demonstrated not only the ineffectiveness but the disempowering effects of the territorial divisions outlined in the Oslo Accords. "[T]his existing political arrangement, in which Palestinian communities exist in mere enclaves of villages and cities, makes economic, political, and social development for a future state extremely difficult" (MA'AN 2012, 5; see UN OCHA 2017).

This political and economic geography of occupied Palestinian territory (oPt) presents significant constraints to Palestinian livelihoods. And yet the story of many Palestinian communities is not one of resignation but of steadfastness and resistance. This chapter will explore the ways in which this resistance is rendered visible or invisible, with particular attention to the ways in which the violence of Israel's settler colonial occupation is rendered invisible through its linkage to concepts of sovereignty—concepts of sovereignty and the state that erase bodily violence and bodily resistance to that violence (via the state's claims of sovereignty).[3]

It explores this conversation with particular attention to Mbembe's (2003) description of sovereignty as "the capacity to dictate who may live and who must die" (11) alongside Seth's (2011) reference to sovereignty as "the name and form of a capacity to impose and stabilize meanings" (182). Particular attention is given to how religion and religious identity presents challenges to the liberal state and its claims. The point is not to present religious identity and religious community as an alternative to the state, but to point out the secular–religious binary that the state's claims to sovereignty rest upon, and destabilize that binary so as to decenter the state and center embodied political agency.

In this way, this chapter will examine the state decentered as an actor in international politics while attempting to center the "everyday" in a way that renders bodies, bodily resistance, and embodied political agency visible. This also aids in the recognition of how transnational solidarities constitute (civil society) actors presenting alternatives to the state. By interrogating the state and the state's claims to sovereignty particularly in the context of settler colonial occupation, we can see additional landscapes or maps of resistance. This resistance is rendered invisible because the violence—of the state—is invisible. This is what sovereignty does. It erases its own violence while rendering others like Palestinians as violent, as something they cannot not be. The claim this chapter makes is that a focus on bodies helps us visibilize, helps us see the violence and the resistance as embodied subjectivity. Attention to embodied subjectivities not only challenge the centrality of the state in our political and geographic imaginations but also takes the embodied experiences of Palestinians as a starting point for talking about political claims and resistance.

State (Sovereign) Maps, Borders, and Violence

The Secular Bias, the Erasure of Bodies, and the Postsecular Challenge

In his essay "The Aftermaths of Sovereignty: Postcolonial Criticism and the Claims of Political Modernity," David Scott looks to histories of communist collapse and liberal triumphalism and argues that we inhabit a "reconfigured cognitive-political space" that requires we rethink the story of liberalism and democracy that has informed our vision of political sovereignty. Put another way, Scott says:

> insofar as this triumphalist story of Western liberalism inscribes the non-Western into its privileged *telos*...it becomes imperative for postcolonial criticism to begin to fold into its practice a criticism that distances itself from the Enlightenment project of both Marxism and liberalism and that constructs a problematized relation to the claims and the categories of political modernity. (1996, 15)

Scott begins to do this by focusing on post-Marxist notions of radical democracy. And observes that, while working to come to terms with this historical moment, they are nonetheless "animated by the view that the ideals of liberal democracy—those of liberty and equality—are an unsurpassable political horizon requiring only better arguments than those so far deployed to secure them" (17). Two problems in particular concern Scott here. The first relates to the normalization of modernity and democracy that emerges in the narrative of radical democracy (in particular its presentation of democracy as a "world-historical plateau" that has displaced all other forms of political order and to which all orders should be judged). The second problem relates to the conception of power on which this story of political modernity depends (namely a conception of power as "indeterminate," emerging in "empty space").

Scott has identified an important line of critical inquiry, and in this chapter I will attempt to extend this critique to an interrogation of the concept of sovereignty and its implications for talking about political violence, resistance, and local dissent. This critical inquiry relates to Talal Asad's (2003) observation that the liberal nation-state is paradoxically required to define the genuinely religious in order to lay claim to the secular. Similarly, William Cavanaugh argues that the religious-secular distinction does not identify facts about the world but rather "authorizes certain arrangements of power in the modern West" (2009, 226). The "myth of religious violence," argues Cavanaugh, replicates "a story of salvation from mortal peril by the creation of the secular nation-state," and the construction of that story identifies "Others and enemies, both internal and external, who threaten the social order and who provide the requisite villains against which the nation-state is said to protect us" (226). The result, suggests Cavanaugh, is that the characterization of religion in this story "legitimizes the direction of the citizen's ultimate loyalty to the nation-state and secures the nation-state's monopoly on legitimate violence" (226).

Mavelli and Petitio (2012) discuss this in terms of the "secular bias" at work within International Relations (IR) that limits the discipline's engagement with the "postsecular." They explain this by pointing to the narrative that surrounds the discipline "with its mythical origin dating back to the peace of Westphalia" (933). This "Westphalian presumption" has inscribed secularism "in the genetic code of the discipline of International Relations, turning secularism into a condition of possibility for IR, rather than an object of its inquiry" (933). One effect of this bias is its reproduction of another binary, the mind/body distinction, and its impact on the categories of critique and resistance that obscure forms of embodied political agency. The postsecular challenge, argues Mavelli (2012), is to move beyond the Kantian-Habermasian cognitive tradition of secularity, giving attention to traditions that articulate "modes of subjectivity beyond the mind/ body dualism" or disclose "the power/ knowledge inscriptions of existing secular formations" (1077).[4]

Mavelli attempts to show that the "postsecular" involves rethinking the mind/body as well as the secular/religious binaries (neither of which are natural divides but are instead both produced by multiple regimes of power and knowledge), offering "a new critical edge to reconsider the very categories of critique and resistance by interrogating and questioning the boundary between the secular and the religious, turning this boundary into a space in which new forms of embodied political agency and imagination may be observed" (1078).

This speaks to the discursive boundaries set by dominant political and economic geographies. As both Cavanaugh and Asad point out, the secular/religious binary is one of many expressions of the us/them, modern/traditional, civilized/uncivilized distinctions that provides a reason for the state. And critical to the state's claims to sovereignty are its claims to violence, or more precisely selectively identifying and condemning certain forms of violence, such as torture, while ignoring or authorizing other horrible forms of violence, particularly those forms deemed essential to the life of the state, namely war (and in Israel's case, settler colonial occupation).

The hegemony of liberalism (and the liberal peace project) as *the* political (and economic) horizon ("end of history") obscures the violence required for its (liberal) peace. This inquiry is relevant because it opens up space for decentering the state. And this is important because the state's centrality is so natural that it presents deep constraints and limitations to our political imaginations, producing categories of sovereignty and resistance that obscure forms of embodied political agency.[5] There are of course many ways to talk about sovereignty, however many turn on these question of violence, bodies, and borders.

Bodies, Borders, and Violence

Paul Kahn's discussion on sovereignty begins with the claim that politics is based on sacrifice, not contract, where terror and torture—reciprocal rituals of pain creating and sustaining political meaning—"press up against the sacrificial character of the state" (2008, 12). This sacrificial character provides both political meaning and power for the sovereign, making torture "a form of sacrifice that inscribes on the body a sacred presence" (25).

A key point for Kahn, which explains why torture is so vigorously debated, are the conflicting social imaginaries we have for establishing political meaning: "an imaginative structure of law, on the one hand, and of sovereignty on the other" (12). Herein lies the question for Kahn: "Does an imagined space remain for a practice of sovereignty beyond law?" If politics creates meaning through sacrifice, Kahn argues, and if political meaning enters the world though the killing and being killed of war, "we take our first step toward torture when we take up arms in defense of the state. This is the step from law to sovereignty" (14). Torture and terror are the necessary instruments of the sovereign's sacred claim over bodies. And attempting to use law to check the sovereign is to engage in self-deception: "We can dream of peace; we can imagine a global order of perfect lawfulness. But we dream of these things from a position deep within the political formation of a state that has its origins in violence, that will maintain itself though violence, and that claims a unique right to demand sacrifice of all its citizens. Before there is terror or torture, there is a political imagination that finds ultimate meanings in acts of killing and being killed" (14).

Achille Mbembe (2003) describes sovereignty as "the capacity to dictate who may live and who must die" (11) and "to define who matters and who does not, who is disposable and who is not" (27).[6] He relates this to what he calls "necropolitics"—the subjugation of life to the power of death. In the era of necropower, weapons are deployed "in the interest of maximum destruction of persons and the creating of *death-worlds*, new and unique forms of social existence in which vast populations are subjected to conditions of life conferring upon them the status of *living dead*" (40). Mbembe identifies this as a key element of late-modern colonial occupation, characterized as it is by the combining of the disciplinary, the biopolitical, and the necropolitical. Important for this discussion is Mbembe's assertion that the "most accomplished form of necropower is the contemporary colonial occupation of Palestine" (27).

Mbembe observes that the late-modern colonial occupation in Gaza and the West Bank presents three major characteristics in relation to the working of the specific terror formation he calls necropower. These characteristics include territorial fragmentation, vertical sovereignty, and splintering occupation. These three characteristics are evidence of a state of siege where "entire populations are the target of the sovereign" (30). So for Mbembe, the Palestinian case illustrates late-modern colonial occupation as a chain of multiple powers—disciplinary, biopolitical, and necropolitical—that results in absolute domination over the inhabitants of the occupied territory.

Kahn's discussion on the sacred and Mbembe's on the necropolitical offer critical perspectives on the articulation of sovereignty by the state—articulated and inscribed in spatial and bodily locations. One way these inscriptions are made known is through borders. Borders are primarily conceptualized as delimiting the scope of state action. However, borders are not a natural phenomenon and only come about as a result of state action. Like other forms of state action, they ultimately depend on the state's monopoly of violence. Borders also, when articulated in terms of security, play both a material and discursive function within global capitalism. Derek Gregory (2004) describes the (large-scale) impact of global capitalism as an aggressively de-territorializing force, "moving ever outwards in a process of ceaseless expansion, furiously tearing down barriers to capital accumulation" (253). Meanwhile colonial modernity is intrinsically territorializing, "forever installing partitions between 'us' and 'them'" (253). What this means is that global capitalism's impact depends on who you are and where you are. "The globe shrinks for those who own it," Homi Bhabha once remarked, but "for the displaced or the dispossessed, the migrant or refugee, no distance is more awesome then the few feet across borders or frontiers" (257). This figure of the refugee, adds Gregory, throws into crisis what Giorgio Agamben called the "originary fiction of sovereignty" because "it calls into question the connective imperative that makes *nativity* the foundation of *nationality* and hence of the sovereign space of the *nation-state*. The refugee is, figuratively and physically, a border figure who, if not excluded or confined, threatens to perforate the territorial integrity of the state" (258).[7]

In summary, this discussion on sovereignty focuses on bodies at a number of levels. First by taking up the postsecular challenge and interrogating the mind/body distinction and its effects, we give attention to modes of subjectivity beyond this dualism that decenter the state and with which new forms of embodied political agency and imagination may be observed. At another level this discussion underscored the violence of the state's claims to sovereignty not least in terms of the manner in which that sovereignty, through borders and barriers, marks flesh and is inscribed on bodies. This interrogation of sovereignty aids in our decentering of the state and the centering of embodied subjectivities as we explore expressions of resistance and local dissent in Palestine.

Counter-Maps, Global Politics, and Transnational Solidarities

The point that global politics and international relations are defined not only by states leads to the consideration of a range of non-state actors that interact with states and international organizations. The term "civil society" is often used to refer to the arena constituted by those non-state actors. The transnational networks that emerge and that structure interactions among those actors can be constituted in a number of ways (see Keck and Sikkink 1998).

This includes transnational solidarities that do not take the state as the reference point, but instead sees that reference point in terms of one's participation in other imagined communities, located on other imagined maps. As Asad has described it in his discussion on complex time and space, these transnational solidarities express a range of multiple and overlapping identities that contest the borders and the claims of the sovereign state.[8]

From a different angle, Michael Hardt (1995) has claimed that we have moved into a "postcivil society"—from a disciplinary society to a society of control—where "new potentialities for contestation and freedom" (41) have emerged. He suggests that to imagine or begin to recognize these new possibilities, we should investigate the form and nature of labor, of creative social practices, in contemporary society. He says:

> The networks of sociality and forms of cooperation embedded in contemporary social practices constitute the germs for a new movement, with new forms of contestation and new conceptions of liberation. This alternative community of social practices (call it, perhaps, the self-organization of concrete labor) will be the most potent challenge to the control of postcivil society, and will point, perhaps, to the community of our future. (41)

In Palestine, what glimpses are there of an "alternative community of social practices" or "the self-organization of concrete labor"? Tariq Dana (2014) hints at this in his discussion of a resistance economy in Palestine. He defines a resistance economy as an "institutionalized form of economic struggle that envisages a transitional reorganization of the economy and social relations to be in harmony with the political requirements and objectives of the Palestinian national liberation process" (1).[9] Decades ago, Raja Khalidi (1985) described "an economy of resistance" in terms of *sumud* or steadfastness.[10] This work challenges a strict political approach to ending the military occupation of Palestine, highlighting the necessary political and economic elements of the situation—and any solution—in Palestine.

More recently, in his discussion contentious politics and economics,[11] Alaa Tartir (2015) describes a resistance economy as "a model that understands the development process as a cumulative, complementary, economic, social, and political one that fundamentally seeks to liberate human beings from dependency and humiliation" (489). He also identifies its liberatory potential as:

> a process that sets out to emancipate human beings by freeing them from poverty, inequality, fear, and oppression, empowering them to cultivate their lands, and expanding their options, capabilities, and potentials to ensure their happiness. As such, this socially inclusive model rejects economic unity with the colonizing power and resists attempts to sustain the status of asymmetric containment. In other words, the model

is the opposite of the Paris Protocol, working at dismantling the regime of oppression and acting as a model that is socially inclusive, and that can ultimately play a role in ending the occupation and colonization of Palestine. (489)

The remainder of this chapter will explore this discourse on resistance and local dissent that incorporates elements of land, small-scale farming, settler colonial occupation, neoliberalism, and global solidarity. In addition to drawing from humanitarian reports and policy analyses, this chapter draws from my own fieldwork in Palestine–Israel with interviews conducted across a range of civil society organizations in January and September 2015.[12] My argument is that Palestinian discourses on political economy present alternative maps and narratives of resistance, especially in the context of Israeli settler colonialism, to neoliberal political, economic, and ecological orderings of life in late colonial modernity.

These maps and narratives of resistance and local dissent become visible when we center bodies and embodied political agency and decenter the state as the only actor that matters in international politics. They can be *heard* in the narration of small-scale farmers as a critical front in Palestinians' struggle for freedom, presenting alternative development models based on economies of resistance and steadfastness. They can be *seen* in the efforts of Palestinian social solidarities that work to link popular, grassroots work and the struggle to defend land—underscoring the central role that land plays in settler colonial struggles—and their "everyday" efforts that attempt to defend political, social and economic rights and reinforce international solidarity with their struggles.

"Improving People's Lives Is Resistance"

Palestinian Land Defense Coalition

Al-Walajah is a village in the West Bethlehem area in Palestine. Several years ago I along with members of the local popular committee visited a house that sits on the path of the Wall that was to be surrounded on all four sides by a 30-foot high concrete wall.[13] We heard how family and friends will need to obtain Israeli military-issued permits just to visit this family in their home. And what's more, the Israeli military was building a tunnel for the family to move in and out of their house. They will need to pass through a tunnel, underground, to leave and enter their own house. One of the residents asked, "where is the right for our children to live a normal life?"

After we visited with this family, we walked down the dirt road to another home. As we did, one of the popular committee members stopped us and began to describe the old farmer we were about to visit. His name was Abu Nidal. "Abu Nidal, he's an old farmer. But sometimes, when we younger folks, when we are tired and discouraged from resisting, when we feel like we have nothing left, we go to Abu Nidal and he inspires us. After listening to him, we come away determined to continue, to be steadfast." And as we were walking down the dirt path to Abu Nidal's home, I could already see the tenacious character of his steadfast resistance. As we were walking, this popular committee member pointed off to a nearby field that was to soon be cut off from Abu Nidal by the path of the Wall. A field holding the graves of grandparents and other family members. And despite the imminent path of the Wall, what had Abu Nidal done? He had planted scores of fruit trees.

As we sat drinking tea, we listened to Abu Nidal and members from the popular committee describe experiences of injustice, like the family in al-Walajah. And then, at the end, Abu Nidal says, "but I am hopeful." He went on to describe how thieves always live in fear and that this wall is a wall of fear and that their land will be returned some day. I have returned to that area in al-Walajah since then, seen the Wall completed, the land violated. Discouraged. And every time I look down at Abu-Nidal's farm, and see those trees, and remember his unrelenting hope. A hope not rooted in some clever political analysis of a seemingly intractable situation. But rather, it is a hope that is rooted in something much deeper. This tenacity, this hope, constitutes the *sumud* or steadfastness that defines a political economy of resistance.

One Palestinian initiative that works with this understanding and articulation of resistance is the Palestinian Land Defense Coalition. Based in Ramallah, it describes its work as "linking grassroots work and the struggle to defend the land." The Land Defense Coalition is a coalition of popular and grassroots organizations that

> seeks to join forces and efforts and coordinate their work in order to protect small farmers and marginalized social groups, especially agricultural workers, women and youth. We want to defend their political, social and economic rights and reinforce international solidarity with their struggles. (Palestinian Land Defense Coalition, n.d.)

This description reiterates the elements described above of a political economy of resistance: build a broad popular social movement for the defense of the land and rights of the people and strengthen the popular steadfastness of communities in areas threatened by Israeli policies of displacement and confiscation. There is a particular focus on working with youth, women, and farmers, to strengthen the ability of people from villages threatened with forced displacement and confiscation of land through the Wall and settlements, for example South Hebron, the Northern Jordan Valley, the eastern part of Nablus, and Bedouin areas. There is also a focus on Palestinian communities in Area C who are in imminent danger of forced displacement.[14]

The Palestinian Land Defense Coalition emerged as a response to needs across Palestinian social, political, and economic experiences, informing its understanding of popular resistance in terms of how it responds to those needs, involving and mobilizing various sectors like youth, women, trade unions, and farmer unions. As a staff member described:

> The issue is this movement should respond to the people's needs and represent them. So you have the farmers representing farmers issues, workers representing workers issues, struggling either internal or against the occupation, against the legislation of the PA and against the actions, for their needs as well, and also for their own national struggle for land, for rights, for work, against unemployment, for youth participation and decision making, all of these things are on the agenda. So when you talk about resistance, when you talk about movement, it's not going there and throwing stones. It is a wider and more strategic.[15]

The Palestinian Land Coalition grew out of a decade of popular struggle against the Wall. The Wall still cuts through Palestinian land, and so the land has become a more unifying rubric—again a key feature of settler colonial struggles:

> Everybody together, because our struggle is for our existence. So it's for our land. And that's what mainly the occupation is taking from our hands. The land is the main thing that brings us together, to struggle for our homeland. It's our rights.[16]

As mentioned above, the *sumud*, steadfastness, of a political economy of resistance reorients, even rearticulates, the discourse away from what the West wants Palestinians to say—a subaltern subject position which undermines or erases Palestinian political subjectivity—to what Palestinians want to say as they talk about their lives:

> This is how we should connect when we talk about popular resistance: how it responds to the people. It's not as a surface shallow thing that people think of, especially on our side. You don't have to limit yourself to a demonstration that is going on here or there. Resistance touches every part of your life. Going to school is a resistance. Improving people's life is resistance. Stopping demolitions is resistance. Supporting the steadfastness of the communities in their areas is resistance. Providing the means for the farmers to stay on their lands and to keep developing their work and their lands is resistance. The workers to have their rights, this is also resistance. Resistance is not just resistance against the occupation. It's resistance for rights.[17]

Using the language of rights speaks again to the ways this discourse articulates global or transnational elements, with its linkage to a transnational movement to resist neoliberal policies. And as a particular outpost in this global struggle, its expression in Palestine in terms of the rights and the needs of the people, it is articulated as resistance in these various aspects of life, that touches every aspect of Palestinian life, because it aids Palestinians in their struggle to stay on their land. This is why going to school is resistance, farming your land is resistance, because it is keeping people on their land.

Building both local and global social solidarities and networks is heard. The Coalition also works to mobilize popular initiatives, and widen grassroots participation, "to start thinking and strategizing widely beyond organizing a demonstration." It becomes a question of long-term, sustainable practices, "how to stand up with the farmers, how to stand up with the youth, how to stand up with the workers, how to stand up with the women. All these struggles. It's not just organizing an activity here and there."[18] This resonates with the theme of resistance discussed above in terms of building more inclusive, radically democratic institutions, and expanding grassroots network to build the capacity of Palestinians to resist.

There is also a reticence and at times suspicion of referring to this in terms of civil society. As one person put it: "Civil society is this imported NGOization terminology, which I don't know the meaning. I'm talking about grassroots movement." He identified the NGO sector as an "industry" that started "after Oslo and also mainly widely it started to take this shape after the falling of the Soviet Union. It started to replace the parties and the movements in a way or another. In Palestine it did a huge damage to the parties work." He interestingly described it in terms of the dislocation of resistance—a depopularization and de-communalism. And he connected it to the impact of Oslo on volunteerism in Palestinian society:

> Before Oslo, when we were involved in the movements, voluntary work was something basic. We didn't make it a slogan. But was part of our life. We being active in our parties, this is voluntary. Doing the work like olive picking, cleaning the streets, going to schools, popular teaching. It's all voluntary. Nobody asked for a payment. After Oslo it became taken over by NGOs and by new funding…It destroyed in a way the whole soul of voluntary work.[19]

Palestinian Farmers Union

The Land Defense Coalition also talks about its work in terms of resilience. Even here, this discourse articulates a term like resilience—which is increasingly used in international development circles—in terms of resistance. Resilience is understood in reference to *sumud*, steadfastness. "The resilience of the people. It is about something within all the people, not in a selective or a group of people. The resilience way of life."[20] With *sumud* the discursive connection is made to resistance, articulating resilience as something that empowers or equips Palestinians for resistance.[21]

A staff person from the Palestinian Farmers Union (PFU)—a member of the Land Defense Coalition—reiterates the point that resistance is already going on, that Palestinians are on the ground:

> One of them is the grass roots movements, popular resistance and popular grass roots movements, by working and interacting with people on the ground. Not as political leaders…but acting with people on the ground. What is needed now? Help Palestinians with resilience, helping them sustain and stay on their land. Protect their land and live in dignity at least, with a minimum of the requirement of dignity for them on daily basis. And this is what we in the Palestinian Farmers Union are trying to do, we work directly with farmers on the ground, and we know land is the core of the conflict in this area.[22]

In the face of expanding Israeli colonization and confiscation of Palestinian land, he described efforts "to help Palestinians stay on their land, cultivate their land, plant their land, protect their land and live with what they produce from their land." For example, the PFU supports farmers encountering legal problems with lands threatened with confiscations. They assist with establishing and maintaining agricultural roads or irrigation systems. PFU also lobbies and advocates on behalf of farmers to the Palestinian Authority, advocating for agriculture policies that respond to farmers' needs:

> If we want farmers to stay on their lands, they need appropriate policies, supportive laws, and support for their resilience to stay there… And land defense, you know, as part of land defense and as Palestinian Farmers' Union, we want to support farmers, because this is the front, the head front against settlers and occupation is protecting the land.[23]

As with farmers in the West Bethlehem area, food security and food sovereignty are reiterated in a political economy of resistance closely linked with farmers and farmers' presence on Palestinian land. In other words:

> keeping the farmers there, and sustaining our food security in this country. You know, not to destroy it, not to be like slaves, eating from what others produce for us and not from what we produce for ourselves. No. We want to eat the tomato we produce on our land. We want to eat the potato… everything, but from our land. And we have land to cultivate, to plant, and to produce from it. But what we expect from a government is to protect the farmer by adopting proper policies that are responsive, reflective to farmers' needs. And this is not something unique. It's applicable all over the world, wherever you go.[24]

Staff from the PFU underscored that this sort of resistance by Palestinian farmers was peaceful and nonviolent:

> you find them staying there, day and night, because to protect their land from confiscation, they have to be physically there so when settlers come… many of them were injured and some of them were killed. Of course, they believe what they are doing is really resistance. Resistance and protecting their own property. But it's part of the resistance movement. This is what they can do. They have no weapons. And they do not believe in weapons or military action. We don't support even this sector. But this is your land.

And part of peaceful resistance, the nonviolent movement in Palestine, starting from wherever to wherever. Everyone is engaged. Depending on his level of effort. We call it "resistance development," development based on resistance.[25]

Conclusion: The Visibility of Palestinian Resistance

A Palestinian staff person from the United Nations Office for the Coordination of Humanitarian Affairs (UN OCHA) described to me the "invisible occupation," the military occupation that seems to be less severe because of the apparent ease of movement throughout the occupied West Bank. The point he made that was even more salient was that if the occupation is invisible to the rest of the world, Palestinian resistance to the occupation—in its embodied, everyday forms of struggle through steadfastness (*sumud*), going to work, farming, going to school—is also invisible. This is key. If you can't even see the violence being inflicted on Palestinians, how would you see, or at least how would you have any discursive context for understanding and explaining, resistance? This is another reason why when the resistance becomes visible, its origins are obscured, invisible, and so the resistance does not visualize as resistance but as violence, violent aggression.

The impact on (a particular kind of) resistance by the neoliberal trends that have grown over the last decade is an important insight. From one perspective the economic development in Palestine has been a success, a crucial step in the liberalization process necessary for state-building. But this has only entrenched those "invisible" aspects of military occupation, that renders resistance invisible—like the Palestinian farmer who sleeps in their fields, not wanting to risk going back and forth through the checkpoint in the Wall separating him from his own land.

Critical to understanding the context of oPt is this everyday resistance that accompanies and even co-constitutes settler colonial projects. Drawing from Wolfe (2006), Dana and Jarbawi (2017) describe this settler colonialism as:

> fundamentally based on the operative logic of "eliminating the native" and failing to utterly marginalize and "minoritize" him. The vibrant Palestinian presence in the land, the everyday resistance to the colonial order, and the robust Palestinian adherence to their rights all stand as structural obstacles

to the ultimate realization of the "Zionist dream." Despite Israel's relentless colonial power and domination, Palestinian steadfastness means that this project will remain impeded and incomplete, a matter that may lead to its future demise. (197)

A critical feature of the discourse on a political economy of resistance is a reframing or renarrating of the context of Palestinian resistance in global terms, with its accompanying discussion of global neoliberal trends (see Haddad 2016) and transnational networks. This relocation of Palestinian resistance away from a rigid focus on Israel's military occupation expands toward a wider struggle against those neoliberal trends that accompany state-building.[26] This political economy of resistance presents alternative understandings of development as a set of practices for communities to resist instead of accommodating the neoliberal forces that understand them politically and economically as "undeveloped."

Another conclusion is that the category, the idea of political and economic development is always produced, constructed, and inscribes those political and economic trajectories that are acceptable, appropriate, even civilized. And so whatever the activity or practice, we can see it as good or nonviolent if it is aligned, for example, with our liberal values, with civility, or with our institutional, social, or political trajectories. It becomes bad, violent or not nonviolent when it transgresses those values and when it deviates from those trajectories. Then it is incivility. It is not civilized. It is bad. This relates to my opening comments on the religious/secular binary and the work that binaries such as these perform—civility and incivility, violence and nonviolence—and how those binaries are constructed in order to authorize certain kinds of practices and de-authorize other kinds.

Take the above examples of "agro-resistance" in the West Bank, of small-scale farmers as a resistance front (see Tartir et al. 2012; Sansour and Tartir 2014). These are Palestinian farmers who are good, who are not violent inasmuch as they conform to and align with the neoliberal trajectories of agribusiness, industrialization of the West Bank, and general conformity to Israel's domination of Palestinian land. They become bad farmers, bad Palestinians, when they transgress, when they refuse to conform not only to the colonizing impulses of Israel as a state seeking to dominate Palestinian land and resources, or to the PA's state-building agenda, but also when they transgress the larger global neoliberal trends of free markets, multinational business, etc.[27]

Destabilizing these categories have an impact on our observations of what's going on in a place like Palestine, giving attention to the silencing and erasure, the inaudibility and invisibility of resistance and local dissent. It reveals how something so mundane as cultivating farmland, herding sheep, and picking olives becomes a form of resistance embodied by Palestinians. As Rose Shinko (2010) argues, confirming that bodies do matter reinvests autonomy with "the creative and eruptive potential to disturb sedimentations of power that enmesh fleshy and living bodies."[28] These expressions of embodied subjectivity present a powerful challenge to the centrality of the state in our political and geographic imaginations and holds particular relevance, not least in terms of how these discourses open up space for articulations of political subjectivity that are embodied by Palestinians—that take the embodied experiences of Palestinians as a starting point for talking about political claims and resistance.

Notes

1. For more on settler colonialism, see Wolfe (2006) as well as the introduction to this volume by Seidel and Tartir.
2. Within the Oslo framework, questions of both political security and economic issues are subject to joint Israeli–Palestinian committees. In the context of an imbalanced power structure, "these joint committees have proven to simply act as an extension of the quiet control exerted by the Israeli Civil Administration" (MA'AN 2012, 6).
3. For more on this discussion of the political and economic geography of occupied Palestinian territory—and the violence and resistance that it produces—see Seidel (2017). A portion of this chapter is taken from that essay.
4. Mavelli (2012) draws from Foucault's discussion of a critical resistance centered on the body, which challenges the secular/religious divide and the secular as a power/knowledge regime. "In this approach, resistance is no longer the search for universal and transcendental structures to oppose the making and unmaking of power and history, but the endeavor to understand and disclose the inscriptions of power/knowledge regimes of domination onto the body, and to imagine these inscriptions as 'contingencies' which 'have made us what we are', but do not rule out the possibility of different ways of being" (1075).
5. This is another way to talk about sovereignty, i.e. stabilizing meaning. As Seth (2011) describes it postcolonial criticism has played an important role in identifying the role of knowledge "not simply as a 'mirror'

which represents the 'real,' but also as a potent force for shaping what is 'out there'—and has been especially sensitive to the many circumstances in which knowledges born in Europe are inadequate to their non-European object. In this, it should share a certain affinity with any discipline devoted to relationship, interconnection, diversity and discontinuity, such as IR. For 'the international' is a realm where endless and seemingly irresolvable contestations—over meanings and morals as much as resources and power—testify to the fact that few things have become so naturalised that they are not potentially subject to contestation, few presumptions so stabilised that they are not periodically destabilised" (182).

6. Mbembe draws from Frantz Fanon's spatial reading of colonial occupation, explaining that "colonial occupation entails first and foremost a division of space into compartments. It involves the setting of boundaries and internal frontiers epitomized by barracks and police stations; it is regulated by the language of pure force, immediate presence, and frequent and direct action; and it is premised on the principle of reciprocal exclusivity. But more important, it is the very way in which necropower operates: 'The town belonging to the colonized people...is a place of ill fame, peopled by men of evil repute. They are born there, it matters little where or how; they die there, it matters not where, nor how.' In this case, sovereignty means the capacity to define who matters and who does not, who is disposable and who is not" (26–27; quote from Fanon 1963, 39).

7. For more on borders, barriers, and "walls that act upon flesh," see Di Cintio (2014) and Seidel (forthcoming).

8. Since there is no such thing as absolute non-interference, Asad (2003) points out, "no action can be perfectly self-contained, but always impinges upon other people, so that spaces will always in some degree 'complexly' overlap, jurisdictions always in some measure be competing, loyalties remain (perhaps benignly) divided" (178). "One consequence of this fact," Asad says, "is that the sovereign state cannot (never could) contain all the practices, relations, and loyalties of its citizens" (179).

9. Classic works in the field of political economy in Palestine include Sayigh (1979), Zureik (1983), Abed (1989), and Roy (1995). For more recent analyses, see Farsakh (2016), Khalidi and Samour (2011), Turner and Shweiki (2014), Tabar and Salamanca (2015).

10. Jean Zaru (2008) describes the practice of *sumud* in terms of remaining "steadfast on one's land and, more generally, to remain steadfast in service to one's homeland and to the struggle for freedom. For example, given the current grave circumstances, just waking up every morning with the determination to carry on with one's daily routine and to hold fast to one's humanity in spite of the challenges and dangers in movement—walking through military checkpoints to get to work, driving your

children past army tanks to get to school, taking your herd out to graze despite physical and verbal abuse of Israeli settlers—is to practice *sumoud* or to be *samid* or *samida*" (71–72).
11. Drawing from, and expanding on, the concept of contentious politics (Tilly and Tarrow 2007) and Tartir (2015) describes contentious economics as a model that "advances the concepts of freedom and dignity as integral parts in exercising self-determination and in fulfilling and acquiring economic rights…confronting the multiple authorities of repression, oppression, and authoritarianism" (476). In this observation, he acknowledges that, while relevant to the case of Palestine, the concept of contentious economics can be seen in comparable experiences "in other parts of the world, for instance the notions of solidarity and self-reliance in the economies of Brazil, South Africa, Mexico, and even villages in Spain" (476).
12. This fieldwork was made possible by the financial support of Nonviolence International's Randall Research Scholarship and the American University Provost's Office Doctoral Student Research Award.
13. Begun in 2002, much of Israel's 430-mile Wall or Separation Barrier is not built along the Green Line—the internationally-recognized border between Israel and the Occupied Palestinian Territories. Instead, the Wall dips deep into the West Bank, expropriating Palestinian land (including rich agricultural land) in order to encompass illegal Israeli settlements. This has created a "seam zone," which comprises about 10% of the West Bank, and in which Palestinians are caught between the barrier and the Green Line. With the Wall in place, Palestinians must deal with a complicated checkpoint and closure regime in order to access farmland, jobs, schools, and other essential services. In 2004 the International Court of Justice in the Hague handed down an advisory opinion that declared the Wall illegal, violating international law including principles outlined in the United Nations Charter, and called for the immediate stop to construction, dismantle sections already built, and compensate Palestinians for any damages. Israel ignored this and continued with its construction.
14. The Coalition describes how "In 2013 Israel established a committee tasked to transfer Palestinian land previously confiscated as Israeli state land to the settlement blocks. As part of this process, one million dunum of West Bank land, which had been confiscated as 'military zones' is now being transformed into state land. In 2014, 46 thousand dunum of state land have already been transferred to settlements. Additionally, Israel consolidated the fragmentation of the West Bank systematically transforming strategic roads into 'Israeli--only' roads and making movement between the south, center and north of the West Bank ever more difficult if not impossible. Finally, the daily threat of the settlers to the

inhabitants of the threatened villages continues to increase" (Palestinian Land Defense Coalition, n.d.).
15. Interview, Ramallah, September 2015.
16. Interview, Ramallah, September 2015.
17. Interview, Ramallah, September 2015.
18. Interview, Ramallah, September 2015.
19. Interview, Ramallah, September 2015.
20. Interview, Ramallah, September 2015.
21. For a discussion on resilience and development, see Brown (2016). Brown takes a political ecology approach to resilience-based development with a "politicized and systems perspective on environment, development, and change" that highlights the relationships between political, economic, and social factors in applying an analysis of "power and politics, knowledge and knowing, rights, access and justice to understandings and applications of resilience" (13). Resistance becomes a key element for Brown in this approach because it "combines a concern for agency and individuals and collective action, with an understanding of the systemic dimensions of broader drivers and mediators of change…[implying] that the everyday forms of resilience are important, but they must be accompanied and supported by institutional and higher order support" (193). The emphasis on everyday forms of resilience is meant to "de-dramatise and de-centre the neoliberal prospectus, and put emphasis on human agency, collective action and knowledge, and 'everyday know-how'" (194).
22. Interview, Ramallah, September 2015.
23. Interview, Ramallah, September 2015.
24. Interview, Ramallah, September 2015.
25. Interview, Ramallah, September 2015.
26. For an interesting discussion relating human rights and the human right's industry to political subjectivity, nationalism, and state-building, see Perugini and Gordon (2015) and Allen (2013). For example, Allen points out how the human rights system "is one critical structure that mediates contests over the dynamics of nationalism, the nature of the Palestinian state and what kind of citizen should build it, and the national struggle against occupation and what kind of subject should undertake it" (9). Particularly interesting was Allen's exploration of the role of human rights training for PA security forces and how it fits into a larger understanding of the modern state. Here Allen returns to the notion of state as performance, and in this case performance for a particular audience—especially the international states and donors from whom emerge funding and legitimacy. The building of a professional security service is "understood to be a necessary element of within the assumed teleology

of creating a 'modern state'" (116). But the transparency of this bureaucratized attitude is not lost particularly on critics of the PA who find objectionable "the pseudo-state's dangerously denationalized approach to the public and the state-building project" (118).

27. And following Fanon (1963) and Mbembe's (2003) discussion on Fanon and necropolitics in Palestine—it is impossible for Palestinians in that situation to not be violent. Anything they do, however nonviolent you could objectively demonstrate, would be discursively articulated as violent because of their subject position in that dominant discourse.

28. Shinko (2010) identifies in autonomous bodies a space that "opens political pathways for resistance against those disciplinary and repressive forces which would separate us, individuate us and prevent us from recasting our autonomy in more relational terms." Lauren Wilcox (2014) discusses the implications for considering embodied subjectivity. She observes that "contemporary forces of capitalism and militarization have demanded an ever more flexible body, one that can be known and thus intervened upon and made to work 'better' and more productively, while creating other bodies as killable or disposable" (364).

References

Abed, George T. 1989. "The Political Economy of Resistance in the Occupied Territories." *Journal of Refugee Studies* 2 (1): 55–63.

Allen, Lori. 2013. *The Rise and Fall of Human Rights: Cynicism and Politics in Occupied Palestine*. Stanford, CA: Stanford University Press.

Arafeh, Nur. 2018. "Long Overdue: Alternatives to the Paris Protocol." *Al-Shabaka*, February 27. https://al-shabaka.org/briefs/long-overdue-alternatives-paris-protocol/.

Asad, Talal. 2003. *Formations of the Secular: Christianity, Islam, Modernity*. Stanford: Stanford University Press.

Brown, Katrina. 2016. *Resilience, Development, and Global Change*. London: Routledge.

B'Tselem. 2012. "Restriction of Movement: The Paris Protocol." *B'Tselem.org*, September 19. http://www.btselem.org/freedom_of_movement/paris_protocol.

Cavanaugh, William T. 2009. *The Myth of Religious Violence: Secular Ideology and the Roots of Modern Conflict*. Oxford: Oxford University Press.

Dana, Tariq. 2014. "A Resistance Economy: What Is It and Can It Provide an Alternative?" *Rosa Luxemburg Stiftung PAL Papers Series*, November. https://www.rosalux.de/publication/41012/a-resistance-economy-what-is-it-and-can-it-provide-an-alternative.html.

Dana, Tariq, and Ali Jarbawi. 2017. "A Century of Settler Colonialism in Palestine: Zionism's Entangled Project." *Brown Journal of World Affairs* 24 (1): 197–219.

Di Cintio, Marcello. 2014. "The Walls That Hurt Us." *New York Times*, January 23. http://www.nytimes.com/2014/01/24/opinion/the-walls-that-hurt-us.html?_r=0.
Fanon, Frantz. 1963. *The Wretched of the Earth*. Translated by C. Farrington. New York: Grove.
Farsakh, Leila. 2016. "Palestinian Economic Development: Paradigm Shifts Since the First Intifada." *Journal of Palestine Studies* 45 (2): 55–71.
Gregory, Derek. 2004. *The Colonial Present: Afghanistan, Palestine, and Iraq*. Malden, MA: Blackwell.
Haddad, Toufic. 2016. *Palestine Ltd: Neoliberalism and Nationalism in the Occupied Territory*. London: I.B. Tauris.
Hardt, Michael. 1995. "The Withering of Civil Society." *Social Text* 45: 27–44.
Kahn, Paul W. 2008. *Sacred Violence: Torture, Terror, and Sovereignty*. Ann Arbor, MI: University of Michigan Press.
Keck, Margaret E., and Kathryn Sikkink. 1998. *Activists Beyond Borders: Advocacy Networks in International Politics*. Ithaca: Cornell University Press.
Khalidi, Raja. 1985. "The Economics of Political Survival." *Journal of Palestine Studies* 14 (4): 153–154.
Khalidi, Raja, and Sobhi Samour. 2011. "Neoliberalism as Liberation: The Statehood Program and the Remaking of the Palestinian National Movement." *Journal of Palestine Studies* 40 (2): 6–25.
MA'AN Development Center. 2012. "Towards a Just Model of Palestinian Development: Reassessing International Aid Conditions." *MA'AN Development Center Position Paper*, January. http://www.maan-ctr.org/old/pdfs/FSReport/PP/PP-towards.pdf.
Mavelli, Luca. 2012. "Postsecular Resistance, the Body, and the 2011 Egyptian Revolution." *Review of International Studies* 38 (5): 1057–1078.
Mavelli, Luca, and Fabio Petito. 2012. "The Postsecular in International Relations: An Overview." *Review of International Studies* 38 (5): 931–942.
Mbembe, Achille. 2003. "Necropolitics." *Public Culture* 15 (1): 11–40.
Palestinian Land Defense Coalition. n.d. *Land Defense Coalition* [brochure]. http://www.stopthewall.org/sites/default/files/LDC%20brochure.pdf.
Perugini, Nicola, and Neve Gordon. 2015. *The Human Right to Dominate*. Oxford: Oxford University.
Roy, Sara. 1995. *The Gaza Strip: The Political Economy of De-development*. Washington, DC: Institute for Palestine Studies.
Salamanca, Omar Jabary, Mezna Qato, Kareem Rabie, and Sobhi Samour. 2012. "Past Is Present: Settler Colonialism in Palestine." *Settler Colonial Studies* 2 (1): 1–8.
Sansour, Vivien, and Alaa Tartir. 2014. "Palestinian Farmers: A Last Stronghold of Resistance." *Al-Shabaka*, July. https://al-shabaka.org/briefs/palestinian-farmers-a-last-stronghold-of-resistance/.

Sayigh, Rosemary. 1979. *Palestinians: From Peasants to Revolutionaries.* London: Zed Press.
Scott, David. 1996. "The Aftermaths of Sovereignty: Postcolonial Criticism and the Claims of Political Modernity." *Social Text 48* 14 (3): 1–26.
Seidel, Timothy. 2017. "'We Refuse to Be Enemies': Political Geographies of Violence and Resistance in Palestine." *Journal of Peacebuilding and Development* 12 (3): 25–38.
Seth, Sanjay. 2011. "Postcolonial Theory and the Critique of International Relations." *Millennium: Journal of International Studies* 40 (1): 167–183.
Shinko, Rosemary E. 2010. "Ethics After Liberalism: Why (Autonomous) Bodies Matter." *Millennium: Journal of International Studies, Special Issue "After Liberalism?"* 38 (3): 1–23.
Tabar, Linda, and Omar Jabary Salamanca, eds. 2015. *Critical Readings of Development Under Colonialism: Towards a Political Economy for Liberation in the Occupied Palestinian Territories.* Ramallah: Rosa Luxemburg Stiftung Regional Office Palestine and Birzeit University Center for Development Studies.
Tartir, Alaa. 2015. "Contentious Economics in Occupied Palestine." In *Contentious Politics in the Middle East: Popular Resistance and Marginalized Activism Beyond the Arab Uprisings*, edited by F. Gerges (469–499). New York: Palgrave Macmillan.
Tartir, Alaa, and Benoit Challand. 2017. "Palestine." In *The Middle East*, 14th ed., edited by E. Lust, 707–736. Thousand Oaks, CA: CQ/Sage.
Tartir, Alaa, Sam Bahour, and Samer Abdelnour. 2012. "Defeating Dependency, Creating a Resistance Economy." *Al-Shabaka*, February 13. https://al-shabaka.org/briefs/defeating-dependency-creating-resistance-economy/.
Tilly, Charles, and Sidney Tarrow. 2007. *Contentious Politics.* Boulder, CO: Paradigm.
Turner, Mandy, and Omar Shweiki, eds. 2014. *Decolonizing Palestinian Political Economy: De-development and Beyond.* New York: Palgrave Macmillan.
UN OCHA. 2017. "Fragmented Lives: Humanitarian Overview 2016." United Nations Office for the Coordination of Humanitarian Affairs, Occupied Palestinian Territory, May 31. https://www.ochaopt.org/content/fragmented-lives-humanitarian-overview-2016.
Wilcox, Lauren. 2014. "Making Bodies Matter in IR." *Millennium: Journal of International Studies* 43 (1): 359–364.
Wolfe, Patrick. 2006. "Settler Colonialism and the Elimination of the Native." *Journal of Genocide Research* 8 (4): 387–409.
Zaru, Jean. 2008. *Occupied with Nonviolence: A Palestinian Woman Speaks.* Minneapolis: Fortress Press.
Zureik, Elia. 1983. "The Economics of Dispossession." *Third World Quarterly* 5 (4): 775–790.

CHAPTER 4

Active and Transformative *Sumud* Among Palestinian Activists in Israel

Nijmeh Ali

INTRODUCTION

Sumud, translated as "steadfastness" which could be described as a form of infrapolitics or everyday resistance, is the dominant description of the daily reality for Palestinians in Israel. In other words, *Sumud* means the stubborn insistence on continuing on with life despite all the obstacles. After the *Nakba* of 1948, some 167,000 Palestinians remained in the newly established state of Israel. In the following decades, they would become 1.6 million, comprising 22% of the population of Israel today. In 1952 Israel granted Israeli citizenship to its "Arab" inhabitants. However, becoming Israeli citizens and participating in the Israeli election did not prevent Israel from imposing a military rule on its Palestinian citizens between the years of 1948 and 1966 (Pappe 2011).

The military rule[1] was imposed in the areas where Palestinians lived on October 21, 1948, and was based on the Defense (Emergency) Regulations established by the British Mandate in 1945 (Pappe 2011). The governor had the right to arrest people without a warrant and detain

N. Ali (✉)
National Centre for Peace and Conflict Studies,
University of Otago, Dunedin, New Zealand

© The Author(s) 2019
A. Tartir and T. Seidel (eds.),
Palestine and Rule of Power, Middle East Today,
https://doi.org/10.1007/978-3-030-05949-1_4

them without trial, control their movements and expel them from their houses. He could close schools, businesses, and newspapers and prohibit demonstrations or protest (Pappe 2011, 49). Military rule was the central Israeli institutional mechanism that shaped the lives of Palestinian citizens of Israel, and Palestinians were transformed from being the owners of the place, into strangers in. This did not prevent them from perceiving themselves as an indigenous national minority remaining in its homeland, Palestine, after its defeat and the establishment of Israel in 1948 (Jamal 2011). The Palestinians' first struggle in Israel thus focused on the question of citizenship, when ironically, Israeli citizenship was seen to offer permanent status to those Palestinians who resisted in every possible way of becoming refugees. However, under these circumstances, nonviolent resistance through parliamentary activism and cultural resistance seemed to be the most appropriate and safest methods of resistance to remain in their homeland, particularly in the first two decades of living in Israel.

Apart from parliamentary activism, culture became a hidden space for resistance and confrontation, where Palestinian poets and writers wrote about their daily life and their struggles to remain in their homeland.[2] Thus, most of the writing on resistance available in the first years after the *Nakba* of 1948 took the form of literature and poetry, and constructed what is known as *Adab al Moqawmah*, the literature of resistance where words and terminology were challenging and became a "weapon" for the Palestinians in Israel. Therefore, *Sumud* among the Palestinians in Israel has been mostly labeled in terms of cultural resistance (Rijke and Van Teeffelen 2014, 87; Jayyusi 1992; Kanafani [1967] 2013; Pappe 2011). The first study that coined the term "Literature of Resistance," describing this activism among the Palestinians in Israel, was published in 1967 by Ghassan Kanafani, a Palestinian intellectual refugee, who was assassinated by Israel later in 1972. Since then, Kanafani's study "*Resistance Literature in Occupied Palestine 1948–1966*" became a landmark for describing the Palestinians' *Sumud* in Israel.

Sumud, therefore, is a concept that reconstructs and adjusts itself according to the context. This observation invites us, after seventy years of the *Nakba*, to reinvestigate the meaning of *Sumud* among Palestinians in Israel, questioning the monopoly of cultural *Sumud* that has been historically linked to the Palestinian resistance in Israel. This investigation can shed light on the understanding of *Sumud* beyond "remaining" and culture, instead of stress "active *Sumud*" whereby Palestinians in Israel take responsibility for, and initiatives in, constructing their resistance. This chapter therefore aims to open a window for understanding resistance, its terminology, its nature and its potential through the eyes of third-generation Palestinian activists in Israel.

UNDERSTANDING RESISTANCE AMONG PALESTINIAN ACTIVISTS IN ISRAEL

For the purpose of this chapter, research participants consist of Palestinian activists, female and male, who are citizens of Israel and use their activism to challenge the existing power structures. Participants can be independent activists or members of political parties or movements, excluding members of the Zionist parties and politicians who occupy official positions such as the Palestinian Knesset members. They come from different political backgrounds and represent the three religious groups that form Palestinian society in Israel: Muslims, Christians, and Druze. Participants are at least eighteen years old and Arabic speakers and were mainly interviewed in 2016.

The vast majority of activists expressed their strong appreciation of the word *muqawamah* (resistance). Many of them felt uncomfortable using the word *muqawem* (resister) to identify themselves. *Muqawamah* (resistance) was described as meaningful, powerful and significant. Few other words were suggested by activists to describe their activism. Words such as *Jihad* (holy war) are preferred by activists with an Islamic background. *Nidal* (struggle), which is associated with secular aspects of the Palestinian people, has a robust presence in the Palestinian resistance discourse due to the Palestinian revolution that was led by the PLO between 1967 and 1972.[3] *Nidal,* and sometimes *kifah* (struggle), are used by activists interchangeably with resistance. Rabea explains[4]:

> I do not identify myself as a resister. I do love resisters. The first thing that springs into my mind when we speak about resistance is HizbAllah, meaning armed resistance. I prefer using the word *Nidal* (struggle). Resistance is very honorable. Someone who has been arrested and held for three days, for example, cannot be called a resister.

A possible explanation for this attitude is derived from a comparison with other Palestinian prisoners who have spent years behind bars and have been kept in custody for long periods under administrative detention.[5] In other words, resistance is related to the price of adopting particular actions. The outcome in a conflictual context is viewed by activists not only in terms of the potential of resulting social change, but also in terms of the willingness to pay a personal price and to sacrifice. This can be explained by the fact that since resisters or activists, especially in oppressive contexts, cannot be certain of social change, personal sacrifice becomes an element for assessing resistant actions and behaviors. This opens the way for considering personalizing outcomes as another element in defining resistant action among oppressed and powerless groups, which could enrich the ongoing efforts to construct a typology[6] for determining and recognizing actions of everyday resistance. Other activists used the term "political activist"[7] to describe their activism, considering themselves part of a particular resistance context. Raja puts it this way: "I see myself as a political activist and part of a left and national movement. I do not know if I have the mandate to consider myself as a resister or struggler. These words are big."

In addition to the personal price discussed above, there are a few possible explanations for understanding the avoidance of using the word "resistance" openly. The first is related to the actual context of living in Israel, where the word "resistance," or *muqawamah*, is associated with particular groups who practice violent actions, such as Hamas and HizbAllah, and who adopt the word *muqawamah* in their Arabic name. The second is embedded in the notion of being modest as part of Arabic culture. On the surface, it can be understood as underestimate the activism or the actions of the agent. However, it is important to understand the place of terminology and manners in collective societies, such as the Palestinian society.

It is less acceptable to speak about oneself: this explains the use of "we" instead of "I" in the interviews by the participants and myself, which can also be related to the collective nature of Palestinian society. This is very clear in Raja's words, emphasizing that he is not allowed to decide if he is a resister or not. It can also be related to the expectation of contributing more to the collective good. As Fadi explains: "I cannot label myself as a resister—maybe because I expect from myself to give more."

Another reason for avoiding the use of resistance to describe Palestinian activist actions might be related to the fact that resistance is associated in the memory of Palestinians with revolutionary names who have been sanctified, and with events that seem to be far removed from the current reality. When activists were asked to describe the first images that come to their minds when speaking about resistance, most of them mentioned HizbAllah, Arafat, Jerusalem and figures from the Palestinian revolution which are associated with armed resistance. Others mentioned old photos of military training of Palestinian guerrilla groups, the first Intifada, and the Land Day. In addition to famous names and popular armed operations in the Palestinian struggle, ordinary Palestinians were described by some activists as the real resisters, pointing to the generation who survived the *Nakba*.

Other activists mentioned the negative connotations of using the word "resistance," as can be noticed in Sana's words:

> Resistance has a negative connotation. It can be resistance to peace and physical resistance. Thus, I wouldn't choose the word resistance to describe my activism. I prefer the world *Nidal* (struggle). Resistance for me has connotations of violence and I do not believe that armed resistance can solve conflicts.

This can be viewed as proof of commitment to the principle nonviolence, but it also reflects viewing resistance as negative, due to its association with violence in the Palestinian context. This can be explained through the "new" terminology that was adopted after the Oslo agreement, which demanded switching the language of resistance by accusing it as "violent" and interrupting the peace process. Tartir (2017) draws our attention to the fact that this policy led to criminalizing resistance by the Palestinian Authority (PA) itself. In other words, Palestinian resistance has been systematically criminalized by three parties: Israel, the conditional international fund that demanded that the Palestinians be quiet and behave properly to get aid funds, and the PA. Criminalizing resistance, in the Palestinian case is a good example of stripping from the oppressed its ability to challenge the oppressor, and maintaining the subjugation of the weak in an unbalanced power structure in the name of "peace." This also leads to the creation of an illusory "symmetrical" reality that views the oppressed and the oppressor as equal parties.

A different view on resistance and violence can be found in Raja and Wafi's words, who emphasize the instrumental role of resistance, the right to resist and the legitimacy of adopting different forms of resistance, including violence, under certain circumstances. Raja explains:

> Most people view resistance as intervention by military means and violence. I cannot say that I reject violence in an absolute way, because blocking streets, for instance, is a violent action. Thus, I support violence against more violent actions. People suffering from injustice have the right to resist and the right to choose what is viewed as the most appropriate means of resistance. This is supported by international law. The political status of the West Bank and Gaza Strip is identified internationally as an occupation. Accordingly, Palestinians who live there have the right to determine what form of resistance is suitable, either armed or popular resistance or both. In our case [the Palestinians in Israel] our status is not identified as an occupation; thus, our understanding of resistance takes the shape of political and cultural resistance. Resistance is a tool for achieving certain goals. There is no resistance for resistance. Thus, resistance can serve a political goal, but at the same time it can harm others, such as civilian killings. In the end we should remember that the occupation is the main source of injustice and there is a moral responsibility for the killing of both Israelis and Palestinians.

Accordingly, Palestinian activists in Israel view resistance in relation to particular contexts, taking into consideration the particular power structure each Palestinian community is subjected to. This could provide a better explanation for the acceptance of different forms of resistance alongside the Palestinian struggle, rather than viewing them in contrast to each other. For this reason, other activists highlight the legitimacy of all forms of resistance and oppose the delegitimization of certain forms. Foucault's (1978) understanding of power and resistance in which resistance is shaped according to the power applied to it can provide a helpful explanation for this observation.

An additional point is refusing to determine what form of resistance is the most "appropriate," "justified" or "ethical." This decision should be taken by the people on the ground, those who confront the power. This observation is important because it gives the subordinate the power over its choices. Wafi explains:

> As a result of the different categories among the Palestinians, there are also different actions of resistance. Baqaa' and Sumud is one form. Other forms of resistance, where people sacrifice more, are much more sophisticated. Starting from people who adopt armed struggle and ending with choosing the minimum level of resistance which is staying here for example, preserving our language and resisting integration within the Israeli society. I consider my work in the cinema and theatre an important part of resistance.

It is very important for me to refuse to work with Israeli institutions and to reject any funds from Israeli institutions. And I am aware of the price of such a decision. What I want to say is that there have always been different forms of resistance and this is legitimate, and because of this I oppose any delegitimization of particular forms of resistance. No one has the mandate to determine for the people what forms of resistance they should adopt… this is one of our complexities, when political parties or people try to exclude types of resistance and legitimize one kind of action, such as achieving our rights only through the participation in the Israeli parliament or through negotiations.

Resistance is also understood as a popular action. However, some activists differentiate between two types of popular resistance: the accommodative and the challenging form that includes chaos, personal price and challenge power structures. Ahmad put it in this way:

Today I am convinced more of adopting a popular resistance model, but not Abu Mazen's (Mahmoud Abbas: The Palestinian president) model of popular resistance, which does not challenge the Palestinian-Israeli security coordination. I mean popular resistance in terms of disobedience, blocking streets and chaos. This kind of resistance is not easy and the price is heavy.

In contrast to passive *Sumud* and cultural resistance, *Sumud* should become "challenging" on the level of practical action, accompanied by the awareness of its "side effects"—the personal price and a situation of chaos in adopting such a kind of resistance. This observation reflects a clear distinction between civil resistance and transformative resistance, as viewed by Atack (2012). Atack points to civil resistance in defining the principles and institutions associated with liberal democratic states, and transformative resistance, which aims to construct new forms of social and political organization. Jefferess' (2008) understanding of transformative resistance is related to its ability in transforming its reactionary label into a position of being able to transform social relations.

Resistance is also embodied in internal censorship or what Hoy (2005) views as ethical resistance. Many activists emphasize that their resistance is derived from refusing to accept what they view as injustice. Sana explains: "When I see a Palestinian kid from Gaza injured by bombs, I cannot stay calm. I cannot see something wrong and unjust and stay silent. My internal censorship feeds my resistance." Some activists also question what is known as the demographic *Sumud*, as part of a general criticism of the traditional understanding of *Sumud*, drawing our attention to the challenges of resistance under power structures such as capitalism. Ahmad explains:

> We understand Sumud and Baqaa' also as a demographic battle, however we can notice the change among the young generation. In order to have 11 children, I need to have 70,000 NIS as monthly income, which is almost possible. This is one of the consequences of living in a capitalist system.

Yet, according to the predicted demography, we should not underestimate the growing percentage of the Palestinian minority in Israel, which is currently estimated at 30–35%. However, this challenging observation of the demography power can be questioned compared to the past. This can be explained by changes in the nature of the Palestinian population, particularly those who remained after the *Nakba*, who were mostly peasants. Being peasants demanded as many family members as possible to work on the land, and with the land confiscations and the transformation of the Palestinians into a cheap labor force in the Israeli market, the structure of the society was affected. Two other factors which increased this transformation are: the high cost of living in Israel; and the increasingly educated proportion of the Palestinian minority.

Other activists highlight the rise of individualist phenomena, as a direct result of living in a competitive capitalist system where success is measured by individual achievement. This harms the collective sense of responsibility toward the community and the belonging to the Palestinian minority. In Fadi's words: "The values have changed, affecting the sense of belonging to and contributing to society. The meaning of success is materialistic, having a new house, a car and good job without caring for the high percentage of employment and the ongoing discrimination against other Palestinians."

One possible reason for this reality is the construction of a clear hierarchy within the oppressed, something that harms the hard core of the Palestinians' struggle in Israel over their collective rights. However, some activists point to the nature of Arab society as a collective society as a proper response to this challenge.

Resistance in a context of oppression, therefore, does not have a solid definition; instead, it can be understood as a multidimensional expression that describes a variety of different actions, events, and behavior. At the same time, resistance is also what it avoids including, partly because of security reasons and cultural considerations, and this is one of the main reasons why the study of resistance is challenging.

Sumud as Unarmed Resistance

Most of the activists interviewed point to unarmed resistance as the model of resistance that was adopted directly after the *Nakba*, expressing the view that Palestinians in Israel see an armed and violent model of resistance as nonrational, non-responsible and not patriotic. As Abed put it: "Those who were calling for nonrealistic demands were either stupid, or cooperating with the authorities." One possible explanation for this observation could be Israeli oppression of the Palestinian minority, particularly in the first years of living under military rule, and the unstable civic status of the Palestinians in Israel.

In the shadow of military rule, Israeli authorities had the power to expel the rest of the Palestinians from Israel. Any provocative actions which were understood by the authorities as challenging the state would play into the hands of the Israeli authorities and legitimize transfer actions. Another possible explanation for adopting unarmed resistance could be a political decision that had been adopted by the Israeli Communist Party, under whose command most of the remaining Palestinian leaderships operated.

The Israeli Communist Party was by that time the only bi-national anti-Zionist party who represented the interests of the Palestinians in Israel, leading to the battle of dismantling military rule through political avenues, and struggling against continuing Israeli attempts to reduce the number of Palestinians in Israel. One historical point that should be stressed is that the Palestinian Communists accepted the 1947 UN partition plan of Palestine, to prevent what they predicted as the catastrophe of Palestine and the refugee problem. Thus, from the beginning, the Palestinian Communists believed that under the present circumstances, a war would bring calamity to the Palestinians. However, activists who supported these explanations describe that period as the *survival battle* that was led in a clever way.

In contrast, some activists point to the effect of collective trauma as an additional possible explanation for avoiding armed struggle among Palestinians in Israel, as viewed by Ahmad: "Internalizing the defeat on the subconsciousness of the Palestinians in Israel blocked the development of an armed struggle model." This approach reflects the psychological power of internalizing fear and weakness that Fanon et al. (1963) views as a major obstacle for preventing the colonized from adopting direct action against the colonizer. Open armed resistance, according to Fanon, is the only way to end colonialism, and the ultimate channel for practicing resistance by oppressed people. However, in contrast to this view, it seems that internalizing fear and weakness did not prevent oppressed, colonized, powerless Palestinians from adopting an unarmed resistance model, taking the forms of cultural resistance. In Hana's words:

> The only thing we still have is our culture; no one can prevent us from being Palestinians, even if it is not written in our I.D or passport. It is practising our daily life, cooking our food, speaking in our accents. Our culture is also what we produce in literature and poetry. Through Palestinian literature, I learned what I did not learn at school. Resistance literature was the first step in articulating my behavior and my refusal.

In this sense, Scott's (1990) notion of hidden transcripts and infrapolitics provides a valuable theoretical framework for understanding resistance among Palestinians in Israel during military rule, when open and direct confrontation was risky. But not only this: most of the activists used the words "responsibility" and "rationality" to justify the adoption of unarmed resistance. This differs from Scott's major explanation for his hidden transcript, which is presented as the only nonviolent choice for powerless people in risky contexts.

The skeptical view of armed resistance among Palestinians in Israel is still relevant. Activists point to three main reasons for legitimizing their skepticism: organized crime and cooperation with the Israeli authority, a cumulative experience of resistance, and the imbalance of power between Palestinian citizens and the Israeli authorities. As Reem says:

> Armed resistance cannot serve our [Palestinian citizens] demands. Weapons are in the hands of criminal groups and the Shin Bet (Israeli Internal Security Services). In addition to not having an armed heritage, we have experience of political organization…we should also remember that this state in 2000, long after 1948, shot thirteen Palestinian citizens who participated in demonstrations.

It is also notable that Palestinian activists in Israel avoided the model of armed resistance because of practical circumstances. This observation can be understood through Sharp's (1973) pragmatic approach, according to which the motivation behind adopting nonviolent resistance is that nonviolence is the most appropriate model for achieving the desired goals. However, an important finding that should be emphasized is that pragmatic motivation and practice led to the development of an ethical commitment toward unarmed resistance among many Palestinian activists, and which is viewed by Gandhi as the principle approach of nonviolent resistance. In Razi's words:

> I resist militarizing our [Palestinians in Israel] struggle. This is not easy at all, when we live in a violent context. I do not see myself using violence, but I can understand why people can adopt armed resistance. However, I think that as a Palestinian in Israel we grow up in the shadow of human values using the terminology of nonviolence in articulating our demands. After 70 years, I think it has left an effect on our way of viewing and understanding the conflict.

In this way, activists emphasize the challenge of adopting unarmed resistance under circumstances of oppression. As viewed by Reem: "Adopting civil or popular resistance is challenging. It demands energy and stubborn faith in its effectiveness. It demands patience as the outcomes are not immediate and most of the time we cannot witness any change." However, this did not prevent Palestinian activists from developing sympathy for and solidarity with armed resistance in general, particularly toward national struggles, including the Palestinian armed struggle. This observation leads to a questioning of the genuineness of principled nonviolence that was identified before; hence, it is important to clarify this type of solidarity.

Since the Palestinians are leading their national struggle for liberation, they developed solidarity with other national struggles and revolutions, respecting all means of resistance and approaches that are adopted. This includes the Algerian liberation revolution, Vietnam's people's war, the Cuban revolution, until Mandela's struggle and methods of boycotting in South Africa. This variety of international resistance experience has inspired the Palestinians, who adopted methods of protest and resistance into their struggle (Sayigh 1997, 196–202). Thus, instead of a question of the "best" form of resistance, it should be framed as the most appropriate form of resistance. Reem put it this way: "I want my children to connect our struggle with international struggles, and for this reason we have the Cuban and the Catalonian flags in our house beside the Palestinian flag, I want them to know that they are part of wide movement." The passion of linking the Palestinian struggle with other international struggles can be explained through the desire to construct a united front in the face of oppression everywhere. This will help in lobbying for Palestine in different places in the world, and also deepens understanding and analysis of the conflict on the international level.

THE DEVELOPMENT OF *SUMUD*: KEY EVENTS

Since the *Nakba*, Palestinians have been subjected to different political, social and economic contexts, leading to particular experiences for each community. In this sense, Palestinians in Israel have a particular experience based on their direct interaction with Israeli society. Hana put in this way: "As a result of direct interaction with Israelis everyday - at universities, workplaces, on the streets, and in restaurants - we [Palestinians in Israel] has developed different attitudes that allows us to look, analyse and react differently, maybe more deeply and flexibly."

Most of the activists point to the continuing influence of collective events such as the years of military rule in constructing the political behavior of the Palestinians in Israel. This was reflected in the interviews when many activists shared similar incidents related to security, fear, and safety. The vast majority of activists who participated in the study used the sentence "I hope this interview won't go to the *Shabak*."

However, activists view the military rule period in two contrasting ways. The first, as poor years of resistance, while the second vision, which is more popular, views military rule as the harshest years of the Palestinians in Israel, and which entailed a significant ability to survive and *Sumud*. Both visions stress the continuing presence of military rule in the consciousness of the Palestinians until today. In Mouhamad's words:

> The military rule shaped the beginning of our relation with the state. For almost two decades Palestinians were subjected to direct power that controlled every aspect of their lives. I am not underestimating their role [the Palestinians who lived under military rule], but to be frank, I think they internalized the defeat and pass it on to us.

Other collective events, such as the attacks on Gaza between 2008 and 2014, and the war in Lebanon in 2006, were viewed as significant events by the vast majority of Palestinian activists. Other participants highlighted personal events they were involved in as the most influential in understanding resistance. Childhood memories, direct confrontations with the police and the army, political arguments with competitive political groups and active engagement, were all mentioned as milestone events for constructing their understanding of resistance. Rabea shares two events to illustrate this point:

> In 1999 demonstrations broke out in my city, protesting Sharansky's visit, the Minister of Internal Affairs in Israel at the time. The police interfered and started shooting tear gas. I remember myself holding a box full of onions,[8] moving between the people handing onions to the demonstrators. I was 15 years old. At that moment I was not afraid, it was my duty to do something. The fear came the second day when the police started to arrest people. This incident comes to my mind every time I participate in a demonstration. The fear of being arrested, but at the same time the need to stay strong and fulfil my duty. Few years after this incident, two of my closest friends were arrested, being accused of security issues, and since then I had a personal dilemma about cooperating with Israelis, even smiling at an ordinary Israeli while walking in the street became a battle.

For many activists, the conflict is not hidden; rather, it is embedded in their daily life, when confrontation could break out at any moment in the form of a personal or collective battle. This opposes Scott's (1985, 1992) understanding of everyday resistance and its "hidden" nature. Rather, everyday resistance in a conflictual context seems to be an everyday battle that cannot be avoided or practiced only through culture. Daily experiences result in an everyday oppression, which would lead in some way to confrontation. Standing in the line of the supermarket and being overlooked by Israelis, for example, becomes an existential battle for Palestinians, or being selected for being "suspect" by the security. This happens to me often when I speak Arabic in public, in the bus or any place. The immediate thought that springs to my mind is, "it is because I am an Arab." And from there, negotiating power becomes part of the *Sumud*, trying to defend myself as a Palestinian, my dignity as a human being and my rights as an Israeli citizen.

Following from this, internal and direct political arguments are also another example of personal events that influence the understanding of resistance. Hana shares her experience of arguing with Islamic movement activists over the legitimacy of women's voices[9] in public, in addition to participation in demonstrations in Tel Aviv[10] as the most influential events in understanding resistance. Another theater for constructing resistance is activism at universities, which was described by many activists as an opportunity for practicing resistance. Raja points to the "student uprising" in 2000 during the second Intifada as an influential event in his activism. Raja explains that:

> The events of 2000 hit the Palestinian minority in Israel as a shock. I did not imagine a scenario where the state would shoot its citizens, particularly after Oslo and the Peace agreement. What happened in 2000 was clear evidence for how much this state can tolerate us as citizens. We, as students, found ourselves facing Israelis on the campus, when Israeli media were portraying us as criminals and lawbreakers…it was important to bring politics to the campus to mobilize students and to raise our voice.

In sum, activists point to collective and personal events as significant milestones in their understanding of resistance and *Sumud*. Based on this, it should be stressed that *Sumud* seems to be constructed from historical memories which construct "collective memory," and present experiences. *Sumud* cannot be static, but is a lived process that is constructed according to accumulated collective and individual experiences. This observation supports the need for investigating the meaning of *Sumud*, avoiding the simple definition of cultural *Sumud*. In this sense, *Sumud* seems to emerge from the field, not from a particular theory. *Sumud* is a kind of "handmade craft" shaped by the agents, the researcher and the negotiations between them. This also supports the credibility of the grounded constructivist theory in researching *Sumud* that was adopted as the methodological approach for conducting this study. This observation of the ongoing construction of resistance provides a possible explanation for the variety of *Sumud* and resistance understandings as it is reflected by activists.

Another important finding is that *Sumud* contains two elements: confrontation and engagement. Since the *Sumud* of the Palestinians was understood as passive and quiet, taking place in the backyard of the Palestinian society, and since there is a call for examining traditional tools of protest that were adopted within the citizenship framework, mainly through formal channels, the data yields new components of *Sumud*, namely, confrontation and engagement. This will be further discussed in the next section.

Patterns of *Sumud*

Thus, based on the data and the analysis of the material, I recognized four patterns of *Sumud* as everyday resistance in the context of Palestinians in Israel: practical, personal, cultural, and active.

Practical *Sumud*

As mentioned above, the battle of *Baqaa'* did not end in the 1948–1949 war and by Palestinians staying in their homeland. Activists, therefore, emphasize that today's *Baqaa'* has many layers; today, the battle is over maintaining the *Baqaa'* by resisting the continuing oppressing of Palestinians in Israel. Reem put it this way:

> In the Nakba more than 500 Palestinian villages were demolished. Since then we have been witnessing the continuing demolishing of houses for the purposes of illegal building and the refusal to recognize Bedouin villages in the Naqab, despite the fact of Palestinians living in their lands for hundreds of years. However, these actions occur openly in front of Israelis and the rest of the world, using the cover of Israeli legal regulations to legitimize the continuing project of stealing lands.

In other words, activists highlight that controlling Palestinians in Israel is done in a sophisticated way which is carried out under the cover of the law, to make it coherent, logical, and justified. For this reason, many activists point to the need for practical methods of *Sumud* to face these specific policies. Activists point to the battle over planning and building as the main obvious example where Israeli law is used to control Palestinian citizens' life, and Palestinians resist in adopting practical *Sumud*. In Orwa's words:

> Israel does not give permission for Palestinian citizens to build their houses, which only increases unrecognized building in Arab villages and results in clashes with Israeli authorities when it comes to demolishing houses. Others simply choose to build vertically, but this increases internal tensions within the family and community. In extreme cases, we witness internal displacement towards the city, which restructures Palestinian society and weakens social mechanisms such as al-hamoula (familial support structure).

Thus, resistance in this case aims to make these policies of discrimination clear and obvious, opening the way to question the nature of Israeli power structure, and the most effective strategy to resist it.

Scott's (1985, 1990) understanding of everyday resistance can explain hidden resistance in extreme contexts, such as dictatorships, but it is problematic for understanding resistance to hidden or unclear power structures in particular contexts such as Israel when discrimination is masked by laws and policies. Since it is important for Israel to maintain its image of being "the only democratic country in the Middle East", discrimination is also hidden to outsiders who are not familiar with cultural and social nuances. Discrimination adopts different forms, some through written legislation, others through unwritten actions which are recognized only by locals. Certain conditions, such as age limitations on work, education, and military and civic service, are essential for acceptance and gaining other privileges, and find their way into Palestinians' daily life in Israel. In Waheed's words:

> When I see a job advertisement, I automatically check the conditions. If it says "over 21 years old,"[11] I know that there is no chance for me! It is worse because we cannot hide ourselves - I don't want to change my Arabic name or my accent to be accepted. Others face problems in renting houses, or not being invited to work interviews, and banned from entering certain places, including entertainment venues.

Some excluding actions are institutionalized in the Israeli system, and others are embedded within Israeli society more generally. Activists point out that this combination of formal and nonformal discrimination, should be challenged through strategies of resistance. This, therefore, opens the way for questioning the type of civil resistance that should be adopted in facing institutionalized discrimination. Is it through adopting institutional channels such as participating in elections, or "breaking the power" from outside the system? This invites us again to consider transformative resistance as a suitable form in the case of the Palestinian minority in Israel.

However, activists also mention the necessity of keeping some patterns of resistance hidden, for security reasons and to maintain the momentum of surprise to ensure the success of the act of resistance. Cooperating with other Palestinian groups, planning for common actions in different locations at the same time, and organizing international flotillas to break the siege on Gaza, are good examples of hidden resistance, which is partly similar to Scott's hidden nature of resistance, but for different reasons. It is not only out of "risk," but it is to ensure the success of the resistant action and to control the momentum determining when to expose it to the public.

Most activists insist on keeping what they describe as "traditional resistance actions," such as demonstrations and humanitarian campaigns, public and open. It is important to note that the vast majority of Palestinian demonstrations are legal and have police permission.[12] However, one possible explanation for insisting on adopting traditional actions of resistance is involving masses and bringing people together in collective action, which is essential for creating a mass popular movement. An additional explanation could be the motivation of constructing solidarity with other marginalized and oppressed groups in Israel. A third explanation is related to media coverage. Public actions are a golden opportunity for marginalized, powerless and oppressed groups and topics to occupy prime time in the news to reach a wider public. An additional reason is the availability of these methods in the hands of those who are blocked from using other channels to practice protest, such as minorities. Minority resistance, in this sense, can provide a proper answer for those who question the legitimacy of resistance in democratic states.

Practical *Sumud* seems to be a continuing struggle of refusing to blend into Israeli society, which is one of the common means of resistance of indigenous minorities around the world, the fear of vanishing and disappearing. Reem presents a direct political argument against integration by explaining that:

> the demand of the Israeli authority to integrate in order to achieve our civil rights is a big illusion. They are asking us to delete part of our identity from our memory in order to be able to live normally and equally in this state. However, even then I doubt if they [the Israelis] will give us full rights. It is enough to look at the structure of Israeli society for discovering the "fake" promised outcome... because if they [Israelis] are interested in building an equal society, social differences between the Ashkenazi, Mizrahi, and Ethiopians within Israeli society wouldn't exist.

The most contradictory practical method that was mentioned by many activists was participation in Israeli elections. While the vast majority of activists agree on the potential role of the Palestinians in Israel in influencing Israelis, participating in Israeli elections is a point of contention. Some activists, mostly those who are members of political parties suggest practicing *Sumud* through the same channels that have been used since 1948, from within the system, supporting participation in elections, although they admit that this is not an easy process. In Abed's words, "it is like a rock sculpture mission." Others view the situation from another angle. Some activists suggest adopting practical *Sumud,* that challenges what they view as "obedient citizenship." Ahmad explains: "We tried to bring change from within the system. We all know it is not working. Thus, we need to try a different way."

Activities such as boycotting were suggested by many activists, as a promising method for disturbing the Israeli bubble of "a normal and quiet life." Many activists suggest using the economic power of the Palestinians in Israel as a source of political pressure for protesting and imposing policies, but more than this, to bring politics and occupation to the daily life of the Israelis. In Orwa's words: "Our economic power is estimated in millions, imagine how much power we have to affect the Israeli market, and I am not speaking now about the power of our human resource which can be used during strikes to stop normal life in Israel."

Striking is another popular method used by the Palestinians in Israel to protest Israeli policies. However, many activists point to the missed potential of using strikes today, demanding adaptation to the new social structure of Palestinian society. During the 1970s, strikes were very effective due to the fact that most Palestinians citizens in Israel comprised the main working class in Israeli factories, and they effectively influenced the Israeli market. Currently, Palestinians occupy different positions on different levels, such as private companies and public institutions, thus strike action should take into consideration the economic effect on the current society. Waheed put it this way:

> There have been some individual campaigns against some companies which prevented their employees from speaking Arabic on workdays or rejected Arab applications for work. This resulted in huge boycotting campaigns from Palestinian customers. During the war on Gaza, Palestinians in Israel boycotted Israeli malls as an act of solidarity with Palestinians in Gaza, and the loss was estimated in millions. However, there are no plans for turning these individual efforts into a strategy.

An additional method is boycotting, simply refusing to buy Israeli products. However, many activists emphasize the complexity of boycotting within Israel. In Firas' words: "As a result of the absence of alternative products in the market, other activists understand the limitations in boycotting Israeli goods while living in Israel. Therefore, they suggest boycotting settlement products."

This opens the way for understanding the action of selective boycott in the Israeli context as a resistance method adapted to the specific circumstances of living in Israel. Again, pragmatic issues play a central role in determining the resistance methods adopted. The fact of living in Israel and consuming Israeli products, for example, is not easy to avoid or overcome, since there are no alternative or other choices. However, being a customer in the Israeli market seems to be similar to being a citizen in the Israeli political system and can be understood as a powerful stance that could also be used for "breaking the power" economically. This leads to constructing what I identify as the "selective boycott" method, such as boycotting settlement products, companies that supports the Israeli army and companies that discriminate against Palestinian employees.

As part of practical *Sumud*, activists also stressed the importance of resisting internal power structures, mainly the traditional political parties. In Wafi's words:

> On the external level we face the Israeli authority, which is obvious. However, on the internal level we face old parties who are still stuck in their old political vision… most of the people who lead these parties lived under military rule or directly after its end, and so they are not able to articulate a confrontational strategy of Sumud. The differences between the old and the young members of the parties are notable. In these parties there is no suitable articulation of political demands according to the new reality.

Generational clashes between the old conservative leadership and the young, who demand adopting revolutionary approaches of resistance that suit the current Israeli context with acknowledgment of its limitations, could be explained through understanding the life cycle approach. This provides an explanation for adolescent rebellion and attempts to attribute social protest in the 1960s to young people's life cycle characteristics and needs, and to deep-seated emotional conflicts between youth and adults (Erikson 1968; Feuer 1969). In a more structural-functionalist perspective, life cycle theory has given birth to a cohort-generational perspective, in which youth unrest is viewed as a product of a rapidly changing social order and unique growing-up experiences that exacerbate age-group relations and may generate organized protest behaviors. The Arab Spring events provide a useful example for this view. However, practical *Sumud* presents a variety of resistant actions, including combinations of new and old methods. Most activists describe the lack of strategic resistance as a gap that should be bridged, in order to transform power structures and create change. Another important point is the necessity of adjusting resistance methods to the new conditions of the Palestinians in Israel in a way that would allow them to practice their hidden power and explore their hidden potential. In other words, this section invites us to reevaluate the methods that had been adopted, not for stressing the need of "inventing" new methods. Instead, it seems that there is a need for updating and "placing" these methods in a more strategic approach of resistance, and here transformative resistance finds its way.

Personal *Sumud*

Subjection to Israeli educational curricula means subjection to the Zionist narrative, in which Palestine is portrayed as an empty land with only primitive communities. Thus, the vast majority of activists emphasize their personal *Sumud*, by emphasizing their efforts in educating themselves and their children in a way that keeps Palestine as a living presence in their minds.

Sumud enters personal life in different ways, for example, by naming newborn children after Palestinian cities and villages such as Yaffa, Majdal, Carmel, Haifa, Jenin, etc. Firas explains this phenomenon by saying:

> It is kind of inheritance. In the beginning we gave the name Yaffa, which is in the center of Palestine, for my first daughter. Then we named my second child Carmel (North Palestine). And to cover the south, we named Majdal. By this means, we give life to the Palestinian cause, constructing our identity and historical narrative... I have historical Palestine in my house, living, breathing, thinking and growing. No one can take it from me.

Most of the activists describe their physical presence in Israel as *Sumud*, particularly those who have an opportunity to travel abroad and establish a normal life. However, it seems that some activists think differently, suggesting viewing *Sumud* beyond a physical presence, and instead emphasizing it as a commitment to the Palestinian cause. In this way, *Sumud* seems to be a notion that crosses borders, an idea that cannot be dismantled by tanks and bombs. Wafi explains that: "even if I choose to live abroad, I will still have commitment towards my people... immigration and leaving turns problematic when it becomes a collective action. During wartime, large numbers of Israelis leave the country, while we chose to stay, I think it says something."

Some activists use the term "refusal" as a third way of practicing disobedience. Firas describes his personal choice of refusing to receive funds or to interact with Israeli institutions. Firas says: "I refuse to receive any support from Israeli or governmental institution. and I do not have any problem with this. I am convinced of my personal choices. I had to give up my studies as a result of being arrested but I have no regrets. This is normal and it is part of the process."

In contrast to Scott's (1990) underestimating of the importance of intention for determining if a particular action can be recognized as everyday resistance, in the case of the Palestinian activists in Israel who are aware of their life in an oppressive context, resistance becomes a lifestyle of *Sumud* associated with their internal strength, when activists adopt it in their personal lives.

Moral *Sumud*

Another important aspect of personalizing *Sumud* is its moral and ethical dimension. In this sense, many activists share their personal ethical dilemmas of being a Palestinian activist in Israel, which is a very sensitive situation. In order to avoid confusion and being misunderstood, many activists emphasize that they are careful in sharing their ethical dilemmas with Arabs and other Palestinians. Most activists mention what I call the "good morning" complexity, which is presented well through Hana's words:

> Saying "good morning" to my classmates at the university is supposed to be a normal action. But it is not - when my classmate is a settler from Hebron. Every time I say "good morning" - I feel I have betrayed my

people… you are expected to hate but you cannot because simply you don't want to. The other side also is expected to hate you. And we are in this circle.

Others resist developing hate, not only because of moral motivation but also for pragmatic reasons. Fadi explains:

> My first meeting with Israeli authorities was when I was five years old, when Israeli policemen broke into our house to arrest my brother. It was easy for me to choose to develop hatred and to stay home. But the question is - where can this lead me? Is it going to make the life of my family and my people better? In my opinion it is not.

In addition to the mission of convincing other oppressed groups in Israel to construct a unity of oppression despite their national belonging, activists emphasize that resisting radical and racist attitudes which have a sound basis in Israel is the most challenging mission they face. In Abed's words:

> The most difficult thing is to resist radical and fanatical ideas that control people's minds, to resist ignorance and to support powerless groups, such as women's movements and other minorities in Israel - not only the Palestinian minority in Israel - and to convince them and us that despite our different religions and national belonging we can do something together.

Sumud has another face, which is resisting losing faith in activism in the shadow of continuing disappointment and failures. Raja says:

> It is easier to sit in a coffee shop and do nothing, saying that no one deserves my efforts. The most challenging point for an activist is reaching the position that he or she loses faith in the people… I do not want to reach this stage because this is what the system wants. To make me believe that no one deserves my help and that there is no need for activism, pushing you to believe that finding a job and seeking your personal benefit is the most important thing.

Others note that being an activist in Israel is a continuing process of challenging themselves by questioning their sense of humanity, especially in a context when the other side—the vast majority of Israelis—does not see you. In Fakhera's words:

> Israelis exist in the Palestinian minority consciousness, but we [Palestinians] do not. As a result, we have an internal dilemma how to make them see us in the way we want to be seen… we need to have the courage to ask questions and not to wait for the Israelis to ask, answer and decide for us.

These observations reflect the rejection of being hidden and demands from the Palestinians in Israel to "take action," and to locate themselves in the consciousness of the Israelis.

In sum, moral *Sumud* resists adopting the oppressor's tools of marginalizing, delaying and denying, and this can be viewed as breaking the rules of the Israeli game, which work to establish full segregation and separation. One possible explanation for this can be the fact that the Palestinians in Israel are not part of the Israeli military mentality. Their obedience is not based on national elements, but rather on civic elements, which might increase a critical sense among the Palestinian minority in Israel. In addition, their historical position of being in opposition makes them sharper in their reaction and behavior toward Israeli policies and conform less with the Israeli national consensus.

Cultural *Sumud*

The *Nakba* did not end with the excluding of the Palestinians but continued with daily confrontation of the Palestinian minority who tried to preserve their identity and remove the ashes of the *Nakba* from them. Raja put it this way:

> As a result of the Palestinian elite displaced and with the combination of imposing Military Rule, Palestinian resistance literature emerged within the Palestinian citizens in Israel out of necessity, but also as a reaction to the hard oppression that Palestinians suffer from… the nature of the conflict forced the use of particular methods. However, we turned this contradiction of being Palestinian in Israel into an opportunity, for example studying at universities, even though we are aware of the Zionist hegemony and the role of the academy in Israel.

In the shadow of these conditions, one of the most important victories, according to many activists, is continuing to speak fluent Arabic. In fact, culture turned out to be the "glow" between all Palestinian communities in the world. Firas says: "Culture is a bridge between me and

Palestinians from Shatila (Lebanon) and Yarmouk (Syria) refugee camps, culture is our only common space. Our socio-economic and political realities are different and I think also our priorities."

Hall (1977) views culture as a dynamic, rather than static, process of construction. Some activists present the contradiction between culture that aims to preserve tradition and history as part of *Sumud*, and culture that seeks to develop and construct new themes and meanings which reflect the present discourses. In Souher's words:

> There is awareness among the young who seek to preserve the Palestinian heritage through photography, theatre and saving Palestinian embroidery for preserving our past tradition, but at the same time we want to be open and to negotiate some of our problematic traditions such as women's status, and all this is a very challenging mission, because we ask ourselves if by questioning our culture do we harm our national struggle.

In addition to the dilemma of preserving and construction, many activists highlight their fear of losing their Palestinian identity as a result of direct and daily interactions with the Israeli side. Sana emphasizes the behavioral aspect of culture, sharing the concern of the negative impact of the clash between Arab and Israeli culture. In Sana's words:

> We have a very beautiful culture and manners that we should keep. I think that we have had negative influence from Israeli manners, which concerns me. For instance, when we travel, our behavior does not reflect our own culture. And the way of behaving towards others and elderly people is another aspect that I am concerned about.

Others view negative influences through attacks on Palestinian identity by more systematic projects and policies. Ahmad draws our attention to the policy of divide and rule, which aims to divide some sectors from the Palestinian society, such as trying to impose compulsory military service[13] on Christians and civic service projects on all the Arabs. However, activists also express strong confidence in Palestinian identity and culture. As Souher puts it: "We, the Arabs, have confidence and great pride in our culture, while there is no [one] Israeli culture."

The first impression of the debate about whose culture is the best seems on the surface very arrogant. It is important to clarify this point. Palestinians, who are part of the rich Arab culture, feel superior to the Israelis, who migrated from different countries from all over the world.

Activists point to the social role of the Israeli army as a "melting pot" to explain the Israeli cultural gap in this sense. Another significant point is that when Palestinian activists speak about a cultural clash, they are referring to a clash between Western values, which are more individualistic, and native Arab values, which are more collectivist. This can explain the anger of Palestinians in general when they view or witness the use of any element associated with Arab or Palestinian culture, whether it be music, food, architecture, literature on the like, as a continuation of the *Nakba*. In other words, this explains why the Israeli appropriation of *falafel* and *hummus*, well-known Palestinian and Arab food, become a battlefield.

Thus, the continuing process of cultural production, in Amal's words, "makes us more confident and rich with our thoughts." Therefore, many activists point to the importance of being financially independent to ensure free art, music, literature and other aspects of their culture, and to establish a free space away from the Zionist hegemony that rejects the presence of non-Zionist motives in Israel.

Activists also share the concern of what they call "political fund," referring to the hidden agenda behind the financing funds. Reem explains:

> The development of the civil society and the establishing of hundreds of NGOs whom entered to the field of developing capacities, turned activism and resistance to projects that ended when the money ended. This means that we do not have an accumulated developed capacity that could work for liberation; instead, we developed capacities that lead to obedience and enslavement.

Continuing this point, some activists shared their concern about ignorance in Israeli society toward the existence of the Palestinian citizens and the legitimacy of practicing their culture and main rights, such as speaking Arabic in public.[14] In Fakhera's words: "I feel we do not have any legitimacy in Jewish public life, it seems they are erasing us from their consciousness, we do not exist. I am afraid of speaking Arabic on the train and suddenly someone can spy on me, curse me or shout at me."

Other participants mentioned historical ignorance and the reshaping of history as the main element in erasing Palestinian existence in Israel. Mouhamad shares a conversation with two of his Jewish colleagues (originally from Iraq and Europe) who asked about the origins of Mouhamad's family that has been in Palestine at least for the last 200 years. The first reaction of Mouhamad's colleagues was "you are more Israeli than us." In Mouhamad's words:

> Israel has been here only for the last 70 years. It is amazing how people do not ask themselves, what has been here before. Who are the people who used to live in this place? They [Israelis] live in a complete denial of everything that is not Israel, as if we are not in the Middle East and we do not exist.

A more optimistic attitude describes any political, cultural, or economic cooperation at the grassroots level between Jewish and Palestinian citizens, as *Sumud* against the system. In Abed's words:

> We are facing a complete and strong brainwashing system which is the Zionist hegemony. Our existence here is an opportunity to reach some sectors in the Israeli society and providing answers and counter-knowledge to unmask the veil from their eyes by showing the true face of racist Israel. This can be done by political and cultural cooperation. Even if we agree only in 10 percent- this common struggle or resistance creates some particular dynamics that reflects the complexity of our life and that it is not a binary white and black situation.

Other participants describe the ongoing cultural resistance as a battle against "appropriation," when it is not only vanishing cultural elements and motives but is a process of stealing and self-appropriation. Souher says:

> it is not a normal occupation. The French in Algeria did not appropriate the Algerian culture (food, for example). Israeli appropriation of Palestinian culture means initially emptying Palestinian identity and deformatting it. I see the houses with Arab sentences above the door, they don't bother even to remove it... it is stealing your, language and thinking it is "authentic" to have Arabic. The funny thing is that usually it is usually a religious blessing from the Quran combined with the year that the buildings or houses were constructed, it is basically evidence that it is not Israeli property.

Therefore, because of the continuity of oppression, forbidding, and silencing, the task of Palestinian culture has become the agent for negotiation between the everyday and the extreme (Tawil-Souri 2011), between the continuation of having a normal life and a battle against disappearance. In this case, resistance was not only a national duty but also a lifestyle. Therefore, following the *Nakba*, Palestinians found themselves subject to a new reality, one which set the stage for the development of a cultural movement that politicized everything. Words associated with everyday life began to take on new meanings. Words such as *Portuqal* (orange), *zeitun* (olives), *shajar zeitun* (olive trees), *el-hassad* (harvest), and so on—all of these were transformed from agricultural discourse to political discourse describing the *watan* (homeland) and the *sumud* (steadfastness) of *El-jamaheer* (the masses)—presented as the cornerstone of the Palestinian resistance (Ali 2009).

However, activists distinguish between Palestinian culture that was developed among Palestinians outside Israel, and that which was developed among Palestinians in Israel. Souher puts it this way:

> As a result of the dynamic nature of the cultural confrontation, Palestinian culture within the Palestinians in Israel developed differently to that which was adopted among Palestinian refugees. The image of a raped Palestine was transformed into the image of a resistant Palestine, which leads us to ask questions about gender and other taboo issues as part of our developing liberation process... this is not the case among Palestinians abroad. Therefore, the adoption of liberation language saved the Palestinians in Israel from falling into the image of romanticizing Palestine. If we lived outside, we would be stuck with romanticizing the weak and raped Palestine... this would not open the way for lively questioning, including everything such as the masculinity of our society.

This observation can be explained by the influence of direct confrontation and everyday resistance, which leads to a dynamic internal and external discourse among the Palestinians, resulting in constructing critical attitudes toward what is viewed as victimization. The vast majority of activists emphasize their resistance to the position of victimhood, despite their acknowledgment of being historical victims as a result of the *Nakba*. This denial of being victims can explain the demand of moving to active *Sumud*, where Palestinians in Israel can manifest their potential.

Toward the Construction of Active *Sumud*

Documenting the past is one of the most significant actions that reflects *Sumud* of the Palestinians in Israel. Firas says: "History and memory are important weapons for creating solid resistance and ensuring commitment to our struggle." Continuing this point, activists highlight additional reasons for the act of documentation, which relate to the unstable political situation of the Palestinians in Israel. Yet, Imad emphasizes that documenting the present is not less important than documenting the past. In Imad's words: "we do not know what will happen to us in the coming years. It is not enough to document the past as part of constructing our stolen history, there is an urgent need to document the everyday actions of our life here [in Israel], especially because of our blurry future."

In this way, Imad and others draw attention to political uncertainty and the urgent need of adopting active *Sumud*, which takes into consideration possible scenarios in the future. In other words, activists suggest adopting strategic *Sumud*, to reflect the nature of active *Sumud*. In Ahmad's words: "We need to transform our Sumud from its conservative role of memorizing tradition and the past, which was important for a significant period …to Sumud that allows me to build vision, for the return, for example."

Active *Sumud* means to take responsibility for the destiny of the Palestinians and to initiate action plans. Ahmad illustrates this point saying:

> I worked with a few Palestinian organizations on a project that aimed to build a future vision for the refugees returning. However, many organizations, particularly those that are led by old people, stressed that it is Israel's responsibility to find solutions, since it is the one that caused it. This is frustrating, because it is sinking in our "disability" and handing our destiny to the Israelis… they will think and we will wait.

Other activists were more optimistic, stressing the willingness of people to sacrifice and confront the Israeli authorities when necessary. Firas explains: "In every confrontation with the Israeli police, you will find people on the streets… many people willing to pay the price, either through arrest or paying for lawyers." These two observations reflect the gap between practicing resistance on the ground and planning for resistance on the strategic level.

In this sense, many activists describe the challenge of traditional understanding of *Sumud* as a positive indicator for moving toward active *Sumud*. Orwa explains that:

> Challenging the mainstream of the political parties which comes from the grassroots is very encouraging... my optimism comes from models of resistance that push the political boundaries far from the mainstream, such as the refusal of the Bedouins in the Naqab to leave their villages despite the harsh living conditions: over 100,000 Palestinian citizens in Israel live with no water, electricity or proper infrastructure, yet they refuse to leave their tents.

One possible explanation for Orwa's optimism can be related to the challenging of the obedient position of the Palestinian leadership, as it was described by many activists, which falls between two categories of political behavior: "accepted" or "not accepted," and "safe" or "dangerous."

As part of constructing the future, the vast majority of activists demand moving to active *Sumud*, demanding to construct a strategy of *Sumud* where people know they are part of an overhaul of the struggle. In Amal's words: "If we want to occupy the streets we should know what our concrete aims are, what is the plan... despite this, our resistant actions will be a waste of energy and time that won't take us anywhere."

As part of challenging the political mainstream, some activists point to the necessity of fighting the neoliberal and capitalist system. Basel and others go against the existing systems, that in their opinion, cause enslavement for the people. In Basel's words: "We should boycott the banks and stop watching TV. Boycott the political system and the election... this will drive them crazy because we won't be under their direct control and supervision, only by refusing to play their game according to their rules can we challenge the system." The same point was raised by Souher, who says: "For many years we were told that the problem is us, not the system. I think that today we are not afraid to say that the problem is institutionalized in the system... and once we understand this and break our obedience, we cannot regret it or stay calm."

Identifying the Israeli system with the "system" reflects the definition of an oppressed people, who view oppression in a multidimensional way, not only in terms of national or civic status. This observation affects the strategy of resistance that would be suggested, the aspects that would be included and doubtless, the methods.

Summary

This chapter has explored various understandings of *Sumud* through the eyes of Palestinian activists, those of the third generation after the *Nakba* who tried to establish a link between *Sumud* and transformative resistance through providing information on patterns of *Sumud* that challenge power structures, either Israeli or Palestinian. A few points should be stressed. First, the vast majority of activists emphasize the necessity of keeping *Sumud* in the context of the Palestinians in Israel as unarmed resistance, both for pragmatic and principled reasons. A second observation which paves the path for a new definition of *Sumud* is emphasizing that *Sumud* is constructed from both individual and collective experiences that took place in the past and still do so. In this way, *Sumud* is viewed as a phenomenon that develops into an ongoing process of construction, something that explains the variety of *Sumud* actions and behaviors of the Palestinian struggle.

However, it also opens the way for understanding the demands of updating and adjusting *Sumud* to present conditions in order to make it effective. This leads to a third observation that was stressed by most of the activists: the need to move toward active *Sumud* in order to transform social and power relations in Israel. "Active" means taking responsibility, constructing future initiatives, and moving from the traditional understanding of cultural *Sumud* in the context of the Palestinians in Israel, toward a transformative *Sumud* which includes the four patterns of *Sumud*: practical, personal, cultural and active. By this, activists challenge the monopoly of *Sumud* as a cultural resistance and demand moving to active *Sumud* as a political act that allows the Palestinians in Israel to fulfill their potential away from romanticizing their physical remaining in their homeland.

Notes

1. Military rule was imposed mainly in rural areas, while the urban centers were put under tight civilian monitoring and control. In my city, Haifa, the remaining Palestinians were concentrated in one main neighborhood, *Wadi al Nisnas*. In Jaffa, Palestinians were concentrated in *al Ajami*. Politically, the military rule unit functioned under the Ministry of Defense on the one hand and the Israeli secret service, the *Shabak*, on the other. For more information, see Ilan Pappe, *The Forgotten Palestinians* (New Haven: Yale University Press, 2011), 46–93.

2. Israel targeted Palestinian intellectuals in general. Some like Ghassan Kanafani were assassinated, others like Mahmoud Darwish, were arrested and others were exiled. Israel used the term "black list," particularly during the years of Military Rule, for political pursuit against intellectuals, writers and teachers.
3. There is disagreement on determining the years of Palestinians' Revolution. *Fateh*, for instance, refers to 1965 as the first year of the Revolution, whereas others refer to the years between 1967 and 1982 as the Palestinian Revolution. However, I am following Yezid Sayigh's determination in his book *Armed Struggle and the Search for State* (1997), since it spans an entire epoch in the history of the contemporary Palestinian national movement, from the *Nakba* of 1948, to the PLO-Israel accord of 1993.
4. Throughout the chapter, I opted to use a first name for activists whom I interviewed. This does not necessarily mean that they are their real names. First names are used throughout the text to simplify the text instead of giving a description to every single actor interviewed as the common dominator between all of them is that they are engaged activists.
5. Administrative detention, as it is used in Israeli terminology is a procedure that allows the Israeli military to hold prisoners indefinitely on secret information without charging them or allowing them to stand trial. Administrative detention is used almost exclusively to detain Palestinians from the occupied Palestinian territory (oPt), which includes the West Bank, East Jerusalem, and the Gaza Strip (see Addameer 2017).
6. There is a discussion between scholars over determining everyday action as everyday resistance. Some emphasize the outcome in terms of bringing change, while others prefer emphasizing the intention of the agent. Personal price is used to describe avoiding open confrontation in extreme contexts. In contrast, the data suggest "personal price and sacrificing" as another indicator for determining everyday action as resistance. Yet, in the Palestinian context, it seems that there is a distinct hierarchy based on this. The more you sacrifice and pay a high personal price, the more you are eligible to gain the title of resistance; otherwise, different words can describe your actions.
7. The word activist, *Nashit* in Arabic, gained popularity with the emergence of the NGO's terminology which was developed after the Oslo Accord, replacing the terminology of revolution which it was viewed as a violent one.
8. Onions neutralize the effect of tear gas and are an integral part of Palestinian demonstrations.
9. According to some Islamic approaches, the voice of women is forbidden in public. This has been an argument with less conservative and

secular groups and feminists, who view this prohibition as another way of oppressing women.
10. Usually most of the demonstrations take place in Arab villages, some of them in Haifa which is a mixed city. Demonstrations in Tel-Aviv are rare, and for some activists are important because they symbolize direct confrontation with the Israeli street and Israelis who live in the "Tel-Aviv battle," in the center away from marginalized places.
11. Since Arabs in general do not serve in the Israeli army, which is three years after finishing high school, from age 18 to 21, the hidden message is that only those who served in the army are eligible to apply for the job.
12. This is done for two reasons. First, to protect Palestinian demonstrators from the right-wing demonstrators who usually protest in front of them (with no need for permission). Second, to protect demonstrators from political and legal prosecution.
13. With the Arab Spring and the chaos in Arab countries combined with attacks on Christians, especially in Egypt, Israeli authorities find it a golden opportunity to promote the idea of Military Service for the Christians. For that, they used some religious figures from the church and established a special unit in the Israeli army to encourage Christians to join the army. However, the vast majority of Palestinian Christians in Israel emphasize their belonging to the Palestinian people and stress that taking part in armed actions oppose their beliefs and religion.
14. While writing this chapter, the Israeli government downgraded Arabic from having the status of an official language, based on the definition of Israel as the "national home for the Jewish people." Before this bill, Arabic was considered an official language from the British Mandate period. This means the disappearance of Arabic from the public sphere and public institutions in an official and legal way. Before that, Arabic appeared on street signs with spelling mistakes, and despite the right of using Arabic in state institution, this did not apply in reality, mainly because of a lack of communication between Arabs and Jews who knew few words of Arabic.

References

Addameer. 2017. "On Administrative Detention." *Addameer.org*, July. http://www.addameer.org/israeli_military_judicial_system/administrative_detention.

Ali, Nijmeh. 2009. "The Role of Music in a Liberation Process: The Palestinian First Intifada." MA diss., The Hebrew University of Jerusalem.

Atack, Iain. 2012. *Nonviolence in Political Theory*. Edinburgh: Edinburgh University Press.

Erikson, Erik Homburger. 1968. *Identity*. New York: Norton.

Fanon, Frantz, Jean-Paul Sartre, and Constance Farrington. 1963. *The Wretched of the Earth*. New York: Grove Press.
Feuer, Lewis S. 1969. *Conflict of Generation: The Character and Significance of Student Movements*. New York: Basic Books.
Foucault, Michel. 1978. *The History of Sexuality. Vol. 1: An Introduction*. New York: Random House.
Hall, Stuart. 1977. "Culture, the Media and the Ideological Effect." In *Mass Communication and Society*, edited by M. Gurevitch, J. Woollacott, and J. Curran, 119–38. London: Arnold Edward.
Hoy, David Couzens. 2005. *Critical Resistance: From Post Structuralism to Post-critique*. Cambridge: MIT Press.
Jamal, Amal. 2011. *Arab Minority Nationalism in Israel: The Politics of Indigeneity*. London: Routledge.
Jayyusi, Salma Khadra, ed. 1992. *Anthology of Modern Palestinian Literature*. New York: Columbia University Press.
Jefferess, David. 2008. *Postcolonial Resistance: Culture, Liberation and Transformation*. Toronto: University of Toronto Press.
Jiryis, Sabrī. 1969. *The Arabs in Israel, 1948–1966 [hā-'Arābīm be-Iiśrā'ēl, engl]*. Translated by Meric Dobson. Beirut: Institute for Palestine Studies.
Kanafani, Ghassan. [1967] 2013. *Resistance Literature in Occupied Palestine 1948–1966*. Cyprus: Rimal Publications.
Pappe, Ilan. 2011. *The Forgotten Palestinians*. New Haven: Yale University Press.
Rijke, Alexandra, and Toine Van Teeffelen. 2014. "To Exist Is to Resist: *Sumud*, Heroism, and the Everyday." *Jerusalem Quarterly* 59: 86–99.
Sayigh, Yezid. 1997. *Armed Struggle and the Search for State: The Palestinian National Movement, 1949–1993*. Oxford: Oxford University Press.
Scott, James C. 1985. *Weapons of the Weak: Everyday Forms of Peasant Resistance*. New Haven: Yale University Press.
Scott, James C. 1990. *Domination and the Arts of Resistance: Hidden Transcripts*. New Haven: Yale University Press.
Scott, James C. 1992. "Domination, Acting, and Fantasy." In *The Paths to Domination, Resistance, and Terror*, edited by C. Nordstorm and J. Martin, 55–84. Berkeley: University of California Press.
Sharp, Gene. 1973. *The Politics of Nonviolent Action: Part 1, 2 & 3*. Boston: Porter Sargent.
Tartir, Alaa. 2017. "Criminalizing Resistance: The Cases of Balata and Jenin Refugee Camps." *Journal of Palestine Studies* 46 (2): 7–22.
Tawil-Souri, Helga. 2011. "Where Is the Political in Cultural Studies in Palestine." *International Journal of Cultural Studies* 14 (5): 467–82.

CHAPTER 5

Who Protests in Palestine? Mobilization Across Class Under the Palestinian Authority

Dana El Kurd

INTRODUCTION

Whether the wave of protests that erupted in 2015, termed the "Third Intifada" (El Kurd 2015), or the protests around the Al-Aqsa mosque more recently—it becomes clear to those observing these events that mass mobilization is common in the Palestinian territories (El Kurd 2017). Mass mobilization is not, however, uniform. While the protests often erupt in contentious areas and refugee camps, many cities remain dormant. Moreover, sustained protest movements thus far only exist in specific villages. The occurrence of protests across the West Bank in a uniform fashion has become increasingly rare. Thus, the question remains: who protests?

There is a wide range of literature that attempts to explain the socioeconomic factors that predict mobilization. A common explanation for who protests is the idea of relative deprivation. This is a particularly common explanation to explain mobilization in the Middle East, and was

D. El Kurd (✉)
Arab Center for Research and Policy Studies,
Doha Institute for Graduate Studies, Doha, Qatar

© The Author(s) 2019
A. Tartir and T. Seidel (eds.),
Palestine and Rule of Power, Middle East Today,
https://doi.org/10.1007/978-3-030-05949-1_5

often used following the Arab Spring. The idea goes that those who protest are more educated middle classes, frustrated at their lack of opportunity. This dovetails with the theory of resource mobilization, i.e. those with more resources (wealth, education, etc.) have greater organizational capacity, and thus mobilize more effectively. These middle classes have more information at their disposal, ability to organize, and political awareness overall.

I argue that there is a clear class differentiation in these protest movements, but not in the direction that the literature would have us expect. While a number of theories would predict middle-class mobilization, in the case of the West Bank, the opposite seems to be true. The middle classes rarely participate in these movements. Surprisingly, those with the expected lowest level of resources (i.e. working classes in rural areas and refugee camps) are those who participate in sustained mobilizations that are both pre-organized and longer-lasting.

Specifically, I argue that the middle class does not mobilize precisely because its interest are tied to the status quo; mainly, the retrenchment of the Palestinian Authority and, unwittingly, the occupation. Mobilization is not determined solely by the availability of resources, both physical and human. Rather, the relation of individuals in society to the status quo regimes determines mobilization. Moreover, the working class has particular types of resources that previous scholarship has not fully considered. It is for that reason specifically that we find mobilization concentrated in areas we would not expect: more rural, less organizational capacity, and with members that do not necessarily have more education or information.

I utilize an original dataset on daily mobilizations in the West Bank, from 2007 to 2015, to assess the pattern of mobilization quantitatively. I find that, as my theory predicts, mobilizations occur overwhelmingly in rural areas and refugee camps. I augment this analysis with case study vignettes of protest movements in the West Bank. I contrast these protest movements with qualitative information on protest capacity in larger cities, using interviews and first-hand accounts.

Class and Democracy

The role of class mobilization has been a crucial factor in the democratization process, but has been highly contested in the literature. Scholars continue to disagree about which class is most relevant to this phenomenon. Many have posited that the middle class is the "bulwark of democracy" (Lipset 1960). As the literature on this topic developed, other scholars introduced some ambiguity to this relationship. Specifically, the argument was that the middle class *could* be the driver of change, if other conditions (particularly the size of the working class) remained small (Rueschemeyer et al. 1992).

The centrality of middle-class mobilization in this dynamic still reemerges frequently, especially with regards to recent events in the Arab world. For instance, scholars such as Acemoglu and Robinson (2009) argue that the middle class is the most crucial to a successful democratization. The argument is that the middle class acts as a buffer between the extremes of the working classes and the elite, and ensures the consolidation of democracy. Much of the analysis of the Arab Spring centered around this explanation as well; many posited that the Arab middle classes were responsible for the uprisings, given their capacity to organize and their frustrations with their regimes (Beissinger et al. 2015). Such explanations for mobilization, as we will see in the next section, do not always stand up to scrutiny.

Explanations for Protest

There are two main theories on mobilization. The first explanation centers on the idea of "relative deprivation." The argument in this vein of literature is that those with high expectations that are not met by their current political contexts are more frustrated, which leads them to be the likely participants of mobilization. A corollary to this general argument is that those with higher education and low achievement are likely to fit this description; mainly, the middle classes. The literature focused on relative deprivation deals with individual, psychological explanations for mobilization. These individuals have grievances related to their class interests, which pushes them to mobilize and engage in contentious politics (Gurr 1970).

Scholars later on noted that while relative deprivation theory perhaps explains psychological motivations for mobilization, it could not capture the whole story. Particularly, it did not address the structural conditions of these individuals and the strategies available to them. For that reason, scholars developed theories of "resource mobilization" (McCarthy and Zald 1977; Tilly 1978). This cluster of work argued that grievances were not a necessary or a sufficient condition for social movements of any form. Rather, the availability of individuals with resources—time, money, labor—was a much more salient determinant. Access to institutional centers, media, information, money, and elite structures are crucial to the emergence of mobilization (Lee 2011). Education in particular leads to greater access to these resources, as well as fosters a national interest, civic duty, and provides greater organizational capacity (Anderson 1983; Wolfinger and Rosenstone 1980). Thus, these arguments still allude to the idea that the middle class will mobilize much more readily than the rural or working classes, given both its physical and human capital.

Another avenue of research has also disproven the original relative deprivation argument posited by the earlier literature. Particularly, research on participation in civil war finds that the original grievance arguments cannot account for who participates in violent conflict or mobilization (Humphreys and Weinstein 2008; Collier and Hoeffler 2004). Rather, structural conditions and the strategies available to participants are more crucial determinants (Fearon and Laitin 2003). Although this research explores a type of mobilization less relevant for our purposes, it still reveals that empirical analysis discounts the earlier explanations of relative deprivation as a factor in mobilization, while providing some proof of the importance of resource mobilization.

Reconsidering the Working Class

Overall, the literature on class mobilization and democracy has relegated the working class to the margins of explanation, although in many places the working class is responsible for the bulk of collective action. In this chapter, I bring class "back in" to the analysis. In that way, we can better understand patterns of collective action, particularly within authoritarian contexts. To do so, I define the working class in opposition to the middle class. As a group, I distinguish the middle class by a set of privileges, beyond their income alone (Yang 2007). These privileges include educational attainment, a particular occupational status, and access to resources—all of which are tied to income level, but not exclusive to it. On that basis, I define the working class as that segment of society *without* those privileges.

Common explanations, outlined above, argue that the working class has fewer resources and thus lower organizational capacity. This reasoning may arise from the fact that the resources of the working class are not entirely recognized, and are thus omitted from analysis. Take for example the role of social networks. Social ties and stronger networks among the working class may substitute for the physical and human capital enjoyed by the middle classes. These social networks can thus sustain working-class mobilization even in the face of repression and high individual costs.

The strength of social networks allows group-level dynamics to become salient and effective; specifically, strong communities allow for the more effective use of "social sanctions" (Taylor 1988). Social sanctions are defined as the manner in which a community enforces particular behaviors and social order through both positive and negative endorsements. When social ties are strong and collective action is seen as necessary for the community, these kinds of sanctions facilitate collective action and allow groups to circumvent the free-rider problem.[1] While the working class may lack educational opportunities as well as brick and mortar institutions with organizational capacity, they may substitute for those resources with the strength of their social networks.[2] Thus, we hypothesize that *working-class communities will have strong social networks and rely more heavily on social ties in moments of collective action.*

Another important factor in working-class mobilization is the working class's weaker ties to the indigenous governing apparatus; in this case, the Palestinian Authority. Since its inception in 1994, the PA has embarked on extensive co-optation campaigns. A large segment of Palestinian society today relies on employment within the PA's institutions for their livelihoods. Even former opposition, such as ex-fighters from the Al-Aqsa Brigades or activists from rural protest campaigns, have been given positions within the PA (International Crisis Group 2008, 14–17). This serves a twofold purpose: tying the relatively educated middle class to the survival of the PA itself, and neutralizing possible opposition to the PA's rule.

However, this co-optation mechanism is not uniform. These measures are at work to a much larger degree among the middle class. After all, would-be bureaucrats have to have a certain level of education and technical skills to assume roles within the PA's institutions, something the working class often cannot offer. These co-optation mechanisms are also most heavily at work in areas under direct PA control, i.e. highly urbanized segments of the Palestinian territories, denoted under Area A. They are less pervasive in areas under partial PA control, such as the rural areas of Area B or the marginalized areas of Area C. Co-optation of the middle class in urban centers helps to tie in their prospects with the survival of the PA, and therefore affects both their capacity and willingness to mobilize. Therefore, we can expect that *affiliation with the PA regime or the Israeli government inhibits collective action efforts in middle-class communities, and a lack of affiliation facilitates collective action efforts in working-class communities.*

Finally, another dynamic that has neutralized the middle class involves the "NGO-ization" of Palestinian politics (Dana 2016). This is the process by which civil society in Palestine has become increasingly tied to foreign aid and foreign approval. As a result, the greater goal of Palestinian liberation has been relegated to small groups focused on narrow issue areas, which remain fragmented and largely demobilized. "Formal" involvement with NGO's and civil society organizations is how the middle class engages in politics, and these organizations coordinate with the PA to remain viable, and avoid any hindrance to their work. Second, these organizations enjoy having a "seat at the table," and so engage with the PA on the basis that they may affect change in their issue areas. On the other hand, the working class does not organize around the creation of NGO's or lobbying for foreign funds; in fact they are often marginalized by these dynamics (Tartir and Sansour 2014). Instead, the working class often relies on grassroots organization and informal institutions, which are more readily available to them. Thus, the theory of class mobilization expects that *working-class communities will engage in formal politics at a lower level than middle-class communities.*

In sum, the difference between the middle class and the working class boils down to the clarity of preferences. In the case of a colonized society such as Palestine, the middle class is tied to the organs of the colonizing state. This has also been the case historically across a number of colonized nations. The long-term interests of the middle class may in fact benefit from an end to the status quo, but their interests in the short term are defined by their *role* in the status quo. The middle class has vested interests in the state's institutions, whatever they may be. If provided with some maneuvering room, the middle class will participate in conventional politics and play by the "rules of the game." Thus their true interests can become distorted and easily co-opted.

This is in direct contrast to the working classes. Those involved in collective action campaigns see little benefit from the PA; they do not enjoy positions in the Palestinian Authority, or through assimilation with the Israeli state. Their interests lie in complete opposition to the continuation of the status quo. This is why these campaigns often demand an end to the apartheid system in its entirety. Overall, the middle class is often channeled into "formal" and "civil" politics, whereas the working class engages with politics at the grassroots level and often through informal institutions.

GENERAL CONDITIONS OF WORKING-CLASS PALESTINIANS

For the purposes of this chapter, we define the working class as those who work in manual labor or service positions, farmers, and those who live in refugee camps. Although conditions for these segments of Palestinian society differ based on particular occupational challenges, they all feature two main characteristics: a lack of ties to Israeli government institutions or PA institutions, and a greater political marginalization.

For example, following the creation of the Palestinian Authority, Palestinian farmers were ignored for much of the 1990s and early 2000s. Attempts to help family farms across the Palestinian territories remain economically viable and independent were limited. In fact, scholars have pointed out that the amount of international aid allocated to Palestinian farmers during this time period was negligible; only 1.4% throughout the whole time period (Tartir and Sansour 2014). Farmers struggled with maintaining control over their land despite Israeli appropriation for the benefit of settlements. They also faced the challenge of subsidized and cheap Israeli products flooding their markets. Finally, they continue to face land appropriation for the sake of building "industrial zones" (Tartir 2013). These zones, instead of achieving economic independence, actually make Palestinian society more dependent on Israeli products, at the expense of the family farm (see Palestinian Economic Policy Research Institute 2005; Environmental Justice in Palestine Team and Al-Haq Organization 2017).

Nevertheless, what is important to note here is that the PA allocates very little of its budget to Palestinian farming communities. On one level, this means these farming communities are generally unrepresented among the PA's institutions and decision-making processes. On the other, however, it means these farming communities are insulated from PA co-optation and intrusion. This has a profound effect on their capacity to engage in collective action and organize around their shared interest.

General Impressions of Mobilization Across the West Bank

Before delving into protest dynamics, it is important to address the unique administrative segmentation that exists today in the West Bank. Following the Oslo accords in 1993, the Palestinian territories were split into three main areas: Areas A, B, and C (Steves 2013). In Area A, the PA is most free to operate as a quasi-state, Area B features limited PA control, and in Area C the PA is not allowed at all. Many Palestinians thus live in areas partially controlled by two regimes. While this was meant to be a temporary measure, with the PA slated to become the government of a future Palestinian state by 1999, the Israeli government never ceded this authority. Instead it utilized the PA to govern the territories while abdicating responsibility for its policies toward Palestinians (Tartir 2016, 2017). Area B and C are both economically and politically marginalized,, consisting of mostly rural villages. Residents of these areas either rely on agriculture or manual labor positions. Of course, the working class and poor communities also exist in parts of Area A; after all, not every resident of Ramallah is middle class or wealthy. Nevertheless the bulk of the working class, as I define it in this chapter, exists in the outskirts of urban areas, rural villages, and camps, which are all often found in Area B and C.

Thus to begin our assessment of who protests, we must first examine the sheer number of mobilizations across the three areas. Using the Institute for Palestine Studies Chronologies, UN OCHA "Protection of Civilians" weekly reports, as well as *Shabakat al-Quds al-Akhbariya* (a Palestinian news network), I created a dataset of political mobilization which covers when protests occur and the location (i.e. whether or not it was in a rural, urban, or refugee camp setting, and exact neighborhood or village).[3] I also collected data on the density of settlements around each neighborhood/village, and whether or not Israeli incursions had occurred in that location at the time of mobilization.

Figure 5.1 illustrates the stark differences between areas; Area A, with the greatest population of middle-class and wealthy Palestinians, features the *least* number of mobilizations by far. Area B and C hold the bulk of protests in the time period examined here (2007–present). This is in spite of the fact that the majority of Palestinians lives in Area A and suffers limitations on mobility, Israeli incursions, and settler violence on a regular basis.

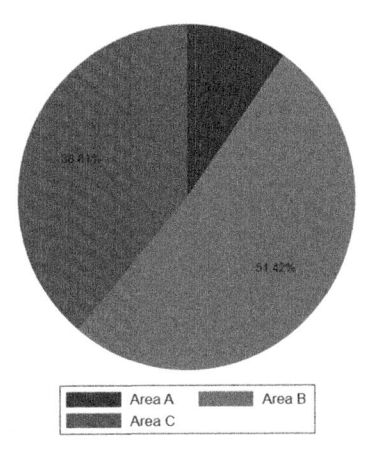

Fig. 5.1 Number of protests by area

Table 5.1 Oneway ANOVA test results

Area	Means and standard deviations	N
A	0.045 (0.305)	11,025
B	0.071 (0.488)	20,071
C	0.058 (0.429)	19,342
	F statistic: 0.0000***	Total N: 50,438

An examination by sheer number may not be the most accurate assessment, so we also use a oneway ANOVA test. This way, we can assess the difference in number of protests across areas is statistically significant. A summary of these results can be found in Table 5.1.

As the *F statistic* in Table 5.1 shows, the difference in number of protests across the three areas is indeed statistically significant (at the highest level of $p < 0.01$). Thus, the difference in number of protests is not due to random variation.

Secondly, I examine the difference in mobilization levels between refugee camps and non-camp areas. Palestinians living in camps suffer poverty, regular Israeli attacks, and lack of access to resources. They should be the least able to mobilize given their precarious conditions, if resource

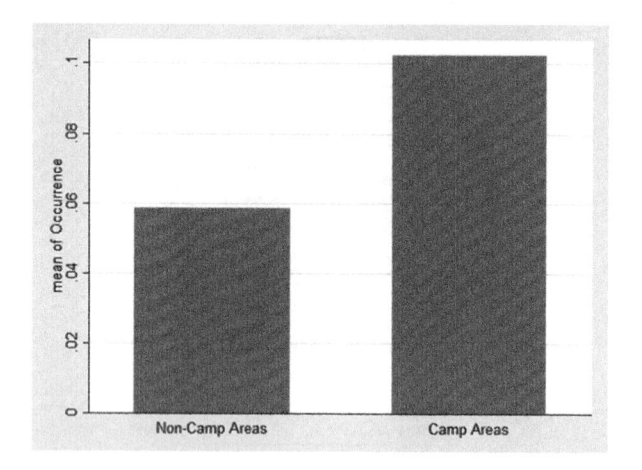

Fig. 5.2 Mobilizations in camp vs. non-camp areas

Table 5.2 T-test of mobilization in camp vs. non-camp areas

	Camp	Non-camp
Mean	0.102	0.058
SD	0.488	0.428
SE	0.011	0.002
N	2080	48,461
p value	0.000***	

mobilization theory is correct. Nonetheless, when we look at the average number of protests in camp areas versus non-camp areas, we find stark differences in the opposite direction of what existing literature would expect (Fig. 5.2 and Table 5.2).

Camp areas have an average number of protest that is significantly higher than non-camp areas. Simple difference of means tests also show a statistically significant difference at the $p<0.01$ level.

Although the difference between areas is statistically significant, it stands to reason that another variable is responsible for this difference, rather than the class dynamic itself. For example, a possible explanation for the differential level of protest across areas is that Palestinians in Area A, under more direct PA jurisdiction, are merely much less aggrieved and have less to protest about. Therefore, I examine the average number of Israeli incursions as a proxy for grievance (Fig. 5.3).

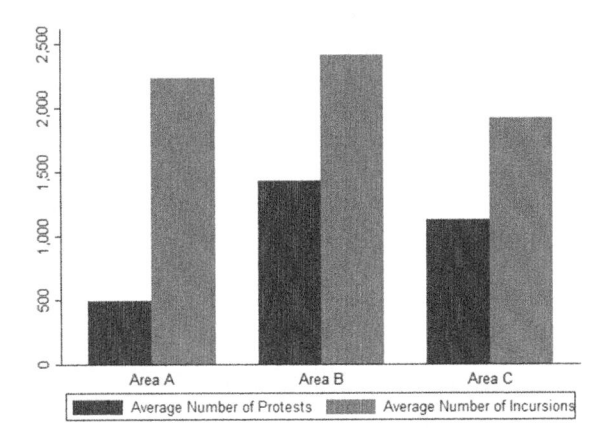

Fig. 5.3 Average number of Israeli incursions compared with average number of protests by area

Clearly, the presence of Israeli incursions does not seem to predict the intensity of protests. The alternative explanation of grievance, either due to IDF incursions or settler violence/activity, does not hold up in the data. The underlying cause of the differentiated nature of protests across the territories today also cannot be explained by an urban–rural divide, given that Area A (the most urban) is often the most acquiescent. In sum, the areas with the highest concentration of the working class are the most active.

Case Studies of Contention

To corroborate the general trends born out of the quantitative assessment, I will demonstrate the theory at work using case studies from the West Bank: the Bil'in protest movement and the Jerusalem protests around the Al-Aqsa compound. I will focus on demonstrating "working-class resources," specifically the role of social ties in the sustainability of these campaigns. I will also examine the role the PA played in each campaign's overall efficacy. And finally, I will demonstrate the each community's strategies, and whether such strategies utilized formal political institutions or remained outside the realm of government oversight.

Bil'in

Bil'in is a rural village of approximately 1800 people in the governorate of Ramallah, located in Area B under dual PA and Israeli jurisdiction. The village epitomizes what we think of when we say working class: manual labor in the Israeli labor market and agriculture are the major sources of employment, and in 2007 only 7.4% of the population has a high school education (ARIJ 2012). In 2005, the Israeli government began work for what they called "the border wall" on the village's lands.[4]

For the villagers dependent on the agricultural sector as a means of survival, this turn of events was unacceptable. The Israeli government was confiscating a full 38% of the village's land (ARIJ 2012). Thus, the people of Bil'in founded a "Popular Committee against the Wall." This committee has since organized a series of weekly protests, conferences, and attempts at negotiation with the Israeli government. They pursued legal strategies, enlisting the assistance of Israeli activists, as well as direct action strategies such as protesting every Friday (Carmeli-Pollak 2006). Their non-violent tactics in the face of repeated repression, as well as their creative strategies, captured the popular imagination worldwide. Bil'in became the site of international solidarity, with a large number of international activists taking part in the protests on a regular basis. Today, Bil'in continues to protest weekly, although their efficacy has waxed and waned throughout the years.

Social Ties

The popular committee in Bil'in village was formed by Iyad Burnat and his social circle, which became deeply involved in the movement since 2005. This popular committee was initiated outside the scope and oversight of the village's official council, unprompted by official institutions. The council is a 9-member body, appointed by the PA, responsible for providing services to the local population. This council did not, however, engage with the issue of the separation wall initially.

Bil'in consists of a few core families—Abu Rahma, Burnat, Ghanim, etc.—and all were represented in the activities and leadership of this committee.[5] The protests were often held right after Friday prayer, an organic assembly point where most of the villagers could participate. They also engaged deliberately in solidarity building exercises so as to, in the words of Emad Burnat, "to encourage us to reach out to other villagers and get them to protest" (Burnat and Davidi 2011). The strong social ties extended outside the village to neighboring areas, such as the village of Nil'in. Whenever protests, incursions, or deaths occurred, Bil'in's residents joined with the other villages to protest in a unified fashion.

Most villagers leaned Fatah in a general sense, but the popular committee did not exclude people from other political groups and did not purport to represent Fatah's positions as a party.[6] Using the committee as a meeting point, villagers utilized their strong social ties to increase their ranks and come to decisions on the basis of consensus around their protest actions, their demands of the Israeli government, and the way they would run their campaign.

PA Involvement

As previously mentioned, the popular committee was formed without the direction of the PA or the official village council. For quite some time, the villagers of Bil'in were even somewhat resistant to visits by PA officials. Attempts at co-opting their movement, through official visits and photo shoots, were met unenthusiastically by the villagers. Iyad Burnat was himself a vocal critic of the PA's political role (Burnat 2013). Over time, however, the PA formulated an institutional arrangement which allowed them to direct and eventually co-opt the Bil'in protest movement.

One way that the PA co-opts political groups involves the *hay'a*, or committee, system. These *hay'as*/committees work under the auspices of a particularly ministry, or are subsumed under the Palestinian Liberation Organization. They are often used to impose PA control over sensitive or popular issues, such as the apartheid wall or popular resistance ("About the *Hay'a*" 2016). The leadership of these *hay'as* often targets existing grassroots organizations and incorporate them into the PA's chain of command.

A *hay'a* centered on opposition to the wall has existed within the PA since 2003. However, after a number of moves, the president assigned jurisdiction of the committee to the PLO in 2014 by presidential decree. This *hay'a* has since inserted itself into the activities of the village's committee, in order to create a "coordinated effort" across the territories. The *hay'a* is not to be confused, however, with the Popular Struggle Coordination Committee, which attempted to accomplish the same task by linking different village movements together at the grassroots level ("The PSCC" 2012). The *hay'a* instead represented the government's official role in the village protest movements.

Many members of the village committee now work within the hay'a, from Ramallah. But, these members report that the *hay'a* has become increasingly ineffective since 2014, and that there is distrust between the villagers and leadership.[7] They complain that it is difficult to sustain the protests, in direct contrast to the early years of the movement. "Even though the *hay'a* tries to coordinate the West Bank protest movements" says one member, "the villagers do not trust us, and we can't get the different popular committees to work together."[8] Today, international participants outnumber the local population in the weekly actions, and attendance overall has tapered off.

We can see from this example that the PA's increased involvement over time had a direct effect on the efficacy of Bil'in's protest movement. Attempting to reorient village activities through formal channels has neutralized the dynamism of Bil'in's popular committee. Moreover, the increased ties to the PA, through employment in the *hay'a* or other institutions, have neutralized particular leaders. Thus, the PA's co-optation mechanism through the *hay'a* system was able to effectively control Bil'in's mobilization, which threatened the PA's role as the prime negotiator between Israel and the Palestinian people. The episode in Bil'in is just one microcosm of this dynamic; many villages and popular committees across the territories shared the same fate in recent years.

Summary

In 2011, after years of protest, Bil'in was successful in pressuring the Israeli government to reroute the segregation wall in a way that allowed the village to regain some of its land (Wilson 2016). What is interesting here is that, although the village succeeded in their demands to some degree, protests continued. The stated purpose of the protests remained an end to Israeli segregation and occupation. For example, in the closing statement of the Bil'in conference of 2013, the villagers reasserted their commitment to the BDS campaign, freedom for all political prisoners, and a unified national struggle (Popular Struggle Coordination Committee 2013). They committed themselves to the Palestinian national cause at its broadest level, even though their immediate demands had been met. Although the Bil'in protest movement struggles to this day with PA intervention and co-optation, the fact that villagers continued to protest at all shows that the working class has a broad, long-term understanding of its preferences. They recognize that a true shift in their living conditions, and a just resolution to the Palestinian struggle, does not come about when they are allowed to use a fragment of their agricultural lands again. Instead, their statements show they believe a shift will only occur once broader Palestinian demands are taken seriously. Their long-term objectives and dynamic strategies garnered concessions from the Israeli occupation; they were only hindered by increased PA intervention.

Jerusalem

The Jerusalem protests of July 2017 present another case study of working-class mobilization. Importantly, these protests were outside the purview of the PA entirely. As such, it allows us to examine how protest movements function without PA intrusion. That way we will be able to gauge how effective the movement was in direct contrast to the case of Bil'in, under PA jurisdiction.

Background on Jerusalem

East Jerusalem was occupied in 1967. Unlike the remainder of the West Bank however, East Jerusalem was not included in the Oslo Accords under the "area" allocations. Instead the issue of Jerusalem was postponed to future negotiations, and East Jerusalem's neighborhoods were classified as J1 (under the Israeli Jerusalem Municipality) and J2 (parts of East Jerusalem ejected from the municipality) (Palestinian Central Bureau of Statistics 2015). Palestinians in Jerusalem were given "permanent residence" in Jerusalem, although these residencies are often revoked for political reasons. Life in both areas is akin to life in Area C, in the fact that both Palestinian institutions and the PA are not allowed to operate. Institutions which organized Palestinians in times of crisis were closed down, and new organizations were not allowed to emerge (Arafeh 2015). The Israeli government took the political vacuum as a green light to pursue aggressive settlement policy in the same areas (Arafeh et al. 2017). The Israelis have also pursued a policy of disenfranchisement in recent years, by way of the segregation wall; predominantly Arab neighborhoods have steadily been cut off by the wall and the greater city (Arafeh 2015). The intention of the Israeli government is to excise the Arab neighborhoods, to maintain a majority Jewish presence in "official" Jerusalem (Agha 2018) (Fig. 5.4).

The excision of Arab neighborhoods has created a unique situation in which particular areas are almost completely lawless. Neighborhoods such as Kufr Aqab, Ar-Ram, Abu Dis, which once were part of Jerusalem are now cut off. While Palestinians in these areas engage in small business and some travel for service work, they remain economically choked. Many who held Jerusalem IDs all their lives now need special permits to enter into the city center (Arafeh 2016). Neither PA officials nor Israeli officials operate in these areas (aside from IDF incursions) or provide services.

Within J1 areas, i.e. Arab neighborhoods that are still under Israeli jurisdiction, Palestinians are struggling economically. Prior to the occupation of Jerusalem, the tourism sector in Jerusalem alone generated 14% of the West Bank's GDP (Arafeh 2016). Today, areas which had depended on seasonal pilgrimages and external tourism have completely dwindled away. Moreover, Palestinians in these areas are also obligated to pay exorbitant taxes to the Israeli municipality even though they are provided with subpar services or none at all (Arafeh 2016). In fact, 90% of Jerusalem city's budget is directed toward Jewish Israeli neighborhoods despite the fact that Palestinians are at least 37% of the population (UNCTAD 2013). Finally, as a result of the wall, people in areas adjacent to the city center of Jerusalem travel elsewhere for basic shopping (Arafeh 2016). These conditions compounded to create economically marginalized communities in J1 neighborhoods such as the Old City. Little educational opportunities are available to them, and they have to rely on low-paid service-sector positions in the Israeli labor market for survival.

Aqsa Protests

The Aqsa Compound lies in the Old City, and has been the site of conflict since the occupation of Jerusalem. Prior to the creation of the state of Israel, the Jewish and Muslim sections of the compound were not separated, and for the most part people worshipped freely (Pappé 2011, 116–117). However, following the creation of Israel and the occupation of Jerusalem in 1967, the compound was segregated between Jewish and Muslim areas. Since that time, Israeli religious extremists have expressed

5 WHO PROTESTS IN PALESTINE? ... 121

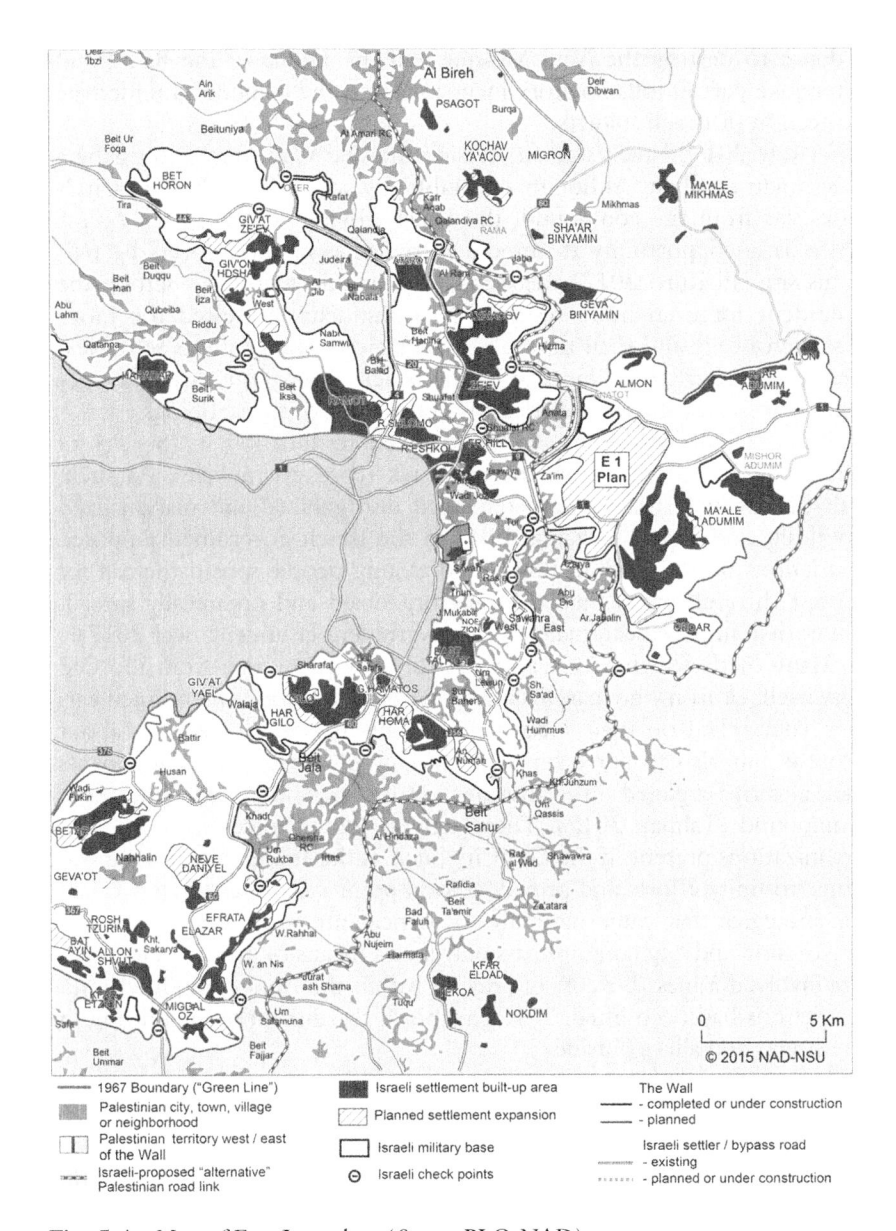

Fig. 5.4 Map of East Jerusalem (*Source* PLO-NAD)

a desire to destroy the Aqsa Mosque and the Dome of the Rock, and often take part in inflammatory incursions into the compound under the protection of Israeli soldiers.

In July 2017, Israeli soldiers outside the Old City were stabbed by a Palestinian assailant. Although the stabbings occurred at the Old City's gates, far from the compound, the Israeli government used the occurrence as an opportunity to impose increased restrictions over the religious site (El Kurd 2017). Recognizing that this action was setting the precedent for even more restrictions, Palestinians protested the move first rhetorically and then through direct action. The goal was to protest the general restrictions imposed by the Israeli occupation, as well as specifically roll back the new restrictions in the wake of the stabbings.

PA-affiliated institutions are not allowed to function in the city of Jerusalem due to the Israeli occupation's repressive policies. As such, Palestinians in Jerusalem have remained disorganized and marginalized politically and kept disorganized. When the Israeli government imposed restrictions on the Aqsa in this period, young people spread the call for protest through social media, locally organized and organically spread, rather than imposed externally or by government entities (Unver 2017).

Many of those who took part in protests either came from the Old City itself, or from the marginalized poor neighborhoods mentioned earlier. They relied on their social ties not only to spread the news about protests but also to agree on tactics. Many of the original participants had already engaged in protesting settler incursions into the Aqsa Compound (Tahhan 2017). These activists joined forces with religious organizations present in the Old City, such as the Islamic Waqf organizations, to unify efforts and provide a focal point for protests. They called for strategies that came naturally to participants, such as protesting at prayer time and engaging in mass prayer as a means of protest. Their tactics involved a mass boycott of praying within the Aqsa compound until restrictions had been lifted. This maximized the disruption by praying in the streets and alleys outside.

Less present at these protests were middle-class Palestinians from comparatively wealthier areas, such as Beit Hanina and Shufat. Middle-class Palestinians often work within the Israeli institutions that service Jerusalem, such as the hospitals and health clinics, or with NGO's and international organizations such as the UN (UNCTAD 2013, 11–13; Palestinian Central Bureau of Statistics 2015, 119–120). They face threats to their livelihoods if they engage in coordinating major protests, and thus often do not participate. In this case, the PA was also slow to react, and did not take a position until a few days of intense activity had passed (El Kurd 2017). Calls for protest from the political parties were also belated, and piggybacked on the existing calls.

Those who were injured or killed during these protests also reveal who actually protested. The young men who died during these protests were all from the areas previously mentioned: Silwan, al-Tur, and Abu Dis. Clearly, most of those who were injured or killed were from neighborhoods which had been subjected to settlement incursions and economic marginalization for years (Al Jazeera 2017).

Summary

Jerusalem's waves of protests have been ongoing in recent years, as economic and political policies of disenfranchisement have taken their toll. What is interesting in the case of Jerusalem is that the Israeli occupation forbids groups with direct ties to the PLO or to the PA from functioning; in fact they target Palestinian organizations generally, even those with no ties to political activity. Despite this prohibition, Palestinians in Jerusalem have been able to depend, somewhat effectively, on their social ties to engage in mobilization campaigns when the need arises. Protests have been organized via independent calls spread through quotidian social networks. These types of protest movements depend on working-class elements in order to succeed, as middle-class elements do not have the incentive to intervene despite the impact Israeli policies bear on their lives. Moreover, the PA's institutions are not involved in the eruption of these protests and are always a step behind. This means that the PA and its co-optation does not have the inhibiting effect it might have in other areas of the territories. Nevertheless, the prohibition on forming sustainable groups means that protest movements in Jerusalem can emerge around narrow issues or particular current events, but cannot be sustained into larger-scale long-term movements.

In the previous sections, I linked increased working-class mobilization to social ties and a lack of affiliation with PA entities. However, an alternative explanation arises: are working-class segments of society protesting because they are simply more aggrieved? Perhaps social ties and a lack of PA affiliation have little to do with a decision to protest. Perhaps the economic stranglehold or political repression on working-class areas is enough to push people to protest.

In answer to this alternative argument, it is important to note: the middle class is not less aggrieved than the working class. After all, the middle class has more to lose as a result of occupation and its subsequent effect on their opportunities. Middle classes, particularly in urban centers, also face a decline in living standards as a result of the occupation's chokehold. Palestinians living in city centers, with more access to education and thus greater expectations for their futures, often find that they are highly limited as a result of the occupation's practices. Perhaps their homes are not immediately endangered, but their livelihoods and future success certainly are. In a recent public opinion poll, 25.4% of Palestinians cited the spread of employment and poverty as the most severe threat facing Palestinian society, closely behind 29.7% of Palestinians who cited the direct threat of land appropriation and occupation (Palestinian Center for Policy and Survey Research 2016).

Thus, the phenomenon of primarily working-class mobilization cannot be accounted for using existing theories related to grievance; in fact, existing theories would predict the exact opposite. With more material and ideational privileges to lose, middle classes should in fact be more aggrieved. And, given their privileges, they should have greater recourse to organizational resources. Nevertheless, what we see in the empirical data is the exact opposite dynamic.

Conclusion

All in all, the assessment of both quantitative and qualitative data shows that existing theories on protest do a poor job of explaining which Palestinians mobilize, and for what reasons. Essentially, the assessment of this chapter is that this can be explained to a large degree by class. The middle class is generally co-opted by the PA's institutions, and the infrastructure of the occupation, whereas the Palestinian working class has been almost entirely marginalized by the PA's development. As such, variation has emerged across class lines regarding political mobilization and protest participation.

This analysis thus helps to explain the patterns of mobilization we see in the Palestinian territories today, as well as the general stagnation in mobilization overall. Judging from this analysis, we can expect protests to emerge in the areas which were not previously centers of protest, given the lack of resources traditionally linked to capacity for mobilization. This chapter also helps to point out the fact that the Palestinian working class has resources not often considered in the literature; specifically, they enjoy strong social cohesion in comparison to middle-class communities, and are therefore able to coordinate more effectively as a community around common goals and shared interests. In sum, future research on this subject would benefit from bringing class "back in" to the analysis, as well as looking at class in new ways and considering new resources.

Notes

1. The free-rider problem is defined here as the situation in which members of a group have an incentive to "free ride," i.e. not contribute to the collective effort, because there is no incentive structure in place to compel true cooperation.
2. One example of this dynamic is that of the Palestinian resistance in the refugee camps of Lebanon. Despite a significant crackdown on resistance networks following the Lebanese civil war, Parkinson (2013) finds that Palestinian resistance was able to sustain itself to a large degree as a direct result of strong social networks. The first intifada is also comparable in these characteristics. Social networks facilitated a sustained resistance movement despite extensive Israeli repression, while mobilizing large segments of society. And this dynamic is replicated within Palestine even today.
3. UN Office for the Coordination of Humanitarian Affairs, Occupied Palestinian Territory (2013–2015), Institute for Palestine Studies Chronologies (2013–2015), Shabakat al-Quds al-Akhbariya (2013–2015), and the Palestinian Central Bureau of Statistics for village-level data.
4. This was misleading term for two reasons. No internationally recognized border exists between Israel and Palestine; only the Green Line exists as a demarcation line following the 1967 war. Although this is now the de facto border, in theory the final drawing of the line is up for debate. Moreover, Israel's wall is not being built along this Green Line; instead, Israel has utilized the "border wall" to confiscate large swaths of land from the West Bank and to maintain a defensive perimeter around illegal Israeli settlements.
5. Interview with Bil'in activist, May 2016.
6. Interview with Bil'in activist, May 2016.
7. Interview with *hay'a* representative, May 2016.
8. Interview with *hay'a* representative, May 2016.

References

"About the *Hay'a*." 2016. Colonization and Wall Resistance Commission, August 21.
Acemoglu, Daron, and James A. Robinson. 2009. *Economic Origins of Dictatorship and Democracy*. Cambridge: Cambridge University Press.
Agha, Zena. 2018. "Israel's Annexation Crusade in Jerusalem: The Role of Ma'ale Adumim and the E-1 Corridor." *Al-Shabaka*, March 26. https://al-shabaka.org/briefs/israels-annexation-crusade-in-jerusalem-the-role-of-maale-adumim-and-the-e1-corridor/.
Al Jazeera. 2017. "Al-Aqsa: Palestinians Killed as Jerusalem Protests Rage." *Al Jazeera*, July 21. https://www.aljazeera.com/news/2017/07/al-aqsa-palestinian-killed-jerusalem-protests-rage-170721113840496.html.
Andersen, Benedict. 1983. *Imagined Communities*. London: Verso.
Arafeh, Nur. 2015. "In Jerusalem, 'Religious War' Is Used to Cloak Colonialism." *Al-Shabaka*, February 3. https://al-shabaka.org/briefs/in-jerusalem-religious-war-is-used-to-cloak-colonialism/.
Arafeh, Nur. 2016. "Economic Collapse in East Jerusalem: Strategies for Recovery." *Al-Shabaka*, November 30. https://al-shabaka.org/briefs/economic-collapse-east-jerusalem-strategies-recovery/.
Arafeh, Nur, Munir Nuseibah, Mouin Rabbani, and Salim Tamari. 2017. "Focus on: Jerusalem." *Al-Shabaka*, March 8. https://al-shabaka.org/focuses/focus-on-jerusalem/.
ARIJ. 2012. "Bil'in Village Profile." Applied Research Institute—Jerusalem. http://vprofile.arij.org/ramallah/pdfs/vprofile/Bi'lin.pdf.
Beissinger, Mark R., Amaney A. Jamal, and Kevin Mazur. 2015. "Explaining Divergent Revolutionary Coalitions: Regime Strategies and the Structuring of Participation in the Tunisian and Egyptian Revolutions." *Comparative Politics* 48 (1): 1–24.
Burnat, Iyad. 2013. "To End the Occupation, Dissolve the Palestinian Authority." *The Electronic Intifada*, December 11. https://electronicintifada.net/content/end-occupation-dissolve-palestinian-authority/12990.
Burnat, Emad, and Guy Davidi. 2011. *5 Broken Cameras* (film). Palestine: Burnat Films.
Carmeli-Pollak, Shai. 2006. *Bil'in Habibti* (film). Tel Aviv: Claudius Films.
Collier, Paul, and Anke Hoeffler. 2004. "Greed and Grievance in Civil War." *Oxford Economic Papers* 56: 563–595.
Dana, Tariq. 2016. "Social Struggle and the Crisis of the Palestinian Left Parties." *Rosa Luxemburg Foundation PAL Papers*, March.
El Kurd, Dana. 2015. "Intifada's Revenge." *Foreign Affairs*, October 22.
El Kurd, Dana. 2017. "Here's What Made Palestinian Protests in East Jerusalem Last Month so Successful." *The Washington Post*, August 17.

Environmental Justice in Palestine Team and Al-Haq Organization. 2017. "Israeli Settlement Industries Polluting Tulkarem, Palestine." *Environmental Justice Atlas.* https://ejatlas.org/conflict/israeli-industries-polluting-palestinian-city-of-tulkarm.

Fearon, James, and David D. Laitin. 2003. "Ethnicity, Insurgency, and Civil War." *American Political Science Review* 97 (1): 75–90.

Gurr, Ted Robert. 1970. *Why Men Rebel.* London: Routledge.

Humphreys, Macartan, and Jeremy M. Weinstein. 2008. "Who Fights? The Determinants of Participation in Civil War." *American Journal of Political Science* 52 (2): 436–455.

International Crisis Group. 2008. "Ruling Palestine II: The West Bank Model?" International Crisis Group Middle East Report No. 79, July 17. https://www.crisisgroup.org/middle-east-north-africa/eastern-mediterranean/israelpalestine/ruling-palestine-ii-west-bank-model.

Lee, Alexander. 2011. "Who Becomes a Terrorist? Poverty, Education, and the Origins of Political Violence." *World Politics* 63 (2): 203–245.

Lipset, Seymour Martin. 1960. *Political Man: The Social Bases of Politics.* Baltimore: Johns Hopkins University Press.

McCarthy, John, and Mayer Zald. 1977. "Resource Mobilization and Social Movements: A Partial Theory." *American Journal of Sociology* 82 (6): 1212–1241.

Palestinian Central Bureau of Statistics. 2015. "Jerusalem Statistical Yearbook, 2015." *Jerusalem Quarterly* 62: 110–124. http://www.palestine-studies.org/sites/default/files/jq-articles/JQ%2062_Jerusalem%20Statistical.pdf.

Palestinian Center for Policy and Survey Research. 2016. "Palestinian Public Opinion Poll #59," March 17–19. http://www.pcpsr.org/sites/default/files/poll%2059%20%20fulltext%20English.pdf.

Palestinian Economic Policy Research Institute. 2005. *The Economics of Agriculture in the Qalqilya and Tulkarem Districts: Improving the Profitability of Farmers Affected by the Separation Wall.* Jerusalem and Ramallah: Palestinian Economic Policy Research Institute (MAS).

Pappé, Ilan. 2011. *The Rise and Fall of a Palestinian Dynasty: The Husaynis, 1700–1948.* London: Saqi.

Parkinson, Sarah Elizabeth. 2013. "Organizing Rebellion: Rethinking High-Risk Mobilization and Social Networks in War." *American Political Science Review* 107 (3): 418–432.

Popular Struggle Coordination Committee. 2013. "Final statement of Bil'in Eighth International Conference: Towards the Mobilization of Popular Resistance: Adopting a Unified Strategy." Bil'in and Bethlehem, October 2–4. https://bilinconference.wordpress.com/.

Rueschemeyer, Dietrich, Evelyne Huber Stephens, and John D. Stephens. 1992. *Capitalist Development and Democracy.* Chicago: University of Chicago Press.

Steves, Rick. 2013. "Palestine's Complicated Borders: Complex as ABC." *The Huffington Post*, May 16. https://www.huffingtonpost.com/rick-steves/palestines-complicated-bo_b_3289084.html.

Tahhan, Zena. 2017. "Israeli Measures at al-Aqsa Will 'Increase Resistance'." *Al Jazeera*, July 22. https://www.aljazeera.com/indepth/features/2017/07/israeli-measures-al-aqsa-increase-resistance-170722080648415.html.

Tartir, Alaa. 2013. "PA Industrial Zones: Cementing Statehood or Occupation?" *Al-Shabaka*, February 7. https://al-shabaka.org/commentaries/pa-industrial-zones-cementing-statehood-or-occupation/.

Tartir, Alaa. 2016. "How US Security Aid to PA Sustains Israel's Occupation." *Al Jazeera*, December 2. https://www.aljazeera.com/indepth/features/2016/11/security-aid-pa-sustains-israel-occupation-161103120213593.html.

Tartir, Alaa. 2017. "The Palestinian Authority Security Forces: Whose Security?" *Al-Shabaka*, May 16. https://al-shabaka.org/briefs/palestinian-authority-security-forces-whose-security/.

Tartir, Alaa, and Vivienne Sansour. 2014. "Palestinian Farmers: A Last Stronghold of Resistance." *Al-Shabaka*, July 1. https://al-shabaka.org/briefs/palestinian-farmers-a-last-stronghold-of-resistance/.

Taylor, Michael. 1988. *Rationality and Revolution*. Cambridge: Cambridge University Press.

"The PSCC." 2012. *Al Mufaqarah R-Exist*, May 23. https://almufaqarah.wordpress.com/the-pscc/.

Tilly, Charles. 1978. *From Mobilization to Revolution*. New York: McGraw-Hill.

UNCTAD. 2013. "The Palestinian Economy in East Jerusalem: Enduring Annexation, Isolation, and Disintegration." http://unctad.org/en/pages/PublicationWebflyer.aspx?publicationid=537.

Unver, Akin. 2017. "What Twitter Can Tell Us About the Jerusalem Protests." *The Washington Post*, August 28. https://www.washingtonpost.com/news/monkey-cage/wp/2017/08/26/what-twitter-can-tell-us-about-the-jerusalem-protests/?utm_term=.a82c61c84271.

Wilson, Nigel. 2016. "Hundreds Mark 11th Year of Protests in Bilin." *Al Jazeera*, February 19. https://www.aljazeera.com/news/2016/02/hundreds-mark-11th-year-protests-bilin-160219161932421.html.

Wolfinger, Raymond, and Steven J. Rosenstone. 1980. *Who Votes?* New Haven: Yale University Press.

Yang, David. 2007. "Classing Ethnicity: Class, Ethnicity, and the Mass Politics of Taiwan's Democratic." *World Politics* 59 (4): 503–538.

PART II

External Intervention and International Aid

CHAPTER 6

More Important Than Other Conflicts: The Uniqueness of the Israeli–Palestinian Conflict in EC/EU Discourse

Anders Persson

INTRODUCTION

This chapter analyzes all EC/EU statements—820 in total[1] published in the *Bulletin of the European Communities* and *Bulletin of the European Union* between 1967 and 2009.[2] Two questions underlie the chapter: how could the EC/EU go from being fully supportive of Israel and uncritical of the occupation in the years after the 1967 war to become supportive of a Palestinian state and one of the leading international critics of Israel's occupation a few decades later and then back again in the 2000s to be more and more critical of the Palestinians and less and less critical of Israel? Which were the major policy departures? And why has the Israeli–Palestinian conflict dominated European foreign policy discourse for over five decades now?[3]

A. Persson (✉)
Department of Political Science, Lund University, Lund, Sweden
e-mail: anders.persson@svet.lu.se

© The Author(s) 2019
A. Tartir and T. Seidel (eds.),
Palestine and Rule of Power, Middle East Today,
https://doi.org/10.1007/978-3-030-05949-1_6

Quantitative and Qualitative Content Analysis

Basic quantitative content analysis enables the researcher to discover the broad pattern in a big material, which is where I start. The method is very useful for finding the manifest in a text, which, at the same time, means that it has a much harder time finding the latent meaning of text (Bryman 2016, 284). It can count the occurrence of the keywords, but the method cannot, at least not without extra coding, say whether one occurrence of a keyword is more important or less important than another. In order to find the more latent meaning of a text, the researcher most go from quantitative to qualitative content analysis. David Altheide and Christopher Schneider (2013, 26) have described qualitative context analysis as being

> systematic and analytic but not rigid. Categories and variables initially guide the study, but others are allowed and expected to emerge during the study, including an orientation to constant discovery and constant comparison of relevant situations, settings, styles, images, meanings, and nuances.

After I have coded the material, I went back into each coded statement to see if there is a latent meaning in it. It could, for example, be a new policy departure or the introduction of new terminology, which are not captured by a quantitative content analysis. Through a qualitative content analysis it is further possible to see how much space the EC/EU has devoted to declarations on this conflict.

As mentioned, the material consists of all EC/EU declarations and other statements on the Israeli–Palestinian conflict published in the *Bulletin of the European Communities* for the period between June 1967 and 1995, and in the *Bulletin of the European Union* for the period 1996–2009, after which the Bulletin ceased to exist. Typically, the Bulletin came out with 10–11 issues each year, including 1–2 double issues, each issue consisting of between 100 and 250 pages. Regarding double issues, I have coded it for the first month; so, for example, a January/February issue was coded only for January and coded zero for February. All and all, the material consists of around 70,000 pages of EC/EU texts.[4] In each issue, I coded four keywords: "Israel" (which includes Israeli, Israelis), "Palest" (which includes Palestine, Palestinian, Palestinians), "Arab" (which was the key term used before Palestinian became accepted EC/EU language and even after that sometimes).

The last key word is "Middle East" (which includes Middle East Peace Process, the conflict in the Middle East etc.). A statement is coded as "1" regardless of its length, regardless if it includes one or several EC/EU positions, regardless if it includes one or several of the keywords. The next such statement is coded as "2" and so on. There is in the material a very striking disconnect between the EU's economic and political dealings with Israel up until the Euro-Mediterranean Partnership (also called the Barcelona Process) was launched in 1995, which is a very important observation and a key point of criticism against the EU at the moment.

The EC and the Middle East After the 1967 War

The six original member countries of the European Community, Germany, France, Belgium, the Netherlands, Luxembourg, and Italy, all enjoyed good relations with Israel in the first decade after the European Economic Community was established in 1957. Right after the June 1967 war had ended, the European Parliament held a debate on what was called "the situation in the Middle East." The rapporteur, Mr Dehousse, deplored the "lack of a politically united Europe," which "was a marvellous opportunity for the then] Six [members] to work out the first elements of a common foreign policy" (Bulletin of the EC 8-1967, 82). Seemingly without exception, parliamentarians from all party groups unanimously supported Israel. There was not one hint of criticism against Israel's acquisition of territory and no demand for Israeli withdrawal in the resolution adopted by the European Parliament. Instead the declaration expressed grave concern at the situation where the existence of Israel was being threatened (Bulletin of the EC 8-1967, 96).

The EC's first major official declaration on the Middle East came in June 1971 at the second EC foreign ministers' conference on political cooperation. It stated that:

> it is of great importance to Europe that a just peace should be established in the Middle East, and they [the foreign ministers] are therefore in favor of any efforts which may be made to bring about a peaceful solution of the conflict, and particularly of the negotiations in which Mr Jarring is involved. They urge all those concerned to ensure that this mission proves successful. They confirm their approval of Resolution No. 242 of the Security Council dated November 22, 1967, which constitutes the basis

of a settlement, and they stress the need to put it into effect in all its parts. (Bulletin of the EC 6-1971, 31)

The term "Palestinian" was not used in the declaration, which is also the case with the UNSC Res. 242. The fact that the EU is still issuing declarations about the conflict almost five decades later indicates that the Union has not been very successful in its efforts to bring peace to this conflict.

Enter Oil, "the Palestinians" and Uneasy Relations with the United States

The nine EC members were dependent on energy supplies from the Middle East, both when it came to stabilizing the price of oil and to ensuring its supply. When the Parliament first debated the situation in the Middle East right after the June 1967 war, the argument was made in the Parliament that Europe depended for 80% of its oil consumption (48% of its supply of power) on the countries of the Middle East, much more than both the USSR and the United States (Bulletin of the EC 8-1967, 83). After the October 1973 war and the subsequent Arab oil embargo, the foreign ministers of the by now nine members of the EC met on November 6, 1973 to discuss the situation in the Middle East. The meeting resulted in a declaration that again emphasized the need for Israel to end the territorial occupation in line with UNSC res. 242 and the newly issued UNSC res. 338. For the first time in an official EU declaration the term "Palestinians" was used and "the Palestinians" were explicitly recognized as a party to the conflict (Bulletin of the EC 10-1973, 106). Furthermore, the declaration went on to recognize "the legitimate rights of the Palestinians" (Bulletin of the EC 10-1973, 106). Emphasizing the early importance of path-dependency in the EC's declarations, it is clear from the moment terms like "just peace" or "Palestinians" are introduced into the discourse, they tend to be mainstreamed very fast.

After the October 1973 war, there were many references in the Bulletin as to how important oil imports from the Middle East were for the EC, how important it was for the EC to form a common foreign policy and how important the conflict in the Middle East was, both when it came to oil imports and forming a common foreign policy. As British PM Edward Heath told the December 1973 Copenhagen Summit Conference

The Community was, in my judgment, entirely correct in concentrating its efforts on a statement of foreign policy, made in the Declaration of 6 November. We can build on that substantial beginning, so that Europe can make the maximum possible contribution to the restoration of peace in the Middle East. It is only by using all the resources of foreign policy that we can hope to give Europe secure access to the oil it needs. (Bulletin of the EC 12-1973, 24)

The EC's declarations on the Middle East after the 1973 war took place against an unprecedented backdrop of West European estrangement from the United states over the war in Vietnam, certain trade policies and strategic defense issues in the light of the period of *détente* (1969–1979). In an important speech in early 1974 titled "Relations between the United States and the Community," the President of the Commission, Francois-Xavier Ortoli, said that:

You cannot applaud the sight of Europe taking wing and at the same time insist that she clips her wings, meaning that she denies herself her concepts and her policy. Europe wants to be adult and mature. This must be understood and acknowledged...It is pointless to cover one's eyes to refuse to see the realities. Europe's dependence on Arab oil (90% of Europe's supply as against only 10% for the United States) is a case in point which, highlighted by its immediacy, shows the measure of the differences...I would like to be quite clear on this point, that the renewal and strengthening of our relations with the United States cannot affect the determination of the Nine to assert themselves as a distinct and original entity. (Bulletin of the EC 3-1974, 7–8)

A week before this speech, US President Richard Nixon had himself delivered a major speech on US–Europe relations. Relating to the EC's involvement in the Middle East, Nixon said

the Europeans cannot have it both ways. They cannot have the United States participation and cooperation on the security front and then proceed to have confrontation and even hostility on the economic and political front... It does not mean that we are not going to have competition, but it does mean that we are not going to be faced with a situation where the nine countries of Europe gang up against the United States–the United States which is their guarantee for their security. That we cannot have. (Nixon 1974)

The second part of 1970s witnessed a dramatic turn in the EC's rhetoric as it drew closer to the Arab/Palestinian narrative of the conflict. The Bulletin described the "Euro-Arab dialogue," launched after the October 1973 war, as an interchange between civilizations (Bulletin of the EC 5-1976, 9). In 1976, the President of the Council of the European Communities, talked for the first time about the Palestinians as a "people" with "legal rights" to "express its national identity in concrete terms" (Bulletin of the EC 11-1976, 96). The June 1977 London European Council further took into account "the need for a homeland for the Palestinian people" (Bulletin of the EC 6-1977, 62). Before that, in early 1977, the EC had condemned Israeli settlements for the first time in an official statement. In the final communiqué of the February 1977 Euro-Arab Dialogue meeting of the General Committee, the EC stated:

> the concern of the [then] Nine [members] over the continued Israeli occupation of Arab territories since 1967. They maintained that the Fourth Geneva Convention was applicable to the occupied territories and opposed the policy of establishing settlements there, which could only prejudice the prospects for peace. (Bulletin of the EC 2-1977, 65)

Later that year, the EC described Israel's settlements as a "policy of colonizing the occupied territories," terminology it would definitely not use today (Bulletin of the EC 11-1977, 111). Two years later, in 1979, the EC explicitly deplored Israel's claim to sovereignty over the occupied territories and stated for the first time that it considered the construction of settlements in these territories as a violation of international law (Bulletin of the EC 6-1979, 93).

The Venice Declaration and the Lost Decade of the 1980s

The rapprochement between the EC and the Palestinians culminated with the seminal 1980 Venice Declaration, which summed up much of the EC's diplomacy toward the conflict during the previous decade. In the Venice Declaration, it was explicitly stated that:

> The nine member states of the European Community consider that the traditional ties and common interests which link Europe to the Middle

East oblige them to play a special role and now require them to work in a more concrete way towards peace. (Bulletin of the EC 6-1980, 10)

The Venice Declaration also stated it was imperative to find a just solution to the Palestinian problem, which the EC did not simply see as a refugee problem. Perhaps most significantly, the EC called for the inclusion of the Palestine Liberation Organization (PLO) in the peace negotiations and stated that the Palestinians must be allowed "to exercise fully its right to self-determination" (Bulletin of the EC 6-1980, 10). One of the big problems though with the Venice Declaration was that it was issued at a time when the EC's actor capacity was being severely reduced by the tightening bipolar structure of the international system. The period of *détente* which had allowed the EU clear room for maneuver was about to be replaced by the *New Cold War* (1979–1986). Because of its dependence on the United States, this more intense phase of the Cold War that followed did not allow the EC many possibilities for an active, alternative policy to that of the United States (Dosenrode and Stubkjaer 2002, 118–119).

The optimism of the Venice Declaration faded away as the problems grew in Lebanon. Israel had launched a major invasion of Lebanon in the summer of 1982, advancing all the way up to Beirut. It is widely recognized in the academic literature that the 1982 Lebanon war marked a negative turning point in Israel's international relations, primarily with the West (see, for example Schiff and Ya'ari 1984, 218). This is clearly visible in the Bulletin, which had never before published declarations and other statements that were harshly critical of Israel's behavior. The Israeli invasion was met with a "vigorous condemnation" by the EC (Bulletin of the EC 6-1982, 16), which stated that it was "horrified by the terrible suffering and damage which were inflicted upon Lebanon and its civil population" (Bulletin of the EC 9-1982, 73). The Bulletin even published a statement by a member of the European Parliament who said that Israel could not solve the Palestinian problem in Lebanon by a "final solution" (Bulletin of the EC 6-1982, 86), something that would never have happened today.

After the 1982 Lebanon war, there is a clear process in the Bulletin of equalizing the rights of the Palestinians to those of Israel, the culmination of a process that had begun after the October 1973 war. In September 1982, right after the Sabra and Shatila massacres (which the EC did not blame Israel for involvement in), the EC stated:

> The [then] Ten [members] remain convinced that two essential principles must be accepted and reconciled: the right to existence and security of all the States and justice for all the peoples. Our commitment to the right of Israel to live in security and peace is absolute and unwavering. So also is our commitment to the right of the Palestinian people to self-determination with all that this implies. (Bulletin of the EC 9-1982, 74)

Israel's most basic demand for security was now equal to the most basic Palestinian demand for justice, while Israel's right to exist was equalized to the Palestinians' right to self-determination. This trend continued in 1985, when the EC called for respecting "the principle of the non-use of force" (clearly meant for the Palestinians) alongside "the non-acquisition of territory by the use of force" (clearly meant for Israel) (Bulletin of the EC 9-1985, 109).

The period between the first intifada, which broke out in 1987 and the signing of the Declaration of Principles (DOP) in 1993, is the period during the past five decades when there were most criticisms of Israel by the EC. The criticism typically included human rights abuses, such as the use of excessive force by the Israel in repressing Palestinian demonstrations (Bulletin of the EC 10-1990, 98), repeated violations of international law (Bulletin of the EC 10-1990, 98), and that Israel had failed to adhere to the Fourth Geneva Convention (Bulletin of the EC 6-1990, 23). At the same time, during all the critique against Israel's behavior, it is important to also highlight that Israel's right to exist and to exist in peace and security was mentioned in basically all EC declarations, even the ones most critical of Israel's behavior. During this period, the EC members voted against a 1975 UNGA resolution equating Zionism with racism (Bulletin of the EC 12-1975, 73). This pattern is repeating itself today with the EU opposing the BDS (Boycott, Divestment and Sanction) movement (see, for example Mogherini 2016).

COMMON POSITIONS AND FORWARD-THINKING

The EPC managed early on to form a common position among the members, and history proved the EC/EU to be forward-thinking in promoting Arab and later Palestinian claims as legitimate demands. Examples of this include promoting the mutual recognition between Israel and the PLO, which later formed the basis of the DOP (also together with other agreements called the Oslo Accords). In 1987, the

EC called on the parties "involved in the Arab/Israeli conflict to open the doors to peace by recognizing each other's rights" (Bulletin of the EC 9-1987, 110). The following year, 1988, PLO recognized UNSC res. 242, which implied acceptance of Israel's right to exist in security. It was warmly welcomed by the EC (Bulletin of the EC 11-1988, 88), as was the American decision to initiate a substantive dialogue with the PLO later that year (Bulletin of the EC 12-1988, 139). In 1989 the EC stated for the first time that the peace negotiations should be based on a "land for peace" principle (Bulletin of the EC 6-1989, 17). Together with the mutual recognition, the "land for peace" principle became the key two formulas of the Oslo peace process during the 1990s. All in all, the EU played an important visionary vanguard role for the Oslo process. When the DOP was finally signed in 1993, it looked much closer to the EC's Venice Declaration of 1980 than to anything the USA, the Israelis or the Arab side, including the Palestinians, had previously outlined.

The DOP was warmly welcomed by the EC. Jacques Delors, the President of the European Commission, expressed his "admiration for the farsightedness and the courage shown by the leaders of the Israeli and Palestinian peoples who have set this historic process in motion" (Bulletin of the EC 9-1993, 58). However, at the same time, from the beginning of the peace process, the EC emphasized the need for regional cooperation to help make the peace process irreversible (Bulletin of the EC 9-1993, 57). The spirit of the time was indeed regional cooperation in what was often at the time referred to as "the new Middle East" (see, for example Peres 1993). While the Israeli–Palestinian conflict was always at the heart of the Oslo peace process, it is almost forgotten today that the peace process of the 1990s also had a Jordanian, a Syrian and a Lebanese track, of which only the first was successful. The Commission also underlined the need for outside third parties, particularly the Community itself, to support the peace process because of its geopolitical location, its close links with all the parties concerned and its historical experience of regional cooperation (Bulletin of the EC 9-1993, 58).

During the Oslo peace process, the EU often highlighted that the 1995 Euro-Mediterranean partnership was the only regional dialogue mechanism that brought together all the states in the Mediterranean (see, for example Bulletin of the EU 1/2-1998, 103). One of many problems with the "regional cooperation approach" though was that the Arab states, including the Palestinians, have historically feared Israel as a regional economic hegemon (see, for example Parsi 2007, 165). When the EU envisioned the 1995 Association Agreement with Israel to act as a driving force in fostering economic and social development in the Middle East region, this scared both the Palestinians and other Arabs (Bulletin of the EU 11-1995, 82).

EC/EU Endorsement of the Need for a Palestinian State

The Venice Declaration had not explicitly called for a Palestinian state and it would take almost another two decades before the EU was ready to support the idea of a Palestinian state. At the Amsterdam European Council of 1997, the EU for the first time called "on the people of Israel to recognize the right of the Palestinians to exercise self-determination, without excluding the option of a State" (Bulletin of the EU 6-1997, 22). This somewhat ambiguous call for a Palestinian state was repeated in The Cardiff European Council of 1998 (Bulletin of the EU 6-1998, 15), but it was not until the Berlin Declaration of 1999 that the EU explicitly endorsed the idea of a Palestinian state, but without recognizing it:

> The European Union reaffirms the continuing and un-qualified Palestinian right to self-determination, including the option of a State, and looks forward to the early fulfilment of this right. It appeals to the parties to strive in good faith for a negotiated solution on the basis of the existing agreements, without prejudice to this right, which is not subject to any veto. The European Union is convinced that the creation of a democratic, viable and peaceful sovereign Palestinian State on the basis of existing agreements and through negotiations would be the best guarantee of Israel's security and Israel's acceptance as an equal partner in the region. The European Union declares its readiness to consider the recognition of a Palestinian State in due course in accordance with the basic principles referred to above. (Bulletin of the EU 3-1999, 21–22)

The strong case for path-dependency in the EC/EU's declarations on the conflict is very clear with the adoption of the need for a Palestinian state, which has been present ever since in basically all EU declarations on the conflict. A year and a half after the Berlin Declaration, just weeks before the second intifada broke out, the EU declared the right of the Palestinian people to build a sovereign, democratic, viable, and peaceful State may not be brought into question. This right is established. There remains the choice of timing which belongs to the Palestinian people. (Bulletin of the EU 9-2000, 69)

It is noteworthy, however, that despite being the leading third party in the Palestinian state-building process and together with the UN, IMF, IBRD, but not the United States deeming the Palestinian Authority technically ready for statehood in 2011 (Ashton 2011), EU recognition of Palestine has yet to happen. Only Sweden has recognized Palestine since becoming member of the EU. Cyprus and Malta have previously recognized Palestine, but that was before they joined the EU. A number of central European member states have also recognized Palestine, when they were part of the Soviet Union. Some of these states (especially the Visegrad four) have today emerged as Israel's closest allies in Europe. In addition, Iceland, Albania, Serbia, Montenegro, Ukraine, and the Vatican have also recognized Palestine, but they are not members of the EU. Israel initially feared that the Swedish recognition would unleash similar recognitions and punitive actions against its occupation of the Palestinian territories. So far it has not happened, most likely because other European states fear the harsh Israeli pushback, but Sweden's recognition did create a certain momentum for the Palestinians, as parliaments in a number of key EU member states (the UK, France, Ireland, Spain, Portugal, Belgium, and Italy) adopted resolutions supporting Palestinian statehood and calling for their governments to recognize Palestine (Persson 2015a). In retrospect, it seems that the harsh response from the Israeli government was part of a deliberate strategy to deter other European states from following Sweden, which, up until now, has been successful.

Recalibrating Criticism After the Outbreak of the Second Intifada

Most pro-Israeli observers would probably not agree that the EU's rhetoric took a somewhat pro-Israeli turn after the outbreak of the second intifada in 2000, but the fact is that there was a shift in the Bulletin's statements toward rebalancing criticism of Israeli and

Palestinian misbehavior after the outbreak of the second intifada, which was actually not referred to as an intifada until December 2001 in the Bulletin (Bulletin of the EU 12-2001, 25). The EU did clearly blame Israel for the outbreak of the intifada, stating that the "lack of progress in the peace process, including the settlements issue, is the source of the Palestinian community's frustration and the violence" (Bulletin of the EU 11-2000, 76). Meanwhile, the European Parliament condemned what it called "Mr Sharon's act of provocation [a visit under heavy security to the Temple Mount/Haram al-Sharif in Jerusalem], which had sparked off the conflict" (Bulletin of the EU 10-2000, 89). There was massive criticism against Israel in the first two years of the second intifada for what the EU called Israel's excessive and disproportionate use of force (Bulletin of the EU 4-2001, 60), extrajudicial killings (Bulletin of the EU 1/2-2001, 101), illegal incursions into PA-controlled territories (Area A of the West Bank) (Bulletin of the EU 4-2001, 60), "the systematic destruction of Palestinian infrastructures, including those financed by the EU" (Bulletin of the EU 10-2002, 92) and the "brutality of occupation for the ordinary people in the Palestinian territories" (Bulletin of the EU 9-2002, 67).

But what was really new here was that for the first time in the Bulletin, there was now also persistent and strong criticism against the Palestinians for their use of "terrorism," in particular suicide bombings. The effects of the 9/11 attacks in the United States and the whole "Global war on terrorism narrative" are very visible in the Bulletin, even if the EU after 9/11 on several occasions expressed that it rejected any equation of terrorism with the Arab and Muslim world. In addition, the EU also called for a dialogue of civilizations with the Arab and Muslim world between equals (see, for example Bulletin of the EU 10-2001, 114). At the peak of the second intifada in 2002, the EU published several statements condemning Palestinian terrorism, including bluntly stating that "[s]uicide attacks do irreparable damage to the Palestinian cause" (Bulletin of the EU 12-2002, 14). Hamas was designated as a terror group by the EU in 2003 (Bulletin of the EU 9-2003, 66). The EU now came to see "the fight against all forms of terrorism" as "paramount in the quest for a just and comprehensive peace in the Middle East" (Bulletin of the EU 7/8-2003, 80).

The EU Tilts Back to a More Uncritical Approach Toward Israel

In the first years after the outbreak of the second intifada, the EU issued declarations saying that it would oppose all parts in the conflict who have recourse to violence and support all those who strive for peace (Bulletin of the EU 10-2003, 18). In retrospect, it is clear that this policy was only applied to Hamas. After Hamas won the 2006 elections in the Palestinian territories, elections deemed "free and fair" by the EU (Bulletin of the EU 1/2-2006, 133), the EU responded by placing three demands on Hamas which the group did not meet: non-violence, recognition of Israel's right to exist and acceptance of existing agreements (Bulletin of the EU 4-2006, 85). Even if the demands on Hamas were not unreasonable in themselves, many in the academic EU literature saw them as unfair and unrealistic, not least since the EU (and the Quartet—the EU together with the USA, the UN and Russia) had never demanded anything similar from the Israeli side, or from many of its other partners in the region (see, for example Smith 2008, 159).

This less Israeli-critical approach of the 2000s, which was already visible during the second intifada, became much clearer during the 2008–2009 Gaza war, which was met with very weak reactions by the EU, almost without any criticism against Israel (Bulletin of the EU 1/2-2009, 151–152). This was in stark contrast to how the United Nations and many human rights organizations reacted to the 2008–2009 Gaza war (see, for example Report of the UN Fact-Finding Mission on the Gaza Conflict 2009). The EU's tilts back to a more uncritical approach toward Israel during the 2000s, which in some aspects resembles the period before the 1973 war, is something that the academic EU literature has yet not sufficiently recognized.

During the 2000s, until 2009, there were no new major policy departures in the EU's declaratory diplomacy toward the conflict. In December 2009, just after the Bulletin had ceased to exist, the Swedish Presidency led the Council to issue a major declaration calling for Jerusalem to be capital of a future Palestinian state, which then quickly became official EU policy (Council of the European Union 2009). In this period, the EU was also heavily involved in peace-building and state-building on the ground through its two CSDP missions (Common Security and Defence Policy) EUBAM Rafah and EUPOL COPPS, and through its massive support for the Palestinian state-building project, which probably made what some Israelis have referred to as "the EU's megaphone diplomacy" (European Jewish Press 2007) more difficult.

CONCLUSION: A UNIQUE CONFLICT FROM EUROPE'S PERSPECTIVE

Israeli government officials often accuse the EU of being obsessed with Israel, while not paying sufficient attention to other, much worse conflicts around the world (see, for example Ravid 2017). Hawkish Israeli analysts also say that being anti-Israeli is the only consistent foreign policy that the EC/EU has ever had (see, for example Glick 2014, 224). As this chapter has shown, there is merit to the first accusation. The EC/EU's over 800 official declarations and other statements on the conflict are simply astonishing. Without having explicitly coded other conflicts, it is still clear through my quantitative and qualitative context analyses of the Bulletin that the Israeli–Palestinian conflict has gotten far more attention in the Bulletin than other conflicts. No other conflict comes even close. At times, the Bulletin's coverage of the Israeli–Palestinian conflict is detailed up to even including statements condemning Israel for evicting a single Palestinian family from their home in East Jerusalem (Bulletin of the EU 11-2008, 125). That is just one example how this conflict is portrayed differently than other conflicts in Europe.

There are multiple reasons for the uniqueness of the Israeli–Palestinian conflict in the Bulletin. Early on, the EC believed that third parties' mediation was necessary that the community could and should make a contribution. The EC/EU's self-perceived "special," "moral," "unique," and "distinctive" role as a peace-builder is a defining feature of its 50-years involvement in the conflict. There are repeated references in the Bulletin of the EC/EU seeing the conflict as lying "at the heart of continuing tension in the Near East" (Bulletin of the EC 9-1987, 110), or being "of the utmost importance to Europe and to the whole world" (Bulletin of the EC 9-1975, 95). Moreover, the EC also believed that its involvement in the conflict would foster integration in the community's emerging foreign policy. Strategic issues like oil, trade, and relations with the United States became major factors for the EC's involvement in the conflict after the October 1973 war. In the EU's security strategy from 2003, resolution of the Israeli–Palestinian conflict is considered as "a strategic priority for Europe" and as the key to deal with other problems in the Middle East (European Security Strategy 2003, 8). However, in the EU's new global strategy from 2016, the Israeli–Palestinian conflict is mentioned only in one passage on pages 34–35, with very weak language:

> On the Palestinian–Israeli conflict, the EU will work closely with the Quartet, the Arab League and all key stakeholders to preserve the prospect of a viable two-state solution based on 1967 lines with equivalent land swaps, and to recreate the conditions for meaningful negotiations. The EU will also promote full compliance with European and international law in deepening cooperation with Israel and the Palestinian Authority. (EUGS 2016, 34–35)

History proved the EC/EU to be forward-thinking in promoting Palestinian claims as legitimate demands and in singling out the issue of settlements as an especially serious obstacle to resolving the conflict. Today, the EU (together with individual European countries) is widely credited in the academic EU literature for having played a key role in legitimizing the Palestinians, the PLO and its leader Yasser Arafat, on the international scene before the DOP were signed in 1993 (see, for example Biscop 2003, 65; Miller 2011, 134; Keukeleire and MacNaughtan 2008, 282). As this analysis has shown, the Israeli accusation that the EU is inherently anti-Israeli has little merit. In fact, the Bulletin's statements were uncritical of Israel up until the October 1973 war. Israel's right to exist within secure borders has always been sacrosanct for the EU, even if that right became equalized over time with the legitimate right of the Palestinians to self-determination and later statehood. Moreover, the EC/EU came out firmly against equating Zionism with racism, and it urged the Arab states over and over again to end its boycott of Israel (Bulletin of the EU 11-1993, 72).

Finally, there is a very strong argument for path-dependency in the material that I have studied. When new terminology is introduced, it often remains. Concepts such as "just peace," references to UNSC res. 242, "Israel's right to exist," "legitimate rights of the Palestinians," "settlements as obstacles to peace," "land for peace," "the need for a Palestinian state," "resolving the conflict through a two-state solution," and "firm condemnations of suicide bombings" have remained ever since they were introduced. Some of these concepts were later adopted by other countries in the international community, most notably by the USA, Israel and, some of the Arab states. Even if the harsh reality on the ground in Israel–Palestine at the present is much stronger than the normative power of the EU's declarations, the ability of the EU to shape discourse and set examples is clearly visible in the Bulletin's statements on the Israeli–Palestinian conflict since 1967 (see further Persson 2015b, 2017). However, with an EU in relative decline and disunity, and with the rise of various right-wing, nationalist or populist governments and parties in Europe in recent years, many of whom are pro-Israeli and anti-Muslim, it is unclear at the moment if the EU can continue to be a "normative power" in the conflict.

Notes

1. Please see the Coding Schedule in the appendix.
2. The Bulletin ceased to exist after its July/August 2009 issue. Today it is much harder to get a comprehensive view of the EU's declarations on the Israeli–Palestinian conflict, as various EU declarations and other official statements are published on several different websites, some of which lacks a proper archive.
3. An article by the author based on the same source material from the Bulletin, but with the focus on EU terminology and changes in how EU speaks about the Israeli–Palestinian conflict, will be published in a forthcoming special issue of the journal *Middle East Critique*.
4. For many years, the Bulletin existed only in libraries, which made quantitative content analysis an overwhelming task for a single researcher. But since 2003, the University of Pittsburgh's Archive of European Integration (AEI) has begun uploading research materials on the topic of European integration and unification, among them many official EC/EU documents, including the *Bulletin of the European Communities* for the period between 1967 and 1995, but not yet the Bulletin of the European Union for the period 1996–2009. For this material, I turned to the online portal EU bookshop. For more info about the University of Pittsburgh's Archive of European Integration (AEI), visit http://aei.pitt.edu/information.html. For more info about the EU bookshop, visit https://bookshop.europa.eu/en/home/.

Coding Schedule

See Table 6.1.

Table 6.1 *Bulletin of the European Communities* and *Bulletin of the European Union* coding schedule

	January	February	March	April	May	June	July	August	September	October	November	December	Total
1967									2	1			6
1968								3					
1969				1									1
1970	2	1							3		1	1	10
1971	1	2		1	1	1	1				1	2	8
1972				1		1		1	1	2	4	3	14
1973	1	1	1		1	1				3		6	18
1974	3		2		1	5	1		1	1	4	3	18
1975				2	4	1			3	2		2	14
1976				2	1						3		6
1977		1				6			1	1	2	1	12
1978						6			2	1	1	1	11
1979			1	1		1			2	2			7
1980				1	1	4	3		2			1	12
1981	1	1				2	2		2		2	2	12
1982	2		1	1		6	1		4		1	1	17
1983	2		1		2	3	1		2		1	1	13
1984	1	1	2				1		1			2	8
1985	1			1	1	1	1		2	1	1	1	9
1986	3	1	1	1					1	3	1	3	14
1987	1	1	1			1	2		3	1	1	3	14
1988	3	1	2	2	4	4	2		1	1	2	2	21
1989	1		1		2	3	2		2	3	1	3	20
1990	5		2	3	2	4			5	6	1	3	31
1991	9			1	5	1	3			2	2	1	24
1992	6		1	1	2	6	1		1	1			18
1993	5		1	1	2	1	4		9	3	4	4	33

(continued)

Table 6.1 (continued)

	January	February	March	April	May	June	July	August	September	October	November	December	Total
1994	1		3	3	3	5	4			4	4	1	28
1995	5			1	2	6	2		8	4	3	4	35
1996	4		5	6	1	3	1		3	4	1	3	31
1997	3		2	4		6	5		3	1	1	3	28
1998	5		1	1	3	5	1		2	3	3	6	30
1999	2		4		1	2	3		2	2		4	20
2000	4			4	3	6			2	5	4		28
2001	6		4	3	3	5	6		1	8	6	6	48
2002	4		4	4	4	4	2		5	1	1	3	32
2003	1		4		2	4	5		3	4	1	3	27
2004			3	1	4					1	3	2	18
2005	8		2	2		2	3			2	5	5	29
2006	5		1	1	1	2	3		3	2	5	1	24
2007	4		3	2	2	6	3		1	3	2	5	31
2008	5		1	1	3	2	2		1	1	4	7	27
2009	7		2		1	2							12
												Total	820

REFERENCES

REFERENCES TO THE LITERATURE

Altheide, David L., and Christopher J. Schneider. 2013. *Qualitative Media Analysis*. Thousand Oaks, CA: Sage.

Ashton, Catherine. 2011. *Remarks by EU High Representative Catherine Ashton After the Donor Coordination Group for the Palestine Territories*. Available at the website of the European Union, http://www.consilium.europa.eu/uedocs/NewsWord/EN/foraff/121525.doc.

Biscop, Sven. 2003. *Euro-Mediterranean Security*. Hants: Ashgate.

Bryman, Alan. 2016. *Social Research Methods*. Oxford: Oxford University Press.

Council of the European Union. 2009. *Council Conclusion on the Middle East Peace Process*. 2985th FOREIGN AFFAIRS Council Meeting Brussels, December 8. Available at the website of the European Union, http://www.consilium.europa.eu/uedocs/cms_data/docs/pressdata/en/foraff/111829.pdf.

Dosenrode, Soren, and Anders Stubkjaer. 2002. *The European Union and the Middle East*. London: Sheffield Academic Press.

EUGS. 2016. *Shared Vision, Common Action: A Stronger Europe*. Available at the website of the EEAS, https://eeas.europa.eu/archives/docs/top_stories/pdf/eugs_review_web.pdf.

European Jewish Press. 2007. "Israel's Ambassador to the EU Praises 'Real Dialogue' Between Israel and Europe." *European Jewish Press*, November 22. Available at the website of EJP, http://www.ejpress.org/article/21980.

European Security Strategy. 2003. *A Secure Europe in a Better World*. Available at the website of the European Union, http://www.consilium.europa.eu/eeas/security-defence/european-security-strategy?lang=en.

Glick, Caroline. 2014. *The Israeli Solution: A One-State Plan for Peace in the Middle East*. New York: Crown Forum.

Keukeleire, Stephan, and Jennifer MacNaughtan. 2008. *The Foreign Policy of the European Union*. Gordonsville: Palgrave.

Miller, Rory. 2011. *Inglorious Disarray: Europe, Israel and the Palestinians Since 1967*. New York: Columbia University Press.

Mogherini, Frederica. 2016. *High Representative/Vice-President Federica Mogherini Speaks with Prime Minister of Israel, Benjamin Netanyahu*. Available at the website of EEAS, https://eeas.europa.eu/delegations/israel/5273/high-representativevice-president-federica-mogherini-speaks-prime-minister-israel-benjamin_en.

Nixon, Richard. 1974. *Question-and-Answer Session at the Executives' Club of Chicago*, March 15. Available at the website of the American Presidency Project, http://www.presidency.ucsb.edu/ws/index.php?pid=%204386.

Parsi, Trita. 2007. *Treacherous Alliance: The Secret Dealings of Israel, Iran, and the United States*. New Haven: Yale University Press.

Peres, Shimon. 1993. *The New Middle East.* New York: Henry Holt.
Persson, Anders. 2015a. "Sweden's Recognition of Palestine: A Possible Snowball Effect?" *Palestine–Israel Journal of Politics, Economics, and Culture* 20 (2/3): 35–41.
Persson, Anders. 2015b. *The EU and the Israeli–Palestinian Conflict 1971–2013: In Pursuit of a Just Peace.* Lanham, MD: Lexington Books.
Persson, Anders. 2017. "Shaping Discourse and Setting Examples: Normative Power Europe Can Work in the Israeli–Palestinian Conflict." *Journal of Common Market Studies* 55 (6): 1415–1431.
Ravid, Barak. 2017. "Israel Slams EU: 32 Humanitarian Crises in the World and Europe's Obsessed with Palestinians." *Haaretz*, April 5. Available at the website of Haaretz, http://www.haaretz.com/israel-news/1.781562.
Report of the United Nations Fact-Finding Mission on the Gaza Conflict. 2009. Available at the website of OHCHR, http://www2.ohchr.org/english/bodies/hrcouncil/docs/12session/A-HRC-12-48.pdf.
Schiff, Ze'ev, and Ehud Ya'ari. 1984. *Israel's Lebanon War.* New York: Simon & Schuster.
Smith, Karen. 2008. *European Union Foreign Policy in a Changing World.* Oxford: Blackwell.

REFERENCES TO THE BULLETIN

Bulletin of the EC (8-1967). Luxembourg: Office for Official Publications of the European Communities.
Bulletin of the EC (6-1971). Luxembourg: Office for Official Publications of the European Communities.
Bulletin of the EC (10-1973). Luxembourg: Office for Official Publications of the European Communities.
Bulletin of the EC (12-1973). Luxembourg: Office for Official Publications of the European Communities.
Bulletin of the EC (3-1974). Luxembourg: Office for Official Publications of the European Communities.
Bulletin of the EC (9-1975). Luxembourg: Office for Official Publications of the European Communities.
Bulletin of the EC (12-1975). Luxembourg: Office for Official Publications of the European Communities.
Bulletin of the EC (5-1976). Luxembourg: Office for Official Publications of the European Communities.
Bulletin of the EC (11-1976). Luxembourg: Office for Official Publications of the European Communities.
Bulletin of the EC (2-1977). Luxembourg: Office for Official Publications of the European Communities.

Bulletin of the EC (6-1977). Luxembourg: Office for Official Publications of the European Communities.
Bulletin of the EC (11-1977). Luxembourg: Office for Official Publications of the European Communities.
Bulletin of the EC (6-1979). Luxembourg: Office for Official Publications of the European Communities.
Bulletin of the EC (6-1980). Luxembourg: Office for Official Publications of the European Communities.
Bulletin of the EC (6-1982). Luxembourg: Office for Official Publications of the European Communities.
Bulletin of the EC (9-1982). Luxembourg: Office for Official Publications of the European Communities.
Bulletin of the EC (9-1985). Luxembourg: Office for Official Publications of the European Communities.
Bulletin of the EC (9-1987). Luxembourg: Office for Official Publications of the European Communities.
Bulletin of the EC (11-1988). Luxembourg: Office for Official Publications of the European Communities.
Bulletin of the EC (12-1988). Luxembourg: Office for Official Publications of the European Communities.
Bulletin of the EC (6-1989). Luxembourg: Office for Official Publications of the European Communities.
Bulletin of the EC (6-1990). Luxembourg: Office for Official Publications of the European Communities.
Bulletin of the EC (10-1990). Luxembourg: Office for Official Publications of the European Communities.
Bulletin of the EC (9-1993). Luxembourg: Office for Official Publications of the European Communities.
Bulletin of the EC (11-1993). Luxembourg: Office for Official Publications of the European Communities.
Bulletin of the EU (9-1995). Luxembourg: Secretariat-General of the European Commission.
Bulletin of the EU (11-1995). Luxembourg: Secretariat-General of the European Commission.
Bulletin of the EU (6-1997). Luxembourg: Secretariat-General of the European Commission.
Bulletin of the EU (1/2-1998). Luxembourg: Secretariat-General of the European Commission.
Bulletin of the EU (6-1998). Luxembourg: Secretariat-General of the European Commission.
Bulletin of the EU (3-1999). Luxembourg: Secretariat-General of the European Commission.

Bulletin of the EU (9-2000). Luxembourg: Secretariat-General of the European Commission.
Bulletin of the EU (10-2000). Luxembourg: Secretariat-General of the European Commission.
Bulletin of the EU (11-2000). Luxembourg: Secretariat-General of the European Commission.
Bulletin of the EU (1/2-2001). Luxembourg: Secretariat-General of the European Commission.
Bulletin of the EU (4-2001). Luxembourg: Secretariat-General of the European Commission.
Bulletin of the EU (10-2001). Luxembourg: Secretariat-General of the European Commission.
Bulletin of the EU (12-2001). Luxembourg: Secretariat-General of the European Commission.
Bulletin of the EU (9-2002). Luxembourg: Secretariat-General of the European Commission.
Bulletin of the EU (10-2002). Luxembourg: Secretariat-General of the European Commission.
Bulletin of the EU (12-2002). Luxembourg: Secretariat-General of the European Commission.
Bulletin of the EU (7/8-2003). Luxembourg: Secretariat-General of the European Commission.
Bulletin of the EU (9-2003). Luxembourg: Secretariat-General of the European Commission.
Bulletin of the EU (10-2003). Luxembourg: Secretariat-General of the European Commission.
Bulletin of the EU (1/2-2006). Luxembourg: Secretariat-General of the European Commission.
Bulletin of the EU (4-2006). Luxembourg: Secretariat-General of the European Commission.
Bulletin of the EU (11-2008). Luxembourg: Secretariat-General of the European Commission.
Bulletin of the EU (1/2-2009). Luxembourg: Secretariat-General of the European Commission.

CHAPTER 7

Neoliberalism as Aid for the Settler Colonization of the Occupied Palestinian Territories After Oslo

Jeremy Wildeman

INTRODUCTION: MIDDLE EAST PEACEBUILDING AFTER OSLO

When the Oslo Accord was signed in 1993, this evoked genuine optimism around the world that peace would soon come to the Middle East. Despite some prominent critiques (Said 1993), voices of doubt were pointedly ignored and drowned out by a vocal majority of observers who wanted to believe that Israelis and Palestinians could establish peace built on the liberal underpinnings of the accord. In order to help nurture the process along, countless state and non-state actors thus began to contribute funding toward Palestinian development aid. This was done on the underlying premise that Palestinians would accept this as a sort of "peace dividend" to abandon violence toward Israel (Le More 2008, 89). The expectation was that Palestinians would take this assistance and donor guidance to build a liberal democratic state, within which they would focus on cooperative free market trade with Israel, in lieu of conflict.

J. Wildeman (✉)
Department of Social and Policy Sciences, University of Bath, Bath, UK
e-mail: j.wildeman@bath.ac.uk

This approach reflected the classical liberal's faith in the innate goodness of the individual (and the market), the capacity for political institutions (and the market) to promote social progress, and the idea that states are capable of meaningful cooperation together (typically through the market). According to this liberal paradigm, rational states will come to realize that their general well-being is inexorably interlinked, because they have more to gain in absolute terms by working together than they are likely to achieve in relative terms on their own. Within this logical framework both Israelis and Palestinians were expected to eventually realize they have more to gain by working together than they do apart in conflict or at war. Over time cooperation would lead to a form of interdependence where security and force matter less than the multiple social and political relationships that formed between them, like shared institutions and accords (Keohane and Nye 1998, 83). This would help nullify the "zero-sum character" of a conflict where economic resources were deemed limited and control of them to be "zero sum" at the expense of the other. Instead of fighting, each side could just trade from their respective strengths, maximizing resources for the benefit of all while resolving any problems through dialogue. In the case of Israel and the oPt, such cooperation would stimulate mutual economic gains, reinforce peace, and lead to yet more economic growth in a virtuous cycle of peace reinforced by economic growth. Oslo was very much an economic peace plan.

However, for this to happen the Palestinians would need a rational government, and for it to be truly rational it would have to be liberal democratic, such as those found in Israel and the rest of the West. Thus, the need immediately arose for the donors to provide Palestinians with a strong governing authority in the occupied Palestinian territory (oPt) that would be able to implement a large-scale, Western-led social engineering program to build a liberal democracy. They were operating on an assumption that Palestinians were an underdeveloped people who, quite unlike Western liberals, were inherently predisposed toward despotism, militancy, and violence. Therefore, that governing Palestinian Authority (PA) would also be necessary to help repress Palestinians' innate violent tendencies, while making them richer and encouraging them to co-habitat in pacific union with Israel. Donors assumed that these changes in the oPt would allow Israel to feel it had the security it needed as the lone liberal democracy in the violent Middle East to then decolonize, and thereby offer the Palestinians breathing room for peace to take hold.

The plan represented a very centralized, top-down variant of liberalism known as neoliberalism. The approach did not reflect the sovereign aspirations of the Palestinians and was laden with prejudiced normative values developed among Israel's Western allies. There they disproportionately left the blame for violence on the weaker, aggrieved party of the violent military occupation; reflected by the constant demand by Western governments that the Palestinians renounce violence and recognize Israel as a state, but never making the same demands of Israel. Nor did the plan account for Israel's hunger for the most existential of all resources, land, while Western policymakers ignored, denied, and simply could not comprehend Israel's settler colonial territoriality. It is in this gross miscomprehension of the actual context of Israel's colonial regime in the oPt that the donors crafted an aid model that was doomed not just for failure but to exacerbate the underlying conditions of colonial occupation, making the economic and human security situation much worse.

This chapter describes how neoliberal development aid has contributed to the settler colonization of the oPt. It does this by first describing what neoliberalism is and its relationship to liberalism. From there the chapter outlines the development aid model applied by donors in the oPt from 1993, and why it is neoliberal. It then provides historical background on aid to the Palestinians and the very top down nature by which the neoliberal aid program has been imposed on them. From there the chapter notes how development was a form of domination controlling the Palestinians while donors specifically ignored the settler colonial context in which the aid program, totally ill-suited to challenge settler colonialism, was imposed. It concludes by noting that liberalism has though had a long historical relationship with colonialism and of helping to reinforce the latter. Thus, that the neoliberal donor development program in the oPt was effectively doing harm to the Palestinians by contributing toward settler colonization was not without precedent, especially in the West.[1]

THE PALESTINIAN AID FRAMEWORK

Neoliberalism in the oPt

As a political philosophy and policy agenda, neoliberalism has always looked to the state to reshape society around its ideals. It is not laissez-faire and instead grants the government a key role in shaping how society and economic freedom is to be defined and instantiated (Davies 2017). It works within a pessimistic "Hobbesian" tradition of political thought arguing for a strong central authority where the absolutist state offers the a priori framework for freedom, "requiring untold reserves of centralized power in order to sustain a civil society" (Davies 2017). It is a particularly strong advocate of the liberal right for the individual to own private property and the right to trade goods internationally. For neoliberals, economic incentives are as important as military concerns, because trade and prosperity based on free market economics are the best antidotes to conflict (Keohane and Nye 1987, 729). They argue that an open trading system offers states ways to transform their positions through economic growth rather than military conquest, and that all states can then benefit from enhanced growth for a positive sum gain for all (Rosecrance 1986, ix). In fact, for neoliberal's trade constitutes the core element for cooperation in world affairs. For this reason, neoliberal belief is very much rooted in, and promotes principles of free market capitalism. Many of the neoliberal faithful even think that capitalism—and democracy—are inherently antithetical to conquest and conflict. It is for this reason that most major donors to the Palestinians believed that democratic state building and free market economics were the key ingredients for peace.

Neoliberal International Relations (IR) theory needs to not be misconstrued as one in the same as neoliberal economic theory, even if the two approaches often complement one another. IR neoliberalism is preoccupied with cooperation among states in world affairs, arguing that states should be concerned foremost with the absolute gains they can accrue by working together. Economic neoliberalism is preoccupied with the proposition that, "human well-being can best be advanced by the maximization of entrepreneurial freedoms within an institutional framework characterized by private property rights, individual liberty, unencumbered markets, and free trade" (Harvey 2007, 22–23). Even if category specialists are quick to explain that each field is unique, perhaps because they address different realms of human interaction, they are nonetheless completely complementary. For instance, IR neoliberalism is a strong proponent of the economic neoliberal theory, while both are the product of liberalism.

As a paradigm neoliberalism is highly influential in US foreign policy, as well as among its Western allies. Neoliberalism and its antecedent liberalism is now so influential and pervasive as an ideology that citizens in

Western states have so fully absorbed their principles and institutions into both their domestic politics and foreign affairs that they are no longer even able to perceive that those are distinctly there (Doyle 1983, 205). Those principles have become the norm, and when you adopt them this has the effect of making you appear to most Western citizens to be nonpolitical.

Neoliberalism has become the norm upon which the Western citizen believes ordinary state, and non-state, life should be organized. Duncan Bell describes this as a situation where little stands outside the "discursive embrace of liberalism" in mainstream Anglo-American politics and academic political theory, such that, "most who identify themselves as socialists, conservatives, social democrats, republicans, greens, feminists, and anarchists have been ideologically incorporated, whether they like it or not" (Bell 2014, 689). As Michael Doyle explains it is an ideology, it has "shaped the perceptions of and capacities for foreign relations of political societies that range from social welfare or social democratic to laissez faire" (Doyle 1983, 206). So, if donors from the West talk about providing "apolitical" assistance, what they really mean—without reflection—is that they are offering a neoliberal value-laden aid package. Thus, when the donor community embarked from 1993 on a mission to endow the Palestinians with modern state institutions modeled on the "civilized" image of the West (Long 1990), this really meant a state patterned precisely on neoliberal Western norms.

A History of Western Aid to the Palestinians

Of the many donors to the Palestinians the biggest have been states. Their governments give either directly through bilateral assistance programs, or indirectly through shared multilateral institutions and nongovernmental organizations (NGOs). Altogether donors have disbursed over $30 billion without any sign of the funding abating (Tartir 2016). Of these donors, Western states have since 1993 dominated the Palestinian aid process financially, politically, and intellectually. This has offered them incredible influence over the Palestinians, especially because Palestinian oPt economic activity collapsed right with the onset of the Peace Process, due to a tightening of the Israeli military occupation, sweeping restrictions on Palestinians' freedom of movement and rapid increases in settlement building on displaced Palestinians' land. This meant that donor aid became the lifeblood of Palestinian economic survival and this offered donors the opportunity to exert incredible influence over the Palestinians through a PA that relied on them for funding.

The attempt by donors to try purchase Palestinian support for peacebuilding, the "peace dividend", was not novel to 1993. It had long-standing precedent in US Middle East policy. For instance, in the 1970s the United States had been using aid as a way to try separately to buy peace in the Middle East, while simultaneously providing Israel with assurances for its own security (Lasensky 2004, 213). This was a neoliberal "security exchange" where the United States was willing to provide different actors in the Middle East with "alternative goods" that would replace concessions that one side was unwilling to offer to the other. It was considered successful model for peacebuilding between Egypt and Israel in the late 1970s, with aid to Egypt playing a key part in that exchange (Lasensky 2004, 213). Though the Carter administration explicitly left Palestinian rights out of the peace negotiations between Israel and Egypt, it did attempt a "depoliticized" solution to the Palestinian "question" in 1978 by adopting policy premised on the idea that "happy" Palestinians who had a job, steady employment, and a functioning administrative structure would be willing to negotiate for a settlement, even under Israeli occupation (Nakhleh 2004, 177).

In the 1980s, the Reagan Administration attempted to find a peace solution by promoting economic issues in lieu of a political settlement (Starr 1989, 4–5). First proposed as a "Quality of Life" initiative in 1983–1984, the United States attempted to promote political reconciliation between Israel and the Palestinians through economic inducements that were "in theory" separate from politics (Nakhleh 2004, 177). The Reagan Administration was attempting to make occupation palatable enough for Palestinians to accept living under the status quo (Nakhleh 2004, 36). That initiative was coached in apolitical technocratic jargon that would come to dominate the discourse on Palestinian development after Oslo. The Quality of Life initiative failed to gain traction though because at the time Israel was wary that Palestinian economic development would embolden their bid for independence. The initiative failed to gain traction with Palestinians, too, who feared any agreement without a political resolution just would reinforce the status quo of Israel's occupation and colonialization of the oPt, a political ploy meant to substitute economics for peace. Despite rejection by both Palestinians and Israelis, the logic of "separating politics" from development survived in US policy circles based on the idea that, "Economics may be politics in the West

Bank and Gaza, but the American government can and should attempt to separate the two for policy purposes" (Starr 1989, 38).

By contrast to US efforts to maintain the status quo in the oPt, from the late 1970s to the 1980s, Arab donors provided substantial financial support for Palestinians to not only survive under Israeli military occupation but also challenge and delay Israel's settler-colonialization of Palestinian land. Following Israel's invasion of Lebanon to target the PLO in the early 1980s, wealthy Palestinians increased their funding for Palestinian resistance (*sumud*) to Israeli rule. Likewise, in that period the USSR acted as a powerful counterbalance for Arabs challenging their former colonizers in the West, and for Palestinians in their confrontation with the West's close regional ally, Israel. That included military support for Palestinian "liberation" groups, which were labeled "terrorist" organizations in the West. This significant Arab and Soviet support for Palestinian resistance stood in stark contrast to US proposals aimed at maintaining the status quo by keeping Palestinians "happy" with a reasonable "quality of life" under occupation.

The Reagan Administration's attempt at maintaining the status quo in Israel and the oPt changed after the First Intifada erupted in late 1987 when "preserving peace", not maintaining the status quo, suddenly became the overriding US concern. Palestinians were at that time successful at challenging Israel through mass mobilizations including street demonstrations and confrontations with the Israeli army, and the economic boycott of Israeli goods, jobs, and tax payments. These all had a deleterious impact on Israel's economy (Gordon 2008, 154–164). The confrontations also severely damaged Israel's international reputation, as it had adopted a violent policy of repression "force, might, and beatings", curfews, closing Palestinian institutions, house demolitions, and the arrest of thousands (Rempel 2006). The Palestinian uprising was succeeding and that led elements of the Israeli government to conclude that ending the uprising should become a top priority. So, in an attempt to contain the Intifada, Israel suddenly opened up to the earlier US-led approaches to buying peace.

Meanwhile, world power dynamics began to change dramatically in the late 1980s when the USSR began rapidly to decline. During this time, it engaged in reforms that included reducing its past support for global guerrilla movements and improving relations with Israel. When the USSR finally dissolved in 1991, a powerful counterforce to US and Israeli interests was removed from the region. This offered space for a Western, US-led vision for Middle East peace to take hold. This led directly to the Oslo Peace Process, a process that would come to be dominated politically by Israel and the United States, underwritten financially by Europe and managed conceptually by the World Bank (Le More 2008, 109). There the United States and its Western allies reinserted the logic of the "Quality of Life" and "happy Palestinian" initiatives to try to maintain quiet in a region considered highly sensitive to US interests, and of their close ally, Israel. This all informed the philosophical rationale of a 1993 World Bank development plan, *An Investment in Peace*, that became the blueprint for donor aid after an October 1993 gathering of several dozen donor states and institutions (World Bank 1993).

Working on the precepts of earlier US models for Palestinian aid, donors oversaw a technical shift in 1993 where development aid replaced humanitarian assistance. In practical terms, that meant a shift from donors who prioritized lifesaving assistance like food, clean water, emergency shelter, and protection from harm; to longer-term assistance meant to help people rebuild their lives, secure jobs and livelihoods, and plan a better future for their families (Gabaudan 2012). Conceptually it depended very much on a political resolution taking hold to ensure enough peace and stability for development to take place. Yet, it was adopted with an explicit aim of undertaking development separate from politics and peacebuilding (Sayigh 2007, 9). This approach was based on the argument that survived in US political circles from the 1980s that politics should be separated from economics, justified based on an argument that development would foster conditions conducive toward peace. As the World Bank stated in *An Investment in Peace*, "Political settlement and peace is a necessary, but not a sufficient, condition for economic development in the OT [oPt]" (World Bank 1993, 13).

The dimensions of Palestinian self-rule radically realigned alongside this shift. Prior to Oslo, international consensus had favored a complete Israeli withdrawal from all the oPt, including East Jerusalem, and supported Palestinian aspirations to create their own state independent of Israeli rule. However, after Oslo, international donors sponsoring the Peace Process largely excluded East Jerusalem from the peacebuilding calculus because it had been annexed by Israel after the 1967 war and its status was politically contentious for their Israeli ally. Other "contentious issues" like final status solutions for Palestinian refugees were largely isolated and left out by donors, while Israeli settlement building and annexations of Palestinian land in the oPt were never seriously challenged, and sometimes implicitly accepted as "facts on the ground". With this new approach Israeli settlements, the status of East Jerusalem, and the (re)settlement of Palestinian refugees were left undetermined and for further negotiation within the framework of a Peace Process sponsored by Western donors who had little appetite for Palestinian demands that might upset Israel. All the while, the Oslo Accord was lauded as an example for what peace making could achieve and Israel was able to reestablish its international legitimacy at a time when much damage had been done to its reputation (Turner 2012, 495).

Top-Down Neoliberal Policy Implementation

The structure laid out by the World Bank for a Palestinian state is similar to all the other "one-size-fits-all" models created by International Financial Institutions (IFIs) for developing world states in the 1990s (Hickel 2012, 2014). The core normative values informing the Palestinian variant emphasized: open markets, economic integration with Israel, regional economic integration, financial liberalization, "good governance," and support for "democracy" (Amundsen et al. 2004; Hanieh 2011). The Bank's natural starting point for change was to work outward from a central authority that "in theory" represents the people who are being developed. In neoliberal development terms, the necessity for the PA was premised on a belief that the political provision of public goods requires one center of authority with responsibility to oversee and ensure that discrimination, utilizing its hierarchy and monopoly to guarantee effective coordination, control, and efficient performance (Landau 1991, 6). That authority would structure policy implementation networks outward and downward to deliver public goods to their people (Brinkerhoff 1996, 1498).

Like other neoliberal policymakers, those at the World Bank and among Western donors were inclined to believe that modernization for an extreme case like the violent Palestinians required, "nothing short of the managed reorganization of state and society to deliver development targets" (Mosse 2004a, 642). In this way social life becomes instrumentalized through policy-driven ideas (buzz words) like social capital, civil society, or good governance; ideas that theorize about relationships between society, democracy, and poverty reduction, extending the "scope of rational design and social engineering from the technical and economic realm to the social and cultural" (Duffield 2001, 9). By this way donor intervention becomes a total intervention into another society where they seek to export Western forms of governance and social organization. Thus, donors prioritized the creation of a PA that could fulfill their policy vision for the Palestinians, all while claiming that their intervention is somehow nonpolitical and very often claiming it was Palestinian led.

Western donors had also early on flagged Palestinian institution building as a key priority area, because at a philosophical level they wanted to turn the oPt into a liberal state which could become a Kantian "moral republic" where power rests in the true consent of its enlightened citizenry (Kant 2007). They believed such a Palestinian political entity would be willing to cohabit in harmony with Israel, the latter already an enlightened "moral republic" naturally predisposed toward peace. The underlying belief of the donors was that they would need to prepare the less advanced Palestinians for independence from Israel in a measured and planned way, to make sure the oPt would grow economically rather than decline suddenly once separated from Israeli oversight, thereby threatening any progress toward peace.

Since donors keep the PA solvent under Israeli military rule, the influence they exert over it and the colonized Palestinian society cannot be understated. The models that they "advise" are much more than advice, and actually shape Palestinian policy. Thus, in its role as a key policy maker, the World Bank ended up laying out the legal framework for Palestinian economic activity and Palestine's economic relations with Israel (Roy 1999, 68). Some aspects of this were even written into Palestinian law. One prominent example is PA Basic Law Article 21, which mirrors the core normative values informing donor state-building in the oPt by stating, "the economic system in Palestine shall be based on the principles of a free market economy."

Development as Domination

The development model applied in the oPt is grounded in age-old tactics where aggressors use the justification of "civilizing forces" for a greater good to carry out some other self-interested end, rarely in the interest of the afflicted. Thus, in the Eighteenth Century Edmund Burke would claim British Imperialism did not have aggressive aims, but a higher noble aim of helping to civilize the savage, chiefly through prolonged exposure to "commerce and Christianity" (Bell 2016, 15). It is a Western political logic articulating a right, or even duty, of self-anointed "advanced" states to remake the world in their own image, undertaken in the name of various related ideals (Bell 2016, 6). It is the same logic by which "democracy building" has been used in contemporary times as a cover for violent intervention in resource rich regions of the world like Iraq or Afghanistan, with commerce remaining a priority but Christianity replaced by the aim to spread liberal democracy.

When Western liberals are confronted with a different culture, they invariably judge that society through "Eurocentric conceptions of what it means to be fully human and/or a legitimate society" (Bell 2016, 8). The prescribed solution is "cognitive, affective, and behavioral transformation" through expert tutelage by "specialists" (Bell 2016, 33), like the technocrats working at the World Bank and other development agencies "advising" the Palestinians. The modernizing ideals remain, "to improve, to civilize, develop, modernize, constitutionalize, democratize, and bring good governance and freedom" (Bell 2016, 6). In its most extreme form, the more "child-like" people are themselves considered the problem, incapable of creating or maintaining a stable and progressive political order. In those cases, total transformation or reorganization is justified. The result is a preordained order within the liberal and neoliberal development discourse, where the world is divided into those who possess reason and are capable of self-government, and those who require tutelage to bring them up to the required standard (Bell 2016, 9).

In reality this represents little more than strong governments exercising dominance over and transposing their systems of belief on the weak for their own ends. This is something empires have always done and European Empires in the West regularly did, masking the more "crude accoutrements of conquest, plunder and territoriality" under the pretenses of spreading civilization for the benefit of those subjected to their rule (Bell 2016, 35). Thus, it is with little coincidence that the word "democracy" is absent from key donor reports on development in the oPt, despite the lead role it has played justifying external intervention into oPt society; or delaying Palestinian independence for fear of what might happen if they were to be released "prematurely" from Israel's democratic oversight. Thus, in 18 World Bank reports from 2009 to 2017 to the powerful Ad Hoc Liaison Committee (AHLC), where the most important donors meet to determine Palestinian bilateral aid, and where the Bank serves as Secretary setting the aid agenda shaping

PA institutions, the words "democracy" and "democratic" appear just 2 times combined in 500 pages of analysis and policy recommendations. Both instances occurred in a June 2010 update to the AHLC and refer to the governance of nongovernmental organizations in the oPt, not of the PA (Bank 2010). This jarring omission hints at how little the donors were actually concerned with Palestinian self-government or democracy.

Though not always wedded to imperialism and domination, liberalism with its "civilizing mission" can form the imperialist logic of liberal political thought (Pitts 2000, 296), and it remained a central feature of imperial ideology well into the twentieth century (Bell 2016, 40). It is through the pretense of spreading civilization for the benefit of all that conquest for gain is rebranded as a moral conquest for the benefit of those who were "lucky enough" to be part of it. By way of this excuse, liberalism has been able to coexist alongside such an illiberal act as state-sponsored colonialism, which is characterized by violent processes of resource theft, conquest, slavery, and the extermination of indigenous peoples on sought-after land (McNally 2014, 28).

Colonizers meanwhile nearly never, if they have ever, acknowledged the historic wrongs they may have carried out against the oppressed. This represents a "sustained denial" cloaked within the pleasant exterior of ideals like a civilizing mission manifested by Western states (Veracini 2010, 107). They steadfastly rationalize and justify their actions until eventually they become "normalized, acceptable, and even righteous," even though colonization ought to be one of the most easily recognized forms of oppression in the world (Waziyatawin 2012, 172). Thus, history as written by the powerful Western states and their academies rarely acknowledges the historic wrongs done to Indigenous people and forgets that the latter never ceded their sovereignty, instead often repurposing the ultimate impact of colonization as one of good (Gordon 2009, 59). It is in this way that the technocrats designing policy for the Palestinians could so completely misunderstand Israel's relationship with the Palestinians, as to assume that Israel was actually developing the oPt after 1967 (Starr 1989, 30). They did this based on economic data, such as GDP indicators, that appeared to provide evidence of such growth (Roy 1987, 59–60) when in reality Israel was bolstering its own economic growth by preying upon and hollowing out the oPt economy in a process of de-development (Roy 1987, 1995, 1999) which undermines or weakens the ability of an economy to grow and expand by preventing it from accessing and utilizing critical inputs needed to promote internal growth beyond a specific structural level (Roy 1987, 56).

Recasting Colonization as Peace

Meanwhile, two seemingly contradictory goals have played an important role in donors' overarching policy design for the Palestinian state and economy. Those were to increase Palestinian economic independence, in order for it to become less reliant on the Israeli economy, while simultaneously encouraging deeper economic integration between the two states. This meant,

> Promoting regional infrastructural networks in electricity, transport, telecommunication, petroleum and gas pipelines and water would offer other opportunities for strengthening interdependence and economies benefitting from complementarities and economies of scale, which may not be available to the OT [oPt] in the absence of such cooperation. (World Bank 1993, 14)

The logic lay on the foundation of peacebuilding through an exchange of goods. It included a key assumption that Israel did not really want to rule over the oPt and would be ready to decolonize once its security concerns were allayed. It reflected the long-standing argument by leading Western policymakers that Palestinians benefit economically from exposure to the superior Israeli economy (Starr 1989, 30).

Thus, from the onset of the Oslo Process, Western policymakers pushed the Palestinians into a customs union between Israel and the oPt. Referred to as the *Paris Protocol*, it formalized a union of Israel and the oPt into a single economic zone with a common currency (Israeli Ministry of Foreign Affairs 1994; B'Tselem 2011). Trade with other countries would continue to be handled through Israeli seaports and airports, or through border crossings controlled by Israel between the oPt with Jordan and Egypt, formalizing by accord a single external border controlled by Israel. Under the protocol, Israel was expected to collect import taxes on goods bound for the oPt and should also transfer to the PA any Value Added Taxes (VAT) collected on goods and services sold in Israel intended for oPt consumption. However, Israel was given the right to unilaterally determine the tax rates imposed on imported goods and allowed to take a significant administrative percentage from those funds. In addition, Israel could continue to choose what gets in and goes out of the oPt economy before then transferring those taxes, at its own discretion, to the PA. The result was a protocol that gave Israel significant leverage over the PA as those taxes comprise, alongside international donor funding, a large percentage of the PA's monthly revenue, which Israel has on many occasions withheld when it felt it needed to punish the PA (UNCTAD 2011, 8).

While Western policymakers had envisaged a Palestinian economy that would rely on export-led growth to propel forward the post-Oslo development model and the Peace Process, Israel instead used control over the oPt's borders to undermine Palestinian trade, mirroring its historical proclivity for blocking and de-developing the Palestinian economy, and undermining oPt economic empowerment (Tartir and Wildeman 2012). Rather than challenging Israeli restrictions, donors would instead opt to prop up the failing oPt economy by funding much of the PA, Palestinian services, and the oPt's enormous trade deficit with Israel (Hever 2010, 145–146). Donors thus also thereby artificially maximized the profit that Israel could extract from the oPt, where a central aspect of settler-colonialism is for the aggressor to extract as much economic value from a conquered people as possible, while also simultaneously removing them from the land (Veracini 2007, 2013; Wolfe 2006, 2012). This relieved Israel of the financial responsibilities of rule over the oPt, but at a profit, making it cost effective to maintain the status quo of colonialism, dispossession, and conflict in lieu of peace. In spite of this, donor policy remained unchanged from change from 1993 onwards (Wildeman and Tartir 2014).

Specifically Ignoring Cause and Effect

From the onset of Oslo, Western policymakers argued that a political solution to the occupation was not a necessary precondition for Palestinian economic growth to take place. Under the rubric of liberal peacebuilding, they argued that peace linkages between Israel and the Palestinians would grow naturally out of the positive conditions created by the oPt development program. This conscious attempt at depoliticization had the effect of causing aid actors to sanitize the language they used to describe conditions in the oPt, shying away from the use of descriptive and accurate terminology like apartheid or ethnic cleansing that were necessary to understand the actual conditions in the oPt (du Plessis et al. 2009). There would be no South African-style truth-and-reconciliation in the oPt under Western donor tutelage, or any acknowledgment of past sins. Preferring to appear neutral and apolitical, technocratic policymakers focused on what they considered "positive dialogue," avoided deconstructive recriminations about past actions by Israel and side-stepped contentious issues, instead focusing on the benefits both sides could attain by moving forward with greater economic integration (World Bank 2012).

Thus, it was possible through this sanitization of the facts for a neoliberal cadre of technocratic policymakers to conceive of an aid model that looked at Palestinian poverty as little more than a "technical problem," which could be solved through well-constructed and nonpolitical policy. Emphasizing the need to solve that "technical problem," those Western aid actors in the 1990s inverted cause and effect, and came to look at Palestinian poverty as the primary issue that needs to be resolved in order to foster political peace between Israelis and Palestinians—rather than the Israeli military occupation and settler colonialism that was actually causing the poverty (Zimmerman 2007, 5). By specifically trying to exclude politics from the development and peace process, aid providers chose to ignore the actual cause of the conflict and poverty in the oPt.

Such technocratic aid providers believe that oPt poverty can be reduced simply through the application of good policy that is neutral (apolitical), rational, and objective (Mosse 2004b, 3–4). They based this on the belief that it is in the best interest of every rational government to adopt "good" policy that provides public goods and open markets for all the people they govern. Thus,

> Those who work in development prefer to focus on technical solutions to the poor's problems, such as forestry projects, clean water supplies, or nutritional supplements. Development experts advise leaders they perceive to be benevolent autocrats to implement these technical solutions. The international professionals perpetrate an illusion that poverty is purely a technical problem, distracting attention away from the real cause: the unchecked power of the state against poor people without rights. The dictators whom experts are advising are not the solution – they are the problem. (Easterly 2014)

For these technocrats there was, and is, no hidden agenda behind policy, and development policy can largely be taken at "face-value" from official documents, public statements, and decision-making records (Mosse 2004b, 3–4). Meanwhile, development writers who suggest that an area suffers from some political trouble, "would not necessarily be censored or suppressed, … but they would find their analyses quickly dismissed and discarded as useless" (Ferguson 1994, 68).

History has though revealed with great consistency that government does not always have at heart the best interests of all the people it rules. This is particularly true of a government engaged in settler colonialism against a group of people it has conquered by force, and whose land it covets for what it considers to be its own citizens. In settler colonialism, land is after all life (Wolfe 2006, 387). Further, in spite of its most progressive elements, liberalism and its contemporary iteration neoliberalism have often been the handmaiden to destructive, autocratic Western imperialism (Bell 2016; Pitts 2000; McNally 2014). Put simply, neoliberal technocrats are unable to cope conceptually with the "irrationalities" of settler-colonialism, particularly by a Western and liberal state like Israel where the government actively seeks to deny public goods and open markets to part of the population it rules. Those technocrats are unable to conceive of the possibility that neutrality is a hallmark of the self-believed "impersonal power" that lies at the heart of the neoliberal state (McNally 2014, 15). Their own inadequacies and the nature of neoliberalism, working alongside rather than challenging settler colonialism, has come at great cost to the Palestinians and broader Middle East peace.

Conclusion: Neoliberalism as the Handmaiden of Settler Colonialism

In its most optimistic iteration the Oslo Process was only ever offering Palestinians more colonial occupation, but coached in the accoutrements of liberalism. Its cooperative liberal element was never meant to be one of interdependence between equals, but of uneven mutual dependence, "an asymmetrical stasis of interdependence" (Nye 1990, 158). Within this system Israel would maintain a preponderance of power over the Palestinians, but it was assumed in the neoliberal discourse that at least each side would benefit from cooperation and this would lead to peace between both when they realized they had more to gain from cooperation than from violent conflict. The open question remains as to what extent policymakers really understood the full measure of this asymmetry or Israel's long-standing settler colonial policies, especially among the neoliberal policymakers who put their faith behind Oslo.

Regardless, the result was that the donors helped formalize the uneven colonial relationship by championing agreements, like the 1994 Paris Protocol, that reinforced and codified the grossly unequal relationship between Israel and the Palestinians (Gerster and Baumgarten 2011, 11). This reinforced deeply unequal trading arrangements, reinventing the conquest of the oPt as a full-fledged union and masking the destructive military occupation in the liberal language of peacebuilding. This gave the occupation new legitimacy and left Israel with full control over oPt Palestinians and their economy. It left unchallenged the matrix of settler-colonial control exercised by Israel over the oPt, which, even if the tactics have adapted over time, has remained strategically consistent dating back to the initial expulsions of Palestinians in 1948 (Pappe 2006; Masalha 2012). This happened because the approach Western aid actors took was decontextualized and ahistorical, ignoring the process of Israeli settler colonialism on Palestinian lands that is at the center of any conflict and the decade's long humanitarian crisis. By ignoring reality and operating on alternative facts, Western policymakers have been able to carry on with neoliberal development projects completely ill-suited to a conflict situation defined by settler colonialism. The hallmark of a totalizing ontology, those neoliberal actors have been completely unable to imagine that a fellow liberal democracy like Israel could be engaged in very illiberal acts of dispossession that are inherent to settler colonialism, even though it for centuries typified the external modalities of their own states/empires in the West.

Thus, it is in the donors' depoliticized alternative reality that they have explicitly chosen to ignore the actual historical context of the Israeli–Palestinian conflict. In the process, they have usurped Palestinians of leadership over their own development process and the right to determine the composure of their own institutions, all while choosing to favor Israel over the Palestinians in the conflict. In many instances they have had the audacity to act as though the oPt Palestinians had been "lucky enough" to benefit from Israeli rule after 1967, just as they should be grateful for Western intervention to develop the oPt making it more advanced and richer. In the process, those donors have violated principles for good practice in development that most had agreed to, such as the Paris Declaration (2005) and Accra Agreement for Action (2008), in addition to cautionary advice offered by the well-respected Do No Harm principle for intervening in a conflict situation (Anderson 1999; OECD 2008, 2010). As a result, Israel has been able to take advantage of the economic and aid arrangements that developed out of the Peace Process, markedly improving its own economic situation after having previously been forced into the Peace Process in 1993 by the first Palestinian uprising. Israel was also able to largely ignore its obligations to the Palestinians under the Accord and dramatically increase its rate of settlement building in the oPt, while donors have picked up the tab for sustaining the Palestinians under occupation, at a profit to Israel.

Palestinians likely had been right in the 1980s to abstain from any agreement that did not include a political resolution to the occupation for fear it would just reinforce the status quo of Israel's occupation and colonialization of the oPt, a political ploy meant to substitute economics in lieu of peace. The Oslo development model has done just that, and in this time Israel's colonial regime has become deeply entrenched at great social and capital cost to the indigenous Palestinians. In this way, the neoliberal approach of the donors has worked in tandem with their Western ally Israel's settler colonialism at the expense of the Palestinians. Though it may be unusual to have so many different states contributing to a colonial enterprise, it is far from being without precedent for liberalism to be the handmaiden of colonialism. The case of the oPt appears just to be a contemporary variant of this relationship.

Note

1. The author would like to acknowledge his external and internal examiners Dr. Adam Hanieh of SOAS and Dr. William Gallois of the University of Exeter for having helped lay the foundations for the argument proposed in this chapter.

References

Amundsen, Inge, George Giacaman, and Mushtaq Husain Khan. 2004. *State Formation in Palestine: Viability and Governance During a Social Transformation*. London and New York: Routledge.

Anderson, Mary B. 1999. *Do No Harm: How Aid Can Support Peace—Or War*. Boulder, CO: Lynne Rienner.

B'Tselem. 2011. "The Paris Protocol." B'Tselem: The Israeli Information Center for Human Rights in the Occupied Territories, January 1. http://www.btselem.org/freedom_of_movement/paris_protocol.

Bell, Duncan. 2014. "What Is Liberalism?" *Political Theory* 42 (6): 682–715.
Bell, Duncan. 2016. "The Dream Machine: On Liberalism and Empire." In *Remaking the World: Essays on Liberalism and Empire*. Princeton: Princeton University Press.
Brinkerhoff, Derick W. 1996. "Coordination Issues in Policy Implementation Networks: An Illustration from Madagascar's Environmental Action Plan." *World Development* 24 (9): 1497–1510.
Davies, William. 2017. "What Is 'Neo' About Neoliberalism?" *New Republic*, July 13. https://newrepublic.com/article/143849/neo-neoliberalism.
Doyle, Michael W. 1983. "Kant, Liberal Legacies, and Foreign Affairs." *Philosophy & Public Affairs* 12 (3): 205–235.
Duffield, Mark R. 2001. *Global Governance and the New Wars: The Merging of Development and Security*. London and New York: Zed Books; Distributed in the USA exclusively by Palgrave.
du Plessis, Max, Fatmeh El-Ajou, Victor Kattan, Michael Kearney, John Reynolds, Rina Rosenberg, Iain Scobbie, and Virginia Tilley. 2009. *Occupation, Colonialism, Apartheid? A Re-assessment of Israel's Practices in the Occupied Palestinian Territories Under International Law*. Cape Town: Human Sciences Research Council.
Easterly, William. 2014. "The New Tyranny." *Foreign Policy*, March 10. http://www.foreignpolicy.com/articles/2014/03/10/the_new_tyranny.
Ferguson, James. 1994. *The Anti-politics Machine: "Development," Depoliticization, and Bureaucratic Power in Lesotho*. Minneapolis: University of Minnesota Press.
Gabaudan, Michel. 2012. "From Emergency Aid to Development Aid: Agencies Are Failing to Connect." *The Guardian*, January 19, sec. Global Development. http://www.theguardian.com/global-development/poverty-matters/2012/jan/19/humanitarian-aid-development-assistance-connect.
Gerster, Karin, and Helga Baumgarten. 2011. "Palestinian NGOs and Their Cultural, Economic and Political Impact in Palestinian Society." Rosa Luxemburg Foundation. http://www.palestine.rosalux.org/news/38136/palestinian-ngos.html.
Gordon, Neve. 2008. *Israel's Occupation*. Berkeley: University of California Press.
Gordon, Todd. 2009. "Canada, Empire and Indigenous People in the Americas." *Socialist Studies/Études Socialistes* 2 (1): 47–75. http://socialist-studies.com/article/view/23795.
Hanieh, Adam. 2011. "Development as Struggle: Confronting the Reality of Power in Palestine." In *Development in the Occupied Palestinian Territory*. Ramallah, Palestine: Birzeit University.
Harvey, David. 2007. "Neoliberalism as Creative Destruction." *The Annals of the American Academy of Political and Social Science* 610 (1): 21–44.

Hever, Shir. 2010. *The Political Economy of Israel's Occupation: Repression Beyond Exploitation*. London: Pluto Press.
Hickel, Jason. 2012. "The World Bank and the Development Delusion." *Al Jazeera*, September 27. http://www.aljazeera.com/indepth/opinion/2012/09/201292673233720461.html.
Hickel, Jason. 2014. "The Death of International Development." *Al Jazeera*, November 20. http://www.aljazeera.com/indepth/opinion/2014/11/death-international-developmen-2014111991426652285.html.
Israeli Ministry of Foreign Affairs. 1994. "Gaza-Jericho Agreement Annex IV-Economic Protocol." Government Ministry—Foreign Policy. Israeli Ministry of Foreign Affairs, April 29. http://www.mfa.gov.il/mfa/foreignpolicy/peace/guide/pages/gaza-jericho%20agreement%20annex%20iv%20-%20economic%20protoco.aspx.
Kant, Immanuel. 2007. *Perpetual Peace*. Minneapolis: Filiquarian Publishing, LLC.
Keohane, Robert O., and Joseph S. Nye. 1987. "Power and Interdependence Revisited." *International Organization* 41 (4): 725–753.
Keohane, Robert O., and Joseph S. Nye. 1998. "Power and Interdependence in the Information Age." *Foreign Affairs*, September 1. http://www.foreignaffairs.com/articles/54395/robert-o-keohane-and-joseph-s-nye-jr/power-and-interdependence-in-the-information-age.
Landau, Martin. 1991. "On Multiorganizational Systems in Public Administration." *Journal of Public Administration Research and Theory* 1 (1): 5–18.
Lasensky, Scott. 2004. "Paying for Peace: The Oslo Process and the Limits of American Foreign Aid." *Middle East Journal* 58 (2): 210–234.
Le More, Anne. 2008. *International Assistance to the Palestinians After Oslo*. London and New York: Routledge.
Long, Norman. 1990. "From Paradigm Lost to Paradigm Regained? The Case for an Actor-Oriented Sociology of Development." *European Review of Latin American and Caribbean Studies* 49 (December): 3–24.
Masalha, Nur. 2012. *Expulsion of the Palestinians: The Concept of 'Transfer' in Zionist Political Thought, 1882–1948*. Washington, DC: Institute for Palestine Studies.
McNally, David. 2014. "The Blood of the Commonwealth." *Historical Materialism* 22 (2): 3–32.
Mosse, David. 2004a. "Is Good Policy Unimplementable? Reflections on the Ethnography of Aid Policy and Practice." *Development and Change* 35 (4): 639–671.
Mosse, David. 2004b. *Cultivating Development: An Ethnography of Aid Policy and Practice*. London: Pluto Press.
Nakhleh, Khalil. 2004. *The Myth of Palestinian Development: Political Aid and Sustainable Deceit*. Jerusalem: PASSIA.

Nye, Joseph S. 1990. "Soft Power." *Foreign Policy* 80 (October): 153–171.
OECD. 2008. "The Paris Declaration on Aid Effectiveness and the Accra Agenda for Action." http://www.oecd.org/dac/effectiveness/34428351.pdf.
OECD. 2010. *Do No Harm—International Support for Statebuilding*. Paris: OECD.
Pappe, Ilan. 2006. *Ethnic Cleansing of Palestine*. Oxford: Oneworld Publications.
Pitts, Jennifer. 2000. "Empire and Democracy: Tocqueville and the Algeria Question." *Journal of Political Philosophy* 8 (3): 295–318.
Rempel, Terry. 2006. "Palestinian Refugees in the West Bank and the Gaza Strip." Folder. Forced Migration Online. http://www.forcedmigration.org/research-resources/expert-guides/palestinian-refugees-in-the-west-bank-and-the-gaza/alldocuments.
Rosecrance, Richard N. 1986. *The Rise of the Trading State: Commerce and Conquest in the Modern World*. New York: Basic Books.
Roy, Sara. 1987. "The Gaza Strip: A Case of Economic De-development." *Journal of Palestine Studies* 17 (1): 56–88.
Roy, Sara. 1995. *The Gaza Strip: The Political Economy of De-development*. Washington, DC: Institute for Palestine Studies.
Roy, Sara. 1999. "De-development Revisited: Palestinian Economy and Society Since Oslo." *Journal of Palestine Studies* 28 (3): 64–82.
Said, Edward. 1993. "The Morning After." *London Review of Books*, October 21.
Sayigh, Yezid. 2007. "Inducing a Failed State in Palestine." *Survival* 49 (3): 7–39.
Starr, Joyce. 1989. "Development Diplomacy: U.S. Economic Assistance to the West Bank and Gaza." Policy Papers 12. Washington Institute for Near East Policy. http://www.washingtoninstitute.org/policy-analysis/view/development-diplomacy-u.s.-economic-assistance-to-the-west-bank-and-gaza.
Tartir, Alaa. 2016. "How US Security Aid to PA Sustains Israel's Occupation." *Al Jazeeera*, December 2. http://www.aljazeera.com/indepth/features/2016/11/security-aid-pa-sustains-israel-occupation-161103120213593.html.
Tartir, Alaa, and Jeremy Wildeman. 2012. "Persistent Failure: World Bank Policies for the Occupied Palestinian Territories." *Al Shabaka*, October 9. http://al-shabaka.org/node/513.
Turner, Mandy. 2012. "Completing the Circle: Peacebuilding as Colonial Practice in the Occupied Palestinian Territory." *International Peacekeeping* 19 (4): 492–507.
UNCTAD. 2011. "Report on UNCTAD Assistance to the Palestinian People: Developments in the Economy of the Occupied Palestinian Territory." Note by the UNCTAD Secretariat. Geneva: United Nations Conference on Trade and Development. http://unctad.org/en/docs/tdb58d4_en.pdf.

Veracini, Lorenzo. 2007. "Settler Colonialism and Decolonisation." *Borderlands E-Journal* 6 (2). http://www.borderlands.net.au/vol6no2_2007/veracini_settler.htm.
Veracini, Lorenzo. 2010. *Settler Colonialism: A Theoretical Overview.* Houndmills, Basingstoke and New York: Palgrave Macmillan.
Veracini, Lorenzo. 2013. "The Other Shift: Settler Colonialism, Israel, and the Occupation." *Journal of Palestine Studies* 42 (2): 26–42.
Waziyatawin. 2012. "Malice Enough in Their Hearts and Courage Enough in Ours: Reflections on US Indigenous and Palestinian Experiences Under Occupation." *Settler Colonial Studies* 2 (1): 172–189.
Wildeman, Jeremy, and Alaa Tartir. 2014. "Unwilling to Change, Determined to Fail: Donor Aid in Occupied Palestine in the Aftermath of the Arab Uprisings." *Mediterranean Politics* 19 (3): 431–449.
Wolfe, Patrick. 2006. "Settler Colonialism and the Elimination of the Native." *Journal of Genocide Research* 8 (4): 387–409.
Wolfe, Patrick. 2012. "Purchase by Other Means: The Palestine Nakba and Zionism's Conquest of Economics." *Settler Colonial Studies* 2 (1): 133–171.
World Bank. 1993. *Developing the Occupied Territories: An Investment in Peace.* Washington, DC: World Bank.
World Bank. 2010. *West Bank and Gaza Update.* Washington, DC: World Bank.
World Bank. 2012. "Towards Economic Sustainability of a Future Palestinian State: Promoting Private Sector—Led Growth." Report No. 68037-GZ. http://siteresources.worldbank.org/INTWESTBANKGAZA/Resources/GrowthStudyEngcorrected.pdf.
Zimmerman, Robert A. 2007. "The Determinants of Foreign Aid." OECD. http://www.oecd.org/dev/40699467.pdf.

CHAPTER 8

Solidarity Donors and Popular Education in the West Bank

Melanie Meinzer

OVERVIEW

Since the 1993 Oslo Accords, the Palestinians have been among the world's highest per capita recipients of non-military foreign aid. This was meant to facilitate the peace process with Israel through humanitarian relief, economic development, Palestinian state-building, and by cultivating a democratic civil society by funding Palestinian non-governmental organizations (NGOs). Yet despite billions of dollars in development aid, the Palestinian economy deteriorated during the Oslo period, and donor support for Palestinian NGOs failed to produce tangible gains for democracy (Roy 1999; Jamal 2009; Taghdisi-Rad 2010). Scholars maintain that Palestinian NGOs' dependence on donors weakens their autonomy and distances them from their grassroots constituents, limiting civil society's ability to challenge the Israeli occupation (Hammami 2000; Hanafi and Tabar 2005; Jad 2007; Taghdisi-Rad 2010; Nakhleh 2012; Merz 2012). They argue that donor-supported developmental and peacebuilding projects undermine Palestinian self-determination,

M. Meinzer (✉)
Environmental Studies Program, Denison University, Granville, OH, USA
e-mail: meinzerm@denison.edu

and that the aid regime functions as a form of counterinsurgency where a docile Palestinian NGOs sector helps maintain the status quo of the occupation (Turner 2015).

Leaders of Palestinian NGOs have been called the "Palestinian globalized elite" and the "missionaries of the new era," who have been co-opted by foreign donors and are complicit in neocolonial and neoliberal projects that undermine Palestinian nationalist resistance under the guise of development (Hanafi and Tabar 2003, 211; Merz 2012, 50; Khalidi and Samour 2011). There is a marked difference between the pre-Oslo era of mass-based civil society movements and the current age of NGO-led development (Dana 2015). Palestinian civic groups led resistance movements during the first *intifada* (uprising from 1987 to 1993), but the subsequent professionalization of civil society after Oslo has separated civic leaders from Palestinian resistance movements (Hanafi and Tabar 2003; Jad 2007; Dana 2015).

Research on aid dependence in the West Bank has thus far overlooked how donors and aid-receiving organizations can resist aid's depoliticizing and demobilizing effects. Studies on aid and NGOs have also overlooked how donor-supported popular education programs can cultivate the values and knowledge that support political resistance. This has left unanswered questions about how Palestinian educational civic organizations use donor funding to raise political awareness and shape group identities, and how these identities translate into different forms of individual and collective political action. Examining Palestinian educational organizations and their donors with this critical perspective in mind can illuminate the relationship between foreign aid, education, and political mobilization in the West Bank.

Building Resistance: The Role of "Solidarity Donors"

Based on findings from the education sector, this chapter introduces the term "solidarity donors" to describe international donors that fund local organizations based on their shared vision of development and education as long-term processes of sociopolitical change. Solidarity donors differ from the larger donors associated with the failed aid regime in the occupied Palestinian territories in three ways. First, solidarity donors are smaller European and American cultural foundations, international NGOs (INGOs) and a subset of progressive governmental development agencies. Second, solidarity donors establish longer-term funding relationships with their recipients, in contrast to short-term project-based funding, which reinforces NGOs' dependence on donors. Third, because solidarity donors share their recipients' critical perspectives on development and education, they commit to being downwardly accountable to these organizations' priorities. Solidarity donors exchange funding for legitimacy, namely to be perceived differently from donors that uphold the status quo of the occupation. Rather than merely employing the language of "ownership," "accountability," "partnership," and "participatory development,"[1] solidarity donors demonstrate their commitment to bottom-up, grassroots practices in education and development. This small-scale success in building a solidarity economy between donors and local organizations in popular education exists within the larger context of the failed aid regime in the occupied territories (Wildeman and Tartir 2014).

The donors in this study are European and North American INGOs and progressive governmental development agencies that follow the German political foundation (*Stiftungen*) model established by West German political parties to support political education after Nazi rule. The earliest party foundations were started by the German Social Democratic Party, which re-established the Friedrich Ebert Foundation in 1947, followed by the Christian Democrats' political academy in 1964, which later became the Konrad Adenauer Foundation.[2] These foundations receive public funding, and expanded internationally to work with labor and trade unions in Latin America and Africa. German political foundations played a significant role in Portugal and Spain's democratic transitions in the 1970s, and Chile's transition in the 1980s (Pinto-Duschinsky 1991). The German model of party and state-funded foundations spread throughout Europe and North America. For example, the US-based National Endowment for Democracy, a major recipient of governmental funding for democracy promotion, was based on the German foundation model (Lloyd 2010). Solidarity donor INGOs working in education and development in the West Bank today include the Rosa Luxemburg Foundation (German Left Party, Die Linke), the Heinrich Böll Foundation (German Green Party), the Olof Palme International Center (Swedish labor movement), and the Gesellschaft für Internationale Zusammenarbeit (a development agency funded by the German government). Solidarity donors' focus on political change through cultural work aligns with the critical educational philosophies and practices of Palestinian educational organizations, but these donors' roles in supporting popular education in the West Bank are little understood.

Solidarity donors' commitment to longer-term funding mitigates some of the financial pressure on local organizations to follow their donors' agendas. This gives local organizations more control over how funding is used, and reinforces the donor's downward accountability to their recipients' goals. Donors' downward accountability is particularly important, given the shift from the pre-Oslo mass-based model of mobilization to the current era of aid-dependent, NGO-led development (Dana 2015). Membership-based organizations (MBOs) represent the pre-Oslo model of mass-mobilization, and include social movements, campaigns and cooperatives that serve, and are often run by, people from marginalized groups (Banks et al. 2015). Some Palestinian MBOs working in education include the Right to Education Campaign, the Jordan Valley Solidarity Organization, Campus in Camps, and the Civic Coalition for Palestinian Rights in Jerusalem. MBOs do not depend on donor funding to survive, and enjoy greater legitimacy than NGOs because they are perceived as more directly accountable to their constituencies, while NGOs, which depend on aid, are viewed as upwardly accountable to donors. A few leading Palestinian educational NGOs in the West Bank include the Tamer Institute for Community Education, the A. M. Qattan Foundation, and the Freedom Theater.

Solidarity donors fund both MBOs and NGOs, but MBOs' relative independence from donors gives them greater freedom than NGOs to espouse more radical political causes, and MBOs tend to have more democratic institutional practices than NGOs (Banks et al. 2015). Palestinian educational MBOs thereby "model" the democratic values, practices, and grassroots connections that Palestinian educational NGOs emulate, and that their solidarity donors seek to support in order to legitimize their interventions in the eyes of Palestinian civil society.

The Palestinian educational NGOs and MBOs in this study work in the tradition of popular resistance education from the first *intifada* (uprising from 1987 to 1993). Previous studies of foreign aid and Palestinian NGOs have overlooked education, despite its role in maintaining collective identity, cultural consciousness and historical memory as a bulwark against the territorial and cultural fragmentation of the West Bank. During the first *intifada*, the Israeli military closed Palestinian schools and universities for weeks to months at a time, fearing that they would become centers for political organizing. These closures prompted neighborhood popular committees to organize ad hoc schools that united education and resistance (Fasheh 1990). In these community spaces, the popular education movement experimented with participatory learning, and taught the Palestinian historical narrative missing from the formal educational system under the occupation.

Popular education recovers what has been lost or rendered invisible or worthless in ways of knowing, learning, and relating to one's own culture (Fasheh 2005, 19). During the *intifada*, these informal schools became alternative spaces for reclaiming power over producing and imparting knowledge. Whereas the didactic "banker's approach" in the formal educational system regards students as receptacles for authoritative knowledge, popular education's focus on participatory learning centers peoples' everyday experiences as a valid source of knowledge about the world (Freire 1993). This egalitarian approach reorients education toward taking action to address the need to build collective memory, identity, and ultimately, a "liberatory consciousness" to sustain popular struggle (Tabar 2015, 145).

After the first *intifada*, several educational activists from this movement founded educational NGOs. The Palestinian educational NGOs and MBOs in this study share a common set of political commitments and pedagogical practices with these earlier educational activists. These organizations adapt aid to continue the work of the popular education movement by working in the informal spaces around the donor-funded Palestinian Authority curriculum to raise political consciousness by reinserting Palestinian history and identity into education (Meinzer 2017).

This chapter is part of a larger project that draws on 44 original interviews with Palestinian educational NGOs, MBOs and their donors, and 240 surveys of Palestinians living in the West Bank, gathered during eleven months of field research between 2014 and 2016 (Meinzer 2017). The overall project traces how Palestinian educational organizations draw on the popular education movement from the first *intifada* to cultivate a critical awareness of Palestinian history and identity, to sustain pre-Oslo forms of social mobilization under the constraints imposed by aid dependence, military occupation, and settler-colonialism in the West Bank. Solidarity donors play a critical role in both enabling and constraining Palestinian organizations' work in this area, and a major objective of the study is to portray the complex empirical reality of aid practice on the ground, through the experiences of solidarity donors and their recipients. This in turn challenges the Manichean narratives of Northern hegemony and Southern passivity in the critical international political economy literature, and what Hobson (2007) called the "West*philian*" tendency of even critical approaches to international relations theory to emphasize Northern power at the expense of Southern agency.

In contrast to previous studies that center around NGOs, this project considers the *network* of relationships around NGOs that constrain and empower NGO autonomy, defined as an organization's ability to advance its own policy preferences regardless of how well these preferences align with its donors (Ohanyan 2009, 477). Palestinian educational MBOs are included because they adhere to the pre-Oslo model of grassroots organizing, as well as the more radical, anti-hierarchical principles and practices of the popular education movement. Many donors, NGOs and MBOs in this study see MBOs as better positioned to articulate and pursue grassroots priorities than NGOs; hence MBOs are perceived as more legitimate representatives of civil society. MBOs are important interlocutors between NGOs, donors and Palestinian communities because MBOs' legitimacy incentivizes NGOs and donors that want to demonstrate their solidarity with grassroots priorities, to be downwardly accountable to these groups (Andrews 2014; AbouAssi and Trent 2016). This pull toward downward accountability resists donor pressure on recipients to be upwardly accountable to their funders. Solidarity donors are usually willing to be held downwardly accountable to NGOs and MBOs, because they value those organizations' connections to grassroots political concerns. In other words, solidarity donors trade funding for legitimacy, to distinguish themselves from the broader aid regime associated with "peacebuilding as counterinsurgency" (Turner 2015). Although donors, NGOs and MBOs do not have equal power in this network, a network approach reveals the symbioses between these actors, as well as recipients' resistances to donors, and their strategies for enforcing downward accountability.

This discussion of the potential of solidarity donors to support progressive change, and of Palestinian organizations' resistance to the constraints placed on their agency, deepens our understanding of the complexity of aid practice on the ground. The failure of the macro-level aid regime in the occupied territories (see Wildeman and Tartir 2013) exists *alongside* the solidarity aid model proposed in this chapter. Palestinian educational organizations draw on this solidarity economy to continue the work of the popular education movement from the first *intifada*, a fact that has been overlooked in our understanding of the current aid regime's failures.

Aid Recipients' Repertoire of Strategic Responses

Resource dependence theory provides a theoretical framework for understanding aid recipients' strategic responses to the restrictions that donors place on their agency. With few exceptions (see, for example Bahdi and Kassis 2016), discussion of NGO agency in Palestinian Studies has been overshadowed by discussion of donors' abilities to co-opt and depoliticize NGO work. Research on NGO agency and resistance to donor demands from other contexts provide a framework for understanding the range of aid recipients' strategic responses in the West Bank.

Aid recipients often *acquiesce* to donor demands, leading to a high degree of institutional isomorphism, where NGOs mimic the practices of financially successful organizations and align themselves with donors' accountability procedures in order to access funding (Ohanyan 2012).

Aid recipients also *compromise*, negotiate, and bargain with their donors. NGOs can leverage their legitimacy as local partners to persuade their donors to follow the NGO's lead (AbouAssi 2013). *Avoidance* describes a category of strategic responses where recipients conceal their work to guard it against donor interference. *Portraying* is a form of avoidance where the NGO pretends to acquiesce to donor demands, while concealing the true nature of their programs. This can manifest as a disconnect between the project as it is described in NGO documents, and the reality of that project on the ground (Oliver 1991; Rauh 2010; Scott 1990). Other avoidance strategies include selecting or rejecting donors, and strategically diversifying funding sources to avoid over-reliance on any one donor (Elbers 2012; Mitchell 2014). For instance, NGOs and MBOs in the West Bank avoid donors that impose political conditionalities on their funding, which they regard as disrespectful and against Palestinian self-determination.

Negotiation and compromise are transparent strategies for maintaining NGO autonomy. Opaque avoidance tactics like buffering (managing the donor's perception of a project or limiting the donor's access to it), and portraying (appearing to acquiesce to donor demands while doing otherwise) are considered to be more active strategic responses (Oliver 1991; Elbers 2012; AbouAssi 2013; Mitchell 2014). Organizations also choose to end or "exit" relationships with donors when compromise is not possible (AbouAssi 2013; Hirschman 1970).

Beyond these established categories, the interviews revealed that unlike NGOs, MBOs strongly preferred to work *without* donor funding.

Choosing to "exit" the donor-supported development paradigm in favor of alternative, more sustainable models of development that can survive without external aid, set the standard for aid (in)dependence as a measure of an organization's autonomy. NGOs and donors admired these organizations, and NGOs frequently expressed their willingness to work without donors when disagreements could not be resolved. These strategies of negotiation, compromise, avoidance and exit strengthened recipients' abilities to demand downward accountability from their donors.

Aid recipients' willingness to disagree with their donors naturally led them toward more sympathetic "solidarity" donors who shared their commitment to critical pedagogy and community-driven change through education. Solidarity donors seek to mitigate the inherent inequalities of the donor–recipient relationship, and intentionally facilitate their recipients' autonomy by providing aid with few conditions, listening to recipients' priorities, and by being transparent about their own upward accountability practices to their parliaments or other funders. Recipients still negotiate with solidarity donors, but since they start from more similar ideological positions, the relationship is less contentious and more frequently cooperative. Solidarity donors are generally well-liked by their recipients, and these donors' interest in being (or at least appearing to be) downwardly accountable to their recipients distinguished them from the broader population of donors in the occupied territories.

Resisting Donor Influence

Palestinian educational NGOs and MBOs maintained their autonomy by employing a range of the strategic responses described above to resist donor interference in their work. Acquiescence, compromise, negotiation, portraying, donor diversification, donor selectivity, exit, and aid independence pressure donors to be downwardly accountable to their recipients. By resisting donor influence, NGOs and MBOs bolster their own legitimacy as representatives of Palestinian civil society, which they can leverage in their relationships with their donors. This section expands upon these strategic responses in order to explain how aid recipients hold solidarity donors accountable.[3]

NGOs and MBOs resist donor influence in similar ways, despite their different views on the legitimacy of using aid to achieve their goals. NGOs and MBOs saw aid recipients' acquiescence to donor agendas and accountability procedures as a problem for other organizations, rather than their own. For instance, an NGO representative in Ramallah insisted that donors did not influence his organization's work, but this was not the case for other NGOs:

> In the aftermath of the Oslo Accords, there was kind of a shift... Most of those NGO leaders are leftists, so they had a revolutionary spirit. They had a mission to free Palestine. After 1993, these organizations were headed by those very effective political leaders, [but] they were driven by the agendas of certain donors. ...they have to obey, or follow the rules... far away from the national agenda.[4]

According to the representative of an NGO that raised most of its funding internally,

> Look at the procedure, the first thing you look at is the [donor's] principles, and what kind of funding they are trying to meet. I'm not saying that it's always the agenda from abroad, but when you have money from others, you will meet their goals.[5]

Donors manipulate aid recipients' agendas by shaping the developmental space of Palestinian civil society, privileging certain actors while excluding others (Challand 2008). According to an NGO representative, "we are in a NGO-ized society...We [have] subconsciously been affected by donor agendas."[6] A representative of a theater NGO described this subtle shaping as the imperative to present projects in donors' terms:

> Very little donor money goes to cultural activities, so the NGO has to present its work in terms of how it will benefit society. We find ourselves trying to talk indirectly, trying to reach the donors, because that's where the money is.[7]

Some degree of acquiescence is necessary to secure donor funding, but organizations can protect the political content of their work when they disagree with their donors. Compromise and negotiation allow recipients to keep their principles without sacrificing their funding. When asked about how donors impacted his NGO, a representative admitted that: "yes, the money changed me, but I keep working." He pointed out that prior to Oslo, funding came from the Soviet Union, and asked "why is this funding good, and this funding is not?"[8] He saw aid as fungible-that how money was used mattered more than its source.

Several organizations offered examples of successful negotiations when concessions were made by the donor, rather than by the recipient. Two theater NGOs and an MBO negotiated to retain terms in their plays and projects that their donors did not like. A representative of a theater NGO said that donors could read their scripts, but not alter them, adding that if donors "have a problem with it… screw them." One of their INGO donors had objected to the NGO's use of the terms "occupation," "apartheid," and "colonialism" in a play. This donor recognized the existence of the Israeli occupation, but not its system of apartheid or the colonization in the West Bank. The NGO ultimately removed the donor's logo from the production at the donor's request, which allowed them to keep their funding *and* retain the controversial terms. The NGO representative acknowledged that "most of the diplomatic missions are in a tough situation, because they themselves usually are very understanding about the actual situation [in Palestine], but they have a mandate to work with, and they have a government that goes between left to right, maybe every two years." In this instance the NGO compromised with the donor, but there were other donors that the NGO refused to work with outright.[9] Donor selectivity led this NGO to a solidarity donor, but they still had to negotiate to keep their original language.

Another theater NGO recalled a time when an INGO donor asked them not to use the term "martyr" in a play:

> [The donor] said 'we will support you fully, but you cannot use the word 'martyr' in what the children have written about what they faced during the war.' They [the children] are talking about what they have lived: it's testimonies. [The donor] is about the rights of children, and they told us 'tell your children not to write the word 'martyrs.'" I was flipping out, I said 'thank you, we don't want your money, keep it for yourself. This is against your mandate, it's not against ours.'[10]

This NGO refused to alter their work based on the request of a donor that had appeared at first to share the NGO's mission. An MBO with a single European governmental donor similarly dismissed criticism about the language they used in a project where the community defined terms and concepts based on their experiences. The MBO representative explained, "of course when you define [terms], you share your story.

You come across some sort of terminology that will totally not please the donor. ...The donor showed us they were unhappy with some materials. And of course for us it was ok, it was not our problem."[11]

In all three examples, recipient organizations refused to make the changes to appease their donors. The first theater NGO agreed to remove the donor's name from the project but retained the funding. The second theater NGO kept the term "martyr" in their play, but lost their donor. In the third case, the MBO refused to accommodate the donor, but kept their funding. These examples show that NGOs and MBOs protect the content of their work, even when it means risking losing funding. Terms like "occupation," "apartheid," "colonialism," and "martyr" are part of the lexicon of critical narratives of the Israeli–Palestinian conflict, a way of framing grievance in relation to larger historical struggles. These terms reflect the politicized awareness of the conflict that resonates with Palestinian audiences; therefore using these terms is vital for the organizations to maintain legitimacy with the public. Even where few alternatives to donor funding exist, these recipients negotiated with donors over the use of these terms, and occasionally rejected donor demands when donors insisted on eliminating particular word choices.

Portraying is another way that aid recipients shield their politics from their donors. Recipients resisted donor depoliticization of their work by appearing to detach their political views from their work in education. Representatives of educational NGOs insisted that their programs were not associated with mobilization or traditional political party work. However, education under occupation cannot be neutral. Popular education subverts the Israeli government's narrative of the conflict, and compensates for donor depoliticization of the Palestinian Authority curriculum. Palestinian NGOs can claim to be apolitical, but their work in popular education shows that they have not abandoned their core political causes.

This played out most clearly in how NGO and MBO representatives talked about the Boycott, Divestment, and Sanctions (BDS) Movement. BDS was launched in 2005 by a coalition of Palestinian civic organizations calling for an international academic, cultural, and economic boycott of Israel. A sign of the movement's strength, Israel's parliament passed a law in March 2017 banning foreign supporters of BDS from entering Israel. The US Congress introduced the Israel Anti-Boycott Act in March 2017, which would similarly criminalize boycotting

Israel. All of the Palestinian organizations interviewed supported BDS, but NGO representatives were quick to distinguish between their personal support for BDS, and their organizations' work. One NGO director said he personally supported the boycott, but that the board did not discuss "political issues," and had not taken a position on BDS.[12] Another NGO director reframed BDS as a question of supporting freedom and resistance and opposing the occupation. Her NGO did not have a boycott campaign, supported the boycott indirectly as a member of the Palestinian NGO Network, which launched BDS. She added that her staff did not use Israeli products at the NGO's activities, and that she encouraged her family to boycott Israeli products.[13] This NGO's employees participated in the boycott, but could not publicly support it through their organization. Representatives from two other NGOs said their organizations openly supported BDS. One refused to work with a donor that funded cultural projects in Israel.[14] Most of the NGOs interviewed would not work with Israeli NGOs.

While NGOs varied in terms of their public support for BDS, all of the MBOs interviewed publicly supported it. Unlike NGOs, MBOs are not expected to present a politically neutral face to donors. One of the MBOs had a BDS campaign as one line of its advocacy work, and another trained university students to teach their peers how to participate in the BDS Movement.[15] The main difference between NGOs and MBOs on BDS is that many NGOs do not support BDS explicitly, even though they support it in practice, while MBOs not only openly support BDS, but also educate and mobilize others to join the campaign. According to the director of a Ramallah-based NGO, her NGO does "not try to mobilize [the students] towards a specific issue… we give them the space to be critical in the way they want."[16] MBOs on the other hand openly connected popular education to specific forms of activism like BDS. The finding that NGOs are more hesitant to connect popular education to activism suggests that although they can resist direct donor interference, NGOs' dependence on donors does constrain their politics. MBOs' distance from donors gives them greater freedom to engage in controversial forms of activism, and NGOs and donors feel the "pull" from MBOs to be more downwardly accountable to grassroots movements. However, NGOs depend on donors to survive, so they are also simultaneously pressured from above to conform (or at least appear) to their donors' politics.

Aid recipients also protect their autonomy through selecting their donors. Organizations strategically diversify their funding portfolios to avoid reliance on a single donor, which gives them more leverage with individual donors (Ohanyan 2009; Mitchell 2014). The interviews found that non-governmental donors generally place fewer restrictions on recipients. NGOs and MBOs both insisted that funding be non-conditional, meaning that donors should not regulate the *political content* of recipients' programs. A representative of a theater NGO described her organization's criteria:

> We're very critical with donors. We do not take money from USAID for example. We do not take money from Europeans if they want us to do something we don't believe in. We don't do it because we want to survive. Money becomes a tool to implement our ideas and beliefs.[17]

Taking aid with fewer conditions allows NGOs to claim that aid is a fungible resource for pursuing their goals, and providing aid with fewer political restrictions portrays donors as downwardly accountable to recipients (AbouAssi 2013).

NGO representatives were often critical of other NGOs' abilities to represent grassroots interests. One NGO described itself as a grassroots organization, meaning that they had "minimal costs. As you see our offices are not fancy. We don't have cars like the fancy organizations. We are a grassroots organization, 100%. We don't accept money with conditions."[18] Whereas most NGOs are located in Ramallah close to their donors, this NGO worked outside of Ramallah, and based their work in community centers rather than at the NGO's headquarters. Several Palestinian educational NGOs in this study embraced the community-based, egalitarian model of popular education from the first *intifada*, and sought to counter the top-down approach to development and education employed by donors and other Palestinian educational NGOs. Defining an NGO as "grassroots" depended less on the amount of aid it received, and more on the organization's efforts to sustain a pre-Oslo mass-based approach to social mobilization, despite their dependence on aid.

NGO representatives also emphasized their independence from donor agendas. An NGO representative recounted his organization's refusal to work with the EU on a project proposal. He objected to the donor's proposed method of reaching a two-state solution saying, "we don't want to be puppets for a political agenda."[19] Another NGO that received donor funding but also provided grants to other Palestinian organizations said that "we want to keep our work independent, especially in education and culture. We are artists and writers, for these people it's about expression and freedom."[20]

Rejecting aid from USAID helped NGOs protect the missions of their organizations. This theater NGO representative explained that the United States was hypocritical for supporting Israel because the United States is:

> ...Against our freedom and sovereignty. The U.S. deliberately stopped Oslo, although it is a bad agreement, what happened after is even worse. The longer it went on, the more colonies there were on the ground, so that's why we don't take their money. We have an Arabic proverb that says 'slap the face, but make the hat look nice,' and this is what they do with us. They give money for roads, but these roads are to separate us even more than before.[21]

USAID's anti-terrorism conditionality (ATC) is particularly unpopular. According to one NGO representative, "eighty percent of the Palestinian people are listed in that statement. Why would I take money and recognize that statement? No, I will not."[22] A representative of another NGO said that the ATC corners NGOs so that they are forced to agree to a condition that no NGO can uphold. He explained, "We don't want to support terrorism. We're also anti-terrorism, you know, and we have a problem with terrorism, mainly from Israel!"[23] The problem is less with the United States as a donor, and more about how the ATC forces Palestinians to accept donors' and Israel's framing of terrorism, which obscures the criminalization of Palestinians living under the occupation. An NGO in Ramallah was working on a EU-funded educational project where the donor asked them to sign an anti-terrorism conditionality. The NGO refused, and the donor allowed the NGO to receive funding without signing the statement.[24] The NGO's willingness to exit the donor relationship helped it escape that conditionality.

MBOs also demanded that aid be given without political conditions. According to an MBO in Ramallah, "if we want to take money from anyone, it should be unconditional, and they should support the full rights of the Palestinian people."[25] For an MBO in Jerusalem, the type of donor (i.e. governmental versus foundation) did not matter, only the absence of political conditionalities. This MBO was funded by the United Nations and said that it would not work with USAID or any donor that required them to sign agreements.[26] By curtailing donor influence, aid recipients can credibly claim that aid is, as one NGO representative described it, "a tool to implement our ideas and beliefs." Aid that does not restrict MBOs' and NGOs' agendas, shifts accountability from donors, toward grassroots political concerns.

NGOs and MBOs were also willing to exit donor relationships. The director of a Ramallah-based NGO detailed an interaction with a duplicitous and incompetent European INGO donor that proposed to send ten Palestinian teachers to Europe for training. When the NGO representative insisted that they use local trainers instead, the donor tried to sweeten the deal by inviting the NGO director to accompany the teachers to Europe. The donor failed to arrange the teachers' visit, but still sent the Palestinian NGO an evaluation form asking them to assess the local impact of the project. "Are you crazy?" the NGO director asked, "where is the project?" When he refused to fill out the evaluation, the donor called his teachers directly. Having had enough, the NGO director called the INGO's funder, the European Commission in Brussels. The Commission asked the donor to return the project money and blacklisted them from receiving future funding.[27] Although this donor-NGO dispute was more about poor donor practices than the politics of education, this example shows that NGOs are willing to not only resist donor demands, but to also use the bureaucratic structure of the aid industry to hold donors accountable.

Aid independence is also a strategic response for maintaining organizational autonomy. Unlike NGOs, MBOs are accustomed to working outside of the aid paradigm, and are perceived as more legitimate representatives of civil society because they resemble pre-Oslo forms of mass-based organizing (Dana 2015). Working without donors frees MBOs from donor agendas. According to an MBO:

> We can never underestimate [the donor's] role in the project... if you have your agenda, we also have our own agenda, and it's not necessarily true that these two agendas will meet. At the end of the day, we'd rather work on our own without money, without the donor. It's always critical.[28]

MBOs emphasized that it was important to be able to sustain their work without donors, because funding outside of Area A is scarce, and occasionally, even solidarity donors do not concede to MBOs' demands. For example, a European INGO donor offered training programs to an MBO working in Area C, but rejected the MBO's requested training (theater training, recycling materials into jewelry as an income generation project for women, and a training on international law).[29] Given the scarcity of funding for Palestinian organizations in Area C, MBOs saw reviving earlier forms of mass-based organizing as a way of making their work more sustainable without aid. An MBO in Ramallah shared this concern about relying on outside funding, and commented, "now we are thinking in a project, an economic project that will provide us with money. [A] collective farm."[30] According to another MBO:

> I think sustainability of projects funded by foreign aid is really important… we are self-funded, so any activity that we want to do, we do right away, because we raise money from amongst ourselves… We went to a workshop about doing documentary film, and we now have a camera from that project. Anytime that we want to do a documentary, we have a camera, and we have the skills. That's sustainability. Instead of giving me a workshop about how to do a documentary, without having the tools to make one.
>
> Another reason we don't want foreign aid is because most of the NGOs in Palestine depend on foreign aid for their projects, so if there's no money, then there are no projects. This will not help us as Palestinians in developing our society. To be a developed society, we need tools of our own to be self-funded. That will help us generate or produce our own thoughts and vision, instead of working on others' agendas. That's why if any international foundation propose or give us money, we need to make sure that this money is being given freely to help us, with no conditions at all.[31]

The clearest way to resist donor influence is to only use donors for material support and minimal training in this case, a video camera and training in documentary film. This example shows that sustainability is an issue of practicality, since in an aid-dependent model, when the aid dries up, projects disappear. This practical argument also has an ideological valence because MBOs are willing to work outside of the aid paradigm (except to carefully exploit it for material resources), they are seen as more legitimate proponents of the Palestinian cause than NGOs, which work closely with donors. Where aid to the Palestinians is seen as ineffective, implicated in dedeveloping the Palestinian economy in depoliticizing development through co-opting Palestinian NGOs, legitimacy (defined as proximity to grassroots priorities) is a commodity that MBOs and NGOs leverage, with some (but not always complete) success with their "solidarity" donors.

Forging Solidarities

NGOs can use their status as local implementers to force donors to be downwardly accountable to them (AbouAssi and Trent 2016). MBOs, in turn, hold NGOs accountable to their causes, in a "chain" of downward accountability (Andrews 2014). Aid recipients' resistance to donor demands can be read as a form of "blocking," or dissent by local actors against donor interventions (Hertel 2006). Donors and recipients participate in a mutual exchange: aid recipients want to access funds with as few restrictions as possible, and donors demonstrate solidarity with their recipients in order to legitimize their interventions.

Solidarity donors were conscious of donor reputations and emphasized that they were different because they listened to their recipients' needs, rather than imposing their own agendas. According to a European INGO donor,

> We are working according to their needs. We never come with a project and tell them 'you will implement this project.' We have discussions about which kinds of problems they can solve through their activities, and what they think each kind of problem they have in the society. We conduct this discussion, and after that we make our program goal. They are the owner of the problems and solutions, not us.[32]

Another European INGO donor that was affiliated with a leftist party saw their mission as supporting other leftist organizations in Palestine. In funding Palestinian educational NGOs, this donor sought to challenge the top-down didactic approach to teaching:

> We are trying to involve students more. We want to push through this mentality of teaching where the teachers are the ultimate source of education, and students are only recipients, where the students are taught to be tame- to receive information, remember it, write it down on the test. You don't think, you don't question, it's not your role. We are trying to break through this through our projects with our partners.[33]

The metaphor of teachers as sources of knowledge and students as recipients corresponds with how these solidarity donors see themselves as simultaneously challenging the hierarchical relationship between donors and recipients in development more broadly.

Although all types of donors draw on the discourses of partnership and local ownership, solidarity donors were especially self-conscious about their power over their recipients, and made a point to emphasize their downward accountability to their recipients. According to a European INGO donor, "it's based on partnership. We are not a donor giving them money. We don't have any conditional funding, but we have values, and when we choose an organization, they have to share these minimum democratic values."[34] Solidarity donors wanted to minimize the appearance of superiority over their recipients, reflecting their awareness of the paternalism inherent in the donor–recipient relationship (Baaz 2005). But, they recognized that they had a limited ability to equalize the donor–recipient relationship. According to the leftist party-affiliated European donor above,

> You want to establish a genuine, democratic, participatory approach. You want to minimize the gap, but you can never escape it. At the end of the day, you are the one who has the money, and who decides to give it to one place or another. We try to have long-term partnerships with our partners. We try to work together with them. The process of proposals- we are obliged to go through all the bureaucracy because ultimately the donor is the government, not us.
>
> We try our best to minimize this power game, this unbalanced structure, by discussing, brainstorming a lot with our partners. Trying to arrive at common ground together, to work out ideas of mutual interest. To develop things together and not to enforce things, and trying to push the Palestinian agenda.[35]

Donors maintain a logical consistency between participatory education and participatory development, however, the donor's power is apparent in the recipient's upward accountability to donors. The donor above continued,

> In terms of monitoring expenditures, we are not at the same level, and we cannot be, because we have to report. We are accountable if there is any form of corruption, [and] are in a higher position in that sense. We are trying to balance. We call them our partners, they call us their partners, but

both of us know we are not entirely equal in this process. You have to be flexible and compromise your principles… we would really appreciate having an equal relationship, but its impossible within this system.[36]

Since it is not possible to put donors and recipients on equal footing, solidarity donors prefer to be transparent about their reporting processes, another way of being downwardly accountable to their recipients. As a European INGO donor explained,

We have power because we have money, but we try to implement [it in a] democratic way, to give an example of how to work. We have a lot of discussion. The same procedure applies for us from [the donor government]. We also explain to them how it works, in international cooperation in [the donor agency], who makes decisions.[37]

Solidarity donors form their relationships with recipients around shared values regarding development and education. A Palestinian foundation run by former educators ran its own educational programs and also funded other NGOs. A representative of this NGO said that at the foundation,

We work together to further our vision for education as an organization. For this reason, we prefer to implement our opinion, ideas, and vision, and we invited people that know about our vision and objectives. We are not just an "agent" or a "funder," we implement our own ideas about education.[38]

This collaborative, network-based approach to finding recipients stands in contrast to the standard approach where donors post a call for proposals and NGOs develop projects to meet the call. The European INGO solidarity donors took a similar approach as this Palestinian foundation in locating Palestinian organizations through their networks that were compatible with their values. One INGO donor said that most of their potential recipients reached out to them and the donor would meet with them to discuss the proposal. Other times, the donor would hear of an organization that matched their educational philosophy and would reach out to them.[39]

The NGO and MBO interviews supported donors' ideal self-perception of the donor–recipient relationship as built on consensus rather than coercion. An educational NGO in Ramallah pointed out that their primary donor, one of the European INGO donors interviewed in this study, shared their emphasis on spreading critical pedagogy in the Palestinian education system. Because of this commonality, he explained that he did not see the donor as imposing their agenda on the NGO:

> We've been dealing with donors who do not have preconditions, they believe in our mission, in our intervention, and they make it part of their intervention in disseminating debate culture, critical pedagogy, and the development of the education system. We do not see [that] they impose their agenda, because we have something in common.[40]

Many NGOs praised their donors, many of whom sought them out based on the NGO's reputation. As one NGO leader commented:

> [Our organization is] lucky in terms of its partnership with the donor community. If you look at the history of our donors, you would find that many of them are long-term partnerships. We do not do lots of fundraising. Usually it's a plus in that they come to [us] more than we go to [them]. This helps our organization reach [its] goals and focus on the content of our work.[41]

A second NGO said that donors sought them out and asked them to write proposals for particular project areas, such as early childhood education.[42] A director of an NGO in Nablus also said it was approached by donors, rather than the other way around. He cited his organization's commitment to grassroots work as the guiding criteria for selecting donors:

> ...We are very proud of our grassroots status, and in general, we are approached by donors. Everybody knows [our organization] now. So when we are approached by donors, we put the conditions. I try to look for donors who are like us. Which means that they have the same principles in regards to grassroots work...when we find donors that share this idea that the money should go where it should be spent, not throwing the money out of the window. Expenditure has to be reasonable, and has to go where it's needed. ...We prefer to work with donors who share this vision, because this is one of the main issues that are problematic with NGOs.[43]

NGOs' strategic responses to donor coercion include selecting donors that do not give conditional aid, negotiating and compromising with donors, and exiting the donor relationship when agreement cannot be reached. The section above demonstrated how NGO's strategic behaviors lead them to sympathetic donors who have an interest in critical pedagogy and are more willing to compromise and negotiate with their recipients.

Downward accountability is important for donors, NGOs and MBOs, because it means being in touch with communities' needs rather than donor priorities. According to an MBO representative, his organization's work is "grounded in our realities. For us, knowledge and whatever we talk about or implement on the ground, comes mainly from the [community] itself. We are conceptualizing our practices."[44] NGOs also try to emphasize their grassroots connections, in order to tap into the legitimacy of representing the community's concerns. An NGO representative in Ramallah described her organization as unique in that it is:

> Transparent with the local community, and we try to take Palestinian priorities into consideration. Sometimes we lose partners or donors because we are very much into slow, unseen change, until maybe years to come. It's not like we are into festivals, and into campaigns... we do what we have to do, not because of partners' requests or donors' requests. More of a community demand.[45]

The NGO shows its deference to community priorities through its willingness to stop working with donors or other organizations that do not share the NGO's vision of transforming education.

The leader of a Ramallah-based NGO provided training and professional development programs that Palestinian teachers designed themselves. A former teacher himself, the NGO leader said that a distinguishing feature of his organization's training programs was that outside experts were expected to go along with the training program the teachers designed, rather than merely providing their own material.[46] NGOs build their legitimacy by being responsive to their constituents' needs.

Solidarity donors were similarly interested in tapping into the legitimacy of grassroots NGO and MBO work. A European INGO donor explained that their accountability procedures with their recipients were very similar to the donor's responsibilities for reporting to their parliament.

We explain that it's not just something special for you [the recipient], we [the donor] have the same. For example, now we are waiting for our auditor, and all of our beneficiary organizations are waiting for auditors. After that, we have auditors in [the donor country]. It's nothing special for them [the recipients], and they appreciate that.[47]

Solidarity donors try to be transparent, and make themselves accessible to their recipients. This donor explained that their office did not require that visitors pass through security, and that recipients had told them they appreciated the atmosphere in the office. The donor said they work in close cooperation with their recipients, who feel that they can call the donor when they want.[48]

An MBO in educational rights advocacy praised their European INGO donors for giving aid without political conditions. This MBO also received UN funding, and remarked that "we are funded by the U.N. because they agree with us that Israeli intervention into our society is not legal, and they want to support us."[49] This MBO had a diverse funding history, including Palestinian foundations and donors from Arab countries. In this case the United Nations was one of their solidarity donors. Another MBO had only one donor, a European government development agency. While they had some trouble reconciling their vision for the organization with the donor's, this development agency nonetheless gave the MBO unrestricted aid.[50]

Like NGOs, MBOs see unrestricted aid as necessary to upholding the mission of their organization. Another MBO praised the Students for Justice in Palestine chapters in the United States that raised funds for the MBO to send Palestinian students to speak at US universities about the Israeli occupation. The MBO representative said that:

> …That's the type of aid that we want to encourage. From students to students, with no conditions and it's really clear why they are giving the money. We don't need 'just give us money to work with you on your agenda here in Palestine.' Give us the money to function, to do any campaign we want. We need money, of course, but the source of the money should align with our vision. They [donors] should not give us money to apply their vision or their agenda.[51]

This MBO representative recounted another time the group used outside funding from an INGO affiliated with a religious group. This donor provided funding for the MBO to buy a video camera and be trained in producing documentaries. The MBO representative praised the donor's hands-off approach:

> ...At the end, they [the donor] watched the film as audience members, not as sponsors. We didn't even put their name on the documentary film. They just gave us the money for a just cause, because they thought we were talking about justice and freedom and this is something that they want to give money to.[52]

The donor's willingness to provide aid and position themselves in the audience (rather than as a sponsor with specific expectations about the product) reflects their respect for, and solidarity with their recipient. Solidarity donors and their recipients recognize their common understanding of the problems in Palestinian education and the aid industry, namely the top-down didactic model of teaching, which is analogous to the hierarchical approach of donor-driven development. This network of funders and civic organizations somewhat mitigates these power imbalances through their dynamic relationships of upward and downward accountability.

IMPLICATIONS FOR THEORY AND PRACTICE

This chapter has demonstrated how Palestinian educational NGOs and MBOs can protect their autonomy by seeking out "solidarity" donors who share their commitment to transforming education and development. By enacting the community-based, egalitarian critical pedagogical practices of the popular education movement from the first *intifada*, these grassroots organizations defend cultural rights by challenging the dominant narratives in popular culture and formal educational settings. Taking a network approach helps map the reciprocities and tensions between donors, NGOs and MBOs, while at the same time revealing the potential and limitations of donor-funded critical pedagogical projects. As one donor put it,

> There is no 'ultimate dependency' or 'ultimate power' from the 'other' over our processes. No, we as Palestinians have a stake- I'm speaking here as a Palestinian, not as a representative of the organization, we have a role, and there are always spaces to maneuver and to push things ahead...[53]

The NGOs and MBOs in this study exploit these spaces of possibility in the aid framework, but are willing to work outside of the aid paradigm to maintain the integrity of their projects. While solidarity donors facilitate NGO and MBO agency by providing unrestricted aid for them to pursue their work largely independently from donors, they nonetheless shape the developmental space of Palestinian education by privileging secular leftist educational NGOs.

One of the primary goals of the *intifada*-era popular education movement was to reconnect education and resistance. Solidarity donors play an essential role in this solidarity economy by supporting Palestinian educational NGOs and their popular education programs, which help maintain collective identity and historical memory under the occupation. But as people at the grassroots level revealed in the interviews central to this study, in the case of the Boycott, Divestment, Sanctions Movement, these same NGOs are less willing to connect education to activism than their MBO counterparts. Further research should evaluate whether even solidarity donors and Palestinian educational NGOs restrict the discursive space for activism in education, thus severing the connection between political consciousness and activism.

Notes

1. These are development buzzwords in the Paris Declaration on Aid Effectiveness (2005), Accra Agenda for Action (2008), and the World Bank's approach to participatory development.
2. These are examples of the German *model* of political party-affiliated NGOs that work internationally. The donor NGOs in this study are institutionally similar to these original party-funded NGOs.
3. A lack of *mutual* accountability, namely donors being held accountable to their commitments to local ownership of development projects, transparency, and meaningful inclusion of civil society are major factors in the failure of the aid industry to achieve its stated goals of peace with Israel and Palestinian economic development in the occupied territories (Tartir and Wildeman 2016).
4. Interview with NGO (Anonymous), October 11, 2015.
5. Interview with NGO/Donor (Anonymous), December 6, 2015.
6. Interview with NGO (Anonymous), May 11, 2016.
7. Interview with NGO (Anonymous), December 2, 2015.
8. Interview with NGO (Anonymous), January 4, 2016.
9. Interview with NGO (Anonymous), May 11, 2016.

10. Interview with NGO (Anonymous), December 2, 2015.
11. Interview with MBO (Anonymous), October 20, 2015.
12. Interview with NGO (Anonymous), January 11, 2014.
13. Interview with NGO (Anonymous), January 8, 2014.
14. Interview with NGO (Anonymous), May 11, 2016.
15. Interview with MBOs (Anonymous), December 10, 2015 and February 3, 2016.
16. Interview with NGO (Anonymous), January 8, 2014.
17. Interview with NGO (Anonymous), December 2, 2015.
18. Interview with NGO (Anonymous), January 20, 2016.
19. Interview with NGO (Anonymous), May 11, 2016.
20. Interview with NGO/Donor (Anonymous), December 6, 2015.
21. Interview with NGO (Anonymous), December 2, 2015.
22. Interview with NGO (Anonymous), January 8, 2014.
23. Interview with NGO (Anonymous), May 11, 2016.
24. Interview with NGO/Donor (Anonymous), December 6, 2015.
25. Interview with MBO (Anonymous), February 3, 2016.
26. Interview with MBO (Anonymous), December 15, 2015.
27. Interview with NGO (Anonymous), January 11, 2014.
28. Interview with MBO (Anonymous), October 20, 2015.
29. Interview with MBO (Anonymous), March 20, 2016.
30. Interview with MBO (Anonymous), February 3, 2016.
31. Interview with MBO (Anonymous), December 10, 2015.
32. Interview with Donor (Anonymous), January 6, 2016.
33. Interview with Donor (Anonymous), November 8, 2015.
34. Interview with Donor (Anonymous), January 6, 2016.
35. Interview with Donor (Anonymous), November 8, 2015.
36. Interview with Donor (Anonymous), November 8, 2015.
37. Interview with Donor (Anonymous), January 6, 2016.
38. Interview with NGO/Donor (Anonymous), December 6, 2015.
39. Interview with Donor (Anonymous), November 8, 2015.
40. Interview with NGO (Anonymous), October 11, 2015.
41. Interview with NGO (Anonymous), January 8, 2014.
42. Interview with NGO/Donor (Anonymous), December 6, 2015.
43. Interview with NGO (Anonymous), January 20, 2016.
44. Interview with MBO (Anonymous), October 20, 2015.
45. Interview with NGO (Anonymous), May 10, 2016.
46. Interview with NGO (Anonymous), January 11, 2014.
47. Interview with Donor (Anonymous), January 6, 2016.
48. Interview with Donor (Anonymous), January 6, 2016.
49. Interview with MBO (Anonymous), December 15, 2015.
50. Interview with MBO (Anonymous), October 20, 2015.

51. Interview with MBO (Anonymous), December 10, 2015.
52. Interview with MBO (Anonymous), December 10, 2015.
53. Interview with Donor (Anonymous), November 8, 2015.

References

AbouAssi, Khaldoun. 2013. "Hands in the Pockets of Mercurial Donors: NGO Response to Shifting Funding Priorities." *Nonprofit and Voluntary Sector Quarterly* 42 (3): 584–602.

AbouAssi, Khaldoun, and Deborah L. Trent. 2016. "NGO Accountability from an NGO Perspective: Perceptions, Strategies, and Practices." *Public Administration and Development* 36 (4): 283–296.

Andrews, Abigail. 2014. "Downward Accountability in Unequal Alliances: Explaining NGO Responses to Zapatista Demands." *World Development* 54: 99–113.

Baaz, Maria Eriksson. 2005. *The Paternalism of Partnership: A Postcolonial Reading of Identity in Development Aid*. London: Zed Books.

Bahdi, Reem, and Mudar Kassis. 2016. "Decolonisation, Dignity and Development Aid: A Judicial Education Experience in Palestine." *Third World Quarterly* 37(11): 2010–2027.

Banks, Nicola, David Hulme, and Michael Edwards. 2015. "NGOs, States, and Donors Revisited: Still Too Close for Comfort?" *World Development* 66: 707–718.

Challand, Benoît. 2008. *Palestinian Civil Society: Foreign Donors and the Power to Promote and Exclude*. London: Routledge.

Dana, Tariq. 2015. "The Structural Transformation of Palestinian Civil Society: Key Paradigm Shifts." *Middle East Critique* 24 (2): 191–210.

Elbers, Wilhelmus Johannes. 2012. *The Partnership Paradox: Principles and Practice in North-South NGO Relations*. [Sl: sn].

Fasheh, Munir. 1990. "Community Education: To Reclaim and Transform What Has Been Made Invisible." *Harvard Educational Review* 60 (1): 19–36.

Fasheh, Munir. 2005. "Al-jame'ah: Learning for All and from All in the Arab region." In *Emerging and Re-emerging Learning Communities: Old Wisdoms and New Initiatives from Around the World*. Paris: UNESCO. http://unesdoc.unesco.org/images/0014/001459/145997e.pdf.

Freire, Paulo. 1993. *Pedagogy of the Oppressed*. New York: Continuum.

Hammami, Rema. 2000. "Palestinian NGOs Since Oslo: From NGO Politics to Social Movements?" *Middle East Report* 214: 16–48.

Hanafi, Sari, and Linda Tabar. 2003. "The Intifada and the Aid Industry: The Impact of the New Liberal Agenda on the Palestinian NGOs." *Comparative Studies of South Asia, Africa and the Middle East* 23 (1): 205–214.

Hanafi, Sari, and Linda Tabar. 2005. *The Emergence of a Palestinian Globalized Elite: Donors, International Organizations, and Local NGOs*. Jerusalem: Institute of Jerusalem Studies.

Hertel, Shareen. 2006. *Unexpected Power: Conflict and Change Among Transnational Activists*. Ithaca, NY: Cornell University Press.

Hirschman, Albert O. 1970. *Exit, Voice, and Loyalty: Responses to Decline in Firms, Organizations, and States*. Cambridge: Harvard University Press.

Hobson, John M. 2007. "Is Critical Theory Always for the White West and for Western Imperialism? Beyond Westphilian Towards a Post-racist Critical IR." *Review of International Studies* 33(S1): 91–116.

Jad, Islah. 2007. "NGOs: Between Buzzwords and Social Movements." *Development in Practice* 17 (4–5): 622–629.

Jamal, Amaney A. 2009. *Barriers to Democracy: The Other Side of Social Capital in Palestine and the Arab World*. Princeton: Princeton University Press.

Khalidi, Raja, and Sobhi Samour. 2011. "Neoliberalism as Liberation: The Statehood Program and the Remaking of the Palestinian National Movement." *Journal of Palestine Studies* 40 (2): 6–25.

Lloyd, Lindsay. 2010. "European Approaches to Democracy Promotion." *International Journal* 65 (3): 547–559.

Meinzer, Melanie. 2017. "Agents of Change? Critical International Relations Theory, Foreign Aid and Political Consciousness in Palestinian Education." PhD diss., The University of Connecticut.

Merz, Sibille. 2012. "'Missionaries of the New Era': Neoliberalism and NGOs in Palestine." *Race & Class* 54 (1): 50–66.

Mitchell, George E. 2014. "Strategic Responses to Resource Dependence Among Transnational NGOs Registered in the United States." *Voluntas: International Journal of Voluntary and Nonprofit Organizations* 25 (1): 67–91.

Nakhleh, Khalil. 2012. *Globalized Palestine: The National Sell-Out of a Homeland*. Trenton, NJ: Red Sea Press.

Ohanyan, Anna. 2009. "Policy Wars for Peace: Network Model of NGO Behavior." *International Studies Review* 11 (3): 475–501.

Ohanyan, Anna. 2012. "Network Institutionalism and NGO Studies." *International Studies Perspectives* 13 (4): 366–389.

Oliver, Christine. 1991. "Strategic Responses to Institutional Processes." *Academy of Management Review* 16 (1): 145–179.

Pinto-Duschinsky, Michael. 1991. "Foreign Political Aid: The German Political Foundations and Their US Counterparts." *International Affairs* 67 (1): 33–63.

Rauh, Karen. 2010. "NGOs, Foreign Donors, and Organizational Processes: Passive NGO Recipients or Strategic Actors?" *McGill Sociological Review* 1 (29): 29–45.

Roy, Sara. 1999. "De-development Revisited: Palestinian Economy and Society Since Oslo." *Journal of Palestine Studies* 28 (3): 64–82.
Scott, James C. 1990. *Domination and the Arts of Resistance: Hidden Transcripts.* New Haven, CT: Yale university press.
Tabar, Linda. 2015. "People's Power: Lessons from the First Intifada." In *Critical Readings of Development Under Colonialism: Towards a Political Economy for Liberation in the Occupied Palestinian Territories.* Ramallah, West Bank: Bir Zeit.
Taghdisi-Rad, Sahar. 2010. *The Political Economy of Aid in Palestine: Relief from Conflict or Development Delayed?* London: Routledge.
Tartir, Alaa and Jeremy Wildeman. 2016. *Mapping of Donor Funding to the Occupied Palestinian Territories 2012–2014/15.* Aid Watch Palestine. https://alaatartirdotcom.files.wordpress.com/2017/11/aidwatchstudy-published.pdf.
Turner, Mandy. 2015. "Peacebuilding as Counterinsurgency in the Occupied Palestinian Territory." *Review of International Studies* 41 (1): 73–98.
Wildeman, Jeremy, and Alaa Tartir. 2013. "Can Oslo's Failed Aid Model Be Laid to Rest?" *Al-Shabaka*, September 18. https://al-shabaka.org/briefs/can-oslos-failed-aid-model-be-laid-rest/.
Wildeman, Jeremy, and Alaa Tartir. 2014. "Unwilling to Change, Determined to Fail: Donor Aid in Occupied Palestine in the Aftermath of the Arab Uprisings." *Mediterranean Politics* 19 (3): 431–449.

PART III

Security Sector Reform, Resistance, and Authoritarianism

CHAPTER 9

Criminalizing Resistance: Security Sector Reform and Palestinian Authoritarianism

Alaa Tartir

INTRODUCTION

Security Sector Reform (SSR) has become a crucial element of any state-building endeavor (Ghani and Lockhart 2008; Chandler and Sisk 2013). Under the leadership of Prime Minister Salam Fayyad from 2007 to 2013, the Palestinian Authority (PA) adopted SSR as a linchpin to its state-building project (Tartir 2016). Besides enhancing the capabilities of security forces through equipment and training, the PA sought to overhaul structures, hierarchies, and chains of command with the stated goal of building up democratic governance and control, in accordance with the demands of its major financial backers in the international donor community (Schroeder et al. 2014). As SSR proceeded (Mustafa 2015), the occupied West Bank became a securitized space and the theater of security campaigns whose ostensible purpose was to establish "law and order."[1]

The reform and effectiveness enhancement of PA security forces (PASF) in particular, and of the security sector in general, were

---

A. Tartir (✉)
The Graduate Institute of International and Development Studies (IHEID), Geneva, Switzerland
e-mail: alaa.tartir@graduateinstitute.ch

© The Author(s) 2019
A. Tartir and T. Seidel (eds.),
Palestine and Rule of Power, Middle East Today,
https://doi.org/10.1007/978-3-030-05949-1_9

conducted under Israeli military occupation and within the context of colonial domination. Given the asymmetric relations of power between Israel and the Palestinians, as well as the preconditions laid down by both Israel and the international donor community, the formulation of the Palestinian security doctrine (Turner 2015) was tantamount to a diktat, whose effectiveness and legitimacy were met with profound skepticism by the Palestinian public in the West Bank. In order to understand the magnitude of the enterprise, it is useful to keep in mind that the Palestinian security sector is today comprised of 83,276 individuals (West Bank and Gaza Strip combined), including 312 brigadier generals—to lend the latter figure perspective, the entire US Army boasts 410 brigadier generals—of whom 232 report to the PA and 80 to Hamas (Tartir 2016). The security sector employs around 44% of all civil servants (United Nations 2013a, b), accounts for nearly $1 billion of the PA budget (Amrov and Tartir 2014a), and is allocated around 30% of total international aid that is disbursed to the Palestinians (Amrov and Tartir 2014b).

In addition to training programs and weapons upgrades, the SSR launched in the wake of the second intifada hinged on security campaigns carried out by US-trained PASF troops in the West Bank. The objectives of the campaigns were to: check the activities of Hamas and Islamic Jihad, as well as their armed wings; contain Fatah-affiliated militants through co-optation, integration into the PASF, and amnesty arrangements; crack down on criminality, and restore public order (International Crisis Group 2008). The governorates of Nablus and Jenin and, more specifically, Balata and Jenin refugee camps in the northern West Bank, which were designated as "bastions of resistance" (*qila'a muqawameh*) and/or "areas of chaos and anarchy" (*manatiq falatan wa fawda*)[2] were selected as the SSR's "pilot projects" (RRT 2008; Giambi 2009).

What ordinary Palestinians thought of these campaigns—whether in terms of security or the broader dynamics of resistance against the occupation—constitutes the main focus of this chapter. The ethnographic data presented is based on a study conducted between August and December 2012 in both refugee camps, using a mix of semi structured interviews and focus groups with youth of both genders. The research sample encompassed a wide variety of social groups and aimed to reflect the voice of subaltern actors that are generally marginalized in mainstream discourse and literature. These included local camp leaders, mid-ranking political faction cadres, armed group members, former fighters, men, women, and youth, as well as individuals who had been detained by the PA in the course of the security campaigns. Ethnographically speaking, the similarities between the camps were striking, and therefore this chapter will not compare and contrast the two but rather use both as one key unit of analysis. At its core, this chapter argues that the overarching goal of the SSR, in general, and the security campaigns, in particular, was to criminalize resistance against the Israeli occupation and to silence opposition to Israel's colonial dominance. As a result, the campaigns can be seen as the early stages of the PA's authoritarian transformation, manifest in the excessive use of arbitrary detention and torture in PA prisons as well as in the narrowing of space for opposition voices or resistance inside the Palestinian polity.

Balata and Jenin Refugee Camps: Setting the Stage

Jenin and Balata camps are located in the north of the occupied West Bank and were established by the United Nations Relief and Works Agency for Palestine Refugees in the Near East (UNRWA) in 1953 and 1950 respectively to house displaced and dispossessed Palestinians in the aftermath of the 1948 Nakba. With a surface area of 0.42 square kilometers, Jenin camp is home to some 16,260 inhabitants, while Balata camp, which is the West Bank's largest in terms of population, stands on an area of only 0.25 square kilometers housing 23,600 inhabitants. Both camps share similar socioeconomic indicators: the average household size is 5.5, around 60% of the population is under twenty-four, and poverty and unemployment rates run at 35–40% (UN OCHA 2008b; UNRWA 2014).

According to UNRWA, high unemployment, overcrowded schools, high population density, and poor water and sewage networks are some of the camps' most pressing problems (UN OCHA 2008a; UNRWA 2014).

In addition to dire living conditions, camp residents have suffered continuous repression and persecution by the Israeli army over the years, including brutal raids and security crackdowns/sweeps. These camps were particularly targeted by Israel because of their active role in armed resistance and in nurturing the emergence of armed groups. The camps also played a major and pioneering role during the popular protests and civil disobedience of the first intifada (1987–1993). During the second intifada (2000–2005), when Israel overran the West Bank, Jenin was the site of an eponymous battle in April 2002 during which, according to Amnesty International and Human Rights Watch, the Israel Defense Forces (IDF) committed war crimes (Amnesty International 2002; Human Rights Watch 2002). In addition to human losses, major parts of the camp were completely destroyed and more than one-quarter of the population was rendered homeless.

The resistance and steadfastness during this battle turned Jenin camp into the second intifada's symbol of resistance, which was celebrated by then Chairman Yasir Arafat as the Palestinians' Stalingrad. "Jeningrad," as Arafat called it, was and remains a major source of pride to both its leaders and inhabitants, and it has been central in shaping the refugee population's collective identity. Balata and Jenin camps witnessed the birth of Fatah's armed wing, the al-Aqsa Martyrs Brigades, during the second intifada. Effectively, the PASF were not allowed to enter the camps as the armed factions controlled the two areas and claimed authority within them.[3] These are a few reasons why these camps have remained a permanent target for Israel, and also why they were the first and main locations to be targeted by the PA's security campaigns.[4]

The security campaigns undertaken in 2007 were offensives carried out using traditional strong-arm tactics. They involved the redeployment of trained and equipped security forces in localities that challenged the PA's authority and control, in particular the PA's objective to establish a monopoly of violence in the security sphere.[5] They were not regular security activities or routine operations, but rather focused offensives with objectives, timelines, methods, and strategies.

On the day the campaigns were launched, well-dressed, well-equipped, well-trained, and mostly masked PASF troops swarmed into Jenin and Balata camps in dozens of new, foreign-bought, military vehicles. Approaching the camps from multiple points the better to establish control, the PASF coordinated their movements and operations with the Israeli military, which remains the ultimate authority in the occupied West Bank. They entered the camp through its narrow lanes, with snipers positioning themselves on the roofs of strategic buildings or close to the center of operations. PASF troops raided homes to arrest targeted individuals and conducted weapons sweeps in which arms caches were uncovered and individual weapons confiscated. Violent clashes ensued, both with armed groups and with camp residents resisting the offensive.[6]

The idea was to cleanse the camps of non-PA weapons, to conduct a disarmament process, to arrest those that challenged the PA's authority, and to send a clear message to camp residents that the PA was the sole governing structure and power allowed. Achieving a monopoly of violence and consolidating power in the security sector were key objectives as the PA's security apparatus had not been allowed into the camps throughout the period of the second intifada, when ultimate power rested with the armed groups. As part of its institutional reform process and state-building project in the aftermath of the Palestinian parliamentary and presidential elections in 2006–2007, and the resulting intra-Palestinian divide, the PA targeted the camps and systematically criminalized resistance (see Tartir 2015a).

The security campaign in Nablus began in November 2007, and was followed in May 2008 by a similar campaign in Jenin that was ironically named "Smile and Hope"—to suggest that the PA was coming to the camps to restore people's happiness and raise their hopes after years of lawlessness (*falatan amni*). From the PA's perspective, the idea behind the campaigns was simple: "We wanted to demonstrate to donors and to Israel that the PA could govern Palestinian society," one high-ranking PA official told me, "even in areas as intractable as Balata and Jenin camps."[7]

The idea of establishing a security reform showpiece was shared at the highest international echelons (Cambrezy 2014). At a dinner with then Quartet Representative Tony Blair and top US diplomats in the region, US general Jim Jones had "proposed a new approach" to peace-making: rather than going for a grand deal with the Israelis, he advocated a piecemeal approach that entailed making a "model" of one place under Israeli occupation and "Pilot Jenin" was born (Calabresi 2009). Described as "an Israeli initiative," Pilot Jenin was a "program currently implemented through direct coordination between the Palestinians and Israel, with limited American involvement. The program is part of the attempt to strengthen the moderate Palestinian camp, led by Abu-Mazen [PA president Mahmoud Abbas], implementing results from the Annapolis Conference" (Israel Defense Forces 2008). As a result, Jenin, one journalist wrote, "gained a reputation as a model security area where armed gangs and warlords have been replaced by organized security forces that respect one chain of command" (Giambi 2009, 33). The former mayor of Jenin later described 2008–2009 as the "Golden Age" (Bronner 2008) and a US journalist referred to it as a "quiet revolution" (Giambi 2009, 33).

Turning Jenin and Nablus into models for other embattled West Bank localities (Zanotti 2010) has been critiqued by a number of scholars.

Linda Tabar has argued that "resistance in Jenin over time was subdued by separately intervening technologies of power, including most notably a long colonial counterinsurgency campaign that was followed by donor-driven projects to revamp the camp and re-establish security collaboration with Israel" (Tabar 2012). In the case of Balata, Philip Leech has argued that the perceived success of the PA in imposing law and order in the camp (and Nablus generally) after 2007, as well as the initial popular consent to the PA's security agenda, did "not demonstrate public endorsement of the PA's legitimacy. Rather, the consent that such measures produced was superficial and, in the long term, the acceleration of the PA's shift toward authoritarianism is likely to be profoundly debilitating for Palestinian society in general" (Leech 2015). In other words, a closer examination reveals that "this consensus was superficial and did not last. In April 2012, polling suggested that the level of popular consent for the Fayyad government was slipping overall" (Leech 2015, 11).

Such critical observations are supported and further amplified by the perspectives of camp residents interviewed for this study. A local Fatah leader from Jenin camp put it as follows during our interview: "There was no phenomenon of security chaos (*falatan amni*). The PA just exaggerated it, which reflects their inability to lead. They used the media machine to portray us as a threat to security, both at the national and community levels." A respondent from Balata camp with left-leaning political views used the following description: "There are three key words to the PA's security campaigns: lies, media, and money (*kizib, i'lam, masari*). The media machine was all over them [the PA], covering their lies; and there is no scarcity of resources when it comes to PA security." A young woman from Balata described the security campaigns as "giving someone paracetamol [Tylenol] to cure cancer."

The apparent gap between the narrative of the people and that of the authorities is striking. In the narrative of the voices from below, the words associated with the PA's post-2007 state-building project are donors, corruption, and police state (*mumawilleen, fasad, dawlat bolees*) (Marten 2014; Sayigh 2011). But more interestingly, these voices focus on resistance as the prism through which to explore the SSR's implications for their lives and their national struggle. In other words, they measure the consequences and effectiveness of the SSR against its impact on people's ability to resist the Israeli occupation. Those interviewed argued that conducting security reform to ensure stability within the context of colonial occupation and without addressing the imbalances of power and revisiting the terms of "peace agreements" can only ever have two outcomes: "better" collaboration with the occupying power, and violating the security and national rights of the Palestinian people by their own government and national security forces.

The PASF's short-term technical successes were seen as fragile, temporary, and conditional upon Israeli goodwill and donor largesse. The consensus from below was that it ultimately came down to power dynamics. "That is what security was all about," as one respondent from Jenin camp put it. The tools that the PA deployed in the process included the use of security coordination as a doctrine; the (ab)use of the judicial system to entrench authoritarian rule rather than mete out justice; the use of informal conciliation mechanisms; and the use of excessive force that perpetuated a culture of fear and discredited resistance to the Israeli occupation.

Mistrust and Crisis of Legitimacy

Despite differences in background, social class, and other demographic variables, the vast majority of people interviewed in both camps shared similar perspectives on the PASF's efficacy and exhibited comparable levels of distrust toward them. The attitudes they expressed and statements they made regarding the security campaigns flew in the face of the authorities' own narrative of glowing rhetoric, highlighting the lack of transparency and local ownership involved.

A female respondent from a women's center in Jenin refugee camp told me: "When the security campaigns began in 2007, we felt somewhat hopeful and optimistic. But then things started to deteriorate: we couldn't understand what they were up to, what kind of weapons they were targeting, why they were arresting local leaders who had headed the intifada or why they were killing others. We used to give them [the PASF] flowers and make them coffee and food, but they thanked us with bullets and by breaking into our houses." A Fatah cadre from Balata camp who had been a local leader during the first intifada argued: "The security campaigns riddled our cause and national struggle with holes, as well as our bodies literally speaking, and the PASF never tried to mend those. With the security campaigns, the PA turned our communities into Swiss cheese …full of holes."

During my fieldwork, the lack of trust between the PASF and camp residents was tangible in the dominant language of othering ("them" and "us"). A youth from Jenin camp concluded that the "camp was targeted not because we're [a] bunch of thugs or criminals, as the PASF portray us, but because we are like a tree full of fruit: everyone wants to throw a stone at the fruit and collect a piece for their selfish benefit." For her part, a female Fatah cadre in Balata camp argued that "when the kids in the camps start to welcome the PASF with flowers and not stones," then there might be a glimmer of hope for bridging the legitimacy gap.

In addition to the operational sphere, the distrust of the PA's security establishment extended to the judicial realms, both formal and informal. In order to lend the process a degree of legitimacy, the PASF had initially relied on local leaders in the camps to facilitate the security campaigns and execute particular operations. These leaders were integral to the disarmament and weapons collection drives and bore witness to the financial compensation paid out when weapons were handed into the PA. Not only did camp residents strongly contest this facilitation role, they also alleged that the local leadership stood to benefit financially from the security campaigns. Ironically, after the taking over, the PASF dismissed the local leaders and arrested many of them. The head of Jenin's Fatah-led camp services committee was anxious to relate the following:

> Once we had handed over Hamas and Islamic Jihad operatives, as well as [regular street] thugs to the PA, it was our (Fatah's) turn next. The PA leadership, aided by its security doctrine and apparatus, dismantled our armed wing, they confiscated our weapons, basically doing us in—and we said OK, we'll accept that. But now, they're rounding us up, trying to get us to renege on our principles and ideals, to change our political beliefs, and they're threatening us with the loss of our jobs on top of it all. In May of this year, after the death of the governor of Jenin, the PA detained and tortured some seven hundred people from the camp. In a nutshell, these unnecessary security operations resulted in the PA losing all legitimacy in the camp—if it ever had any.

In addition, the PASF coerced people to obey the outcomes of informal mechanisms of justice and deterred them from seeking redress through more formal routes (Amnesty International 2013; Human Rights Watch 2014). The PASF committed many human rights violations such as torturing political prisoners, humiliating people publicly, and detaining people without charge, and families and clans were pressured to address these excesses on a personal basis, through traditional mechanisms of tribal conciliation, rather than through courts of law or the formal judicial system. Such matters were settled over "coffee and conciliation" (*finjan qahwa wa 'atwa*), further entrenching the legitimacy gap and amplifying mistrust. A thirty-five-year-old woman from Jenin camp told me:

> My husband was arrested and tortured by the PA for forty-five days. When we wanted to litigate the PA, the elder of the family came to our house—at the PA's behest—with fifty men in tow in order to pressure my husband to resolve the matter on an amicable basis. They killed us and wanted us to solve it amicably! We had no choice. … But, of course, what it means is that we will carry this suffering and humiliation with us until our dying day. I will never forgive anyone who forces us to give up our rights.

The PASF's priority was to consolidate power and guarantee that they had the monopoly on the use of violence in the Palestinian polity, regardless of the implications. Their mission was to establish the rule of "one gun, one law, one authority" (Abbas and Al-Amri 2006), a major electoral slogan of Abbas's 2005 electoral campaign and a cardinal principle of successive Fayyad governments after 2007—even if this came at the expense of people's security, basic human rights, or indeed their ability to resist the occupation. In fact, the implementation of the "one gun, one law, one authority" slogan meant clashing head-on with the notion and practice of resistance, and particularly armed resistance to the Israeli occupation.

Taming Camps, Taming Resistance: Authoritarian Transformation and Arbitrary Detention

The PA's security campaigns were not only illegitimate in the eyes of their targets but they also had detrimental effects on the resistance movement, and it was this message that formed the core of what the voices from below had to say. The PA's "deliberate failure," as one respondent put it, to make a clear distinction between "the weapons of anarchy" and those of the "armed resistance" meant that people were equally targeted whether they were criminals or resistance fighters. As one Balata camp resident eloquently asked: "How can a thief be held in the same jail cell as a *muqawim* (freedom fighter)?"

Criminalizing resistance against the Israeli occupation was a common theme invoked by respondents. A former member of Fatah's al-Aqsa Martyrs Brigades, who was arrested by the PA during the Jenin security campaigns, commented as follows:

> They consider us criminals and bring us before military court judges for resisting the occupation. Is it a crime to resist the occupation? Surely, it is a duty for an occupied people! They just want to subjugate us and strip us of our dignity. ... I was tortured in the PA's Jericho jail for eighty-three days without charge or access to a lawyer. Then they assigned me a lawyer and his advice was that I should confess and sign a form stating that I would refrain from engaging in so-called criminal activity. I'm a freedom fighter, I'm not a thief!

Another former member of the brigades who was also arrested during one of the security campaigns in Nablus was held by the PA for fifty-four days in al-Juneid (Nablus), and then for a further thirty-two days at al-Dhahiriyya Prison in Hebron (from 25 June to 27 July 2012). Although he had successfully integrated into the PA's Civilian Police and was the father of four children, he was held on several charges that were ambiguous and sometimes contradictory. They included: presenting a security threat to his community; being a drug addict and dealer; engaging in criminal activities and corruption; owning weapons and arms dealing; being a follower of Mohammad Dahlan[8]; and even being a member of Hamas! In November 2007, he had handed in two rifles to the PA, a short M16 with an Israeli logo, and a long M16 sporting a Lebanese cedar; he received $18,500 for the two pieces, as well as a conditional Israeli amnesty one month after handing them in. The amnesty document, which he carries with him at all times (and showed me during the interview), states that if he is reported by any other person, or seen in the company of people wanted by the authorities, or carries any type of weapon, including his official PA-issued gun on duty, the amnesty will be canceled.

> It was a "terrorismfest" (*haflet irhab*) in al-Dhahiriyya Prison. There's blood all over the walls and sounds of torture echo through the building— all while being kept blindfolded, you hear people screaming and shouting, doors slamming, the sound of people being slammed against walls. ... Where did they learn all this aggression, I wonder? They enjoyed torturing me. I spent my days in a miniscule cell, 1 meter 20 by 2 meters. One day

they came with a bucket of dirty water and poured it all over the cell. It was a nightmare: torture, interrogation, being hung for hours using the *shabeh* technique,[9] being under constant surveillance with cameras and sound sensors everywhere, sleep deprivation at night, cells being raided after midnight, changing interrogators every day, and on and on—and all of that because they wanted to stop me from resisting the occupation!

Our conversation was interrupted by the sound of a very loud siren, which happened to be the ringtone on his mobile phone. He continued his account, with bitterness in his voice, as his legs shook and he sweated profusely. "Those fifty-four days were the worst of my life. I would have long conversations with the spiders, ants, and mosquitoes in my cell. I kept telling them: take your portion of my blood and please leave me alone! I watched the slow movements of the ants in my cell intensely. … I would feed them and then kill them. This is exactly what the PA is doing with us. They pay us our salaries and then they come and kill us."

He stopped midsentence, gripped his stomach, and said he felt dizzy. Continuing to sweat and to shake, he added: "Whenever I talk about this topic, I get awful pains in my stomach and all over my body." This man was eventually released from jail after President Abbas ordered security amnesties over Ramadan and Eid al-Fitr that year. Fearing that he might go to a human rights organization and sue, the PASF asked him for a fiscal guarantee of JD 7000 (about $10,000) underwritten by the Nablus Chamber of Commerce. They also asked him to sign a commitment, written in Arabic, English, and Hebrew, not to carry any weapons, nor travel or move within the West Bank, and to agree to be held overnight at the main police station in Nablus between 8:00 p.m. and 8:00 a.m. every day.

In our two-hour conversation, one of the leaders of the 2002 Jenin battle, who was on Israel's most wanted list during the second intifada, described his arrest and subsequent detention in the PA's Jericho prison between May and October 2012:

> I received a call from the head of the Civil Police to go and have coffee with him, but when I got there, it was a trap. All of a sudden, a group of Preventive Security forces swarmed into the office, tied my hands behind my back roughly, hooded my head, and dragged me down the stairs to their jeep. They drove me all the way to Jericho, through all the Israeli checkpoints. How ironic that every single Israeli checkpoint was open for

me when I was arrested by the PA! I even heard them [PASF] speaking on the phone in Hebrew saying, "We got him!" I have health issues, I still have five bullets in my legs and four bullets in my back from 2002. A bomb also exploded in my face [in 2002] but they [PASF] refused to allow the doctors to see me at the prison. After being on the dirty and wet cell floor for a week, I got a bacterial infection in my back. Then they started to torture me physically, they would shove me hard against the wall and stretch me on a chair using the *shabeh* technique for three days. After eight days of this, and even though I was entitled to have a mattress, they refused to let me have it if I didn't confess to a crime that I never committed. In my five months in jail, I was not once questioned by the public prosecutor. They made an example of me, to show all the other so-called security prisoners that no one is an exception and that even the leaders of the armed resistance can be arrested and tortured. They blindfolded me, and had me lying on the ground with my head under the interrogator's boots, and they opened the little observation hatch at the top of the door so the other prisoners could see me in that state. It was so humiliating … talking about this upsets me, I feel overwhelmed.

A resident of Balata summed up the consequence of the security campaign on the space available for dissent in the following words: "Since 2007, public gatherings are only allowed on three occasions: weddings, funerals, or prison gatherings." A local field researcher for a major Palestinian human rights organization told me that legal violations were rife; these included "arrests and house raids without legal warrants, prolonged interrogation in a security force compound without charge or trial, appearance in court after weeks of detention without charge, no formal charges, or specific accusations." He added, "Actually, I just received a call from the Preventive Security Force to go and see them, and I am sure they want to question me about the latest report I wrote."

A few weeks after his release, an eighteen-year-old youth from Jenin camp, with the marks of torture still visible on many parts of his body, told me: "I was accused of causing social unrest and threats to public order as the leader of the Devils gang. They accused me of writing a statement and spreading it all over the camp, but the thing is, I can't read or write!"

Standing in his workshop, a sad-faced twenty-four-year-old carpenter told me as his hands and legs shook:

I was arrested and detained three times in PA jails in Jericho and Jenin. I was never ever as humiliated in my life as I was that year. Twelve days without sleep, stretched on a broken and painful chair. The chains in my hand ate into my skin and bones. Seventeen days in solitary confinement in a very cold cell with a rotten and disgusting mattress and the worst possible meals. I thought I was in Guantanamo. In Jericho, the prison is underground and it has twenty-eight cells, three bigger rooms, a kitchen that is often used for torture, and an interrogators' room that includes a so-called health-care unit. It is the same design as in Israeli prisons.

It is clear from these and other similar testimonies that many people in both camps, whether civil society actors or members of local organizations, considered that the security campaigns' objective was the creation of a culture of fear so that the PA could consolidate its power and illustrate its ability to govern notoriously difficult spaces. The dynamics of security coordination with Israel are such that for camp residents, internal, or homegrown, sources of insecurity form yet another layer of fear and humiliation in their experience of the Israeli occupation.

SECURITY COORDINATION: DOMINATION AS COOPERATION[10]

Security coordination with Israel is a defining feature of the PA security doctrine and a major source of tension between the Palestinian people and their leadership (Dana 2014). Although it was an outcome of the 1993 Oslo Accords,[11] it gained both rhetorical and operational dominance once the PA's state-building agenda became paramount and was subsequently entrenched post-2007.[12] However, its detractors view security coordination as having had a detrimental impact on the PA's legitimacy and it is perceived by many Palestinians as a form of national betrayal (Tartir 2015b).

Security coordination between the PASF and the Israeli military manifests in a number of ways, including: the PASF's arrest of Palestinian suspects wanted by Israel; the suppression of Palestinian protests against Israeli soldiers and/or settlers; intelligence sharing between the IDF and the PASF; the revolving door between Israeli and PA jails through which Palestinian activists cycle successively for the same offenses; and regular joint Israeli-Palestinian meetings, workshops, and trainings (Amrov and Tartir 2014b).

In May 2014, President Abbas declared that "security coordination [with Israel] is sacred, [it is] sacred. And we'll continue it regardless of policy difference or agreement" (Abbas 2014). The vast majority of Palestinian people simply disagree, however. A poll of Palestinian residents of the West Bank and the Gaza Strip by the Arab Center for Research and Policy Studies in 2014 showed that 80% of respondents opposed continued security coordination with Israel (Arab Center for Research and Policy Studies 2014).

This fundamental disagreement between the Palestinian public and its official political leadership has given rise to popular anger, eventually leading to protests that were violently suppressed. Such anger is also reflected in the way that the PASF are perceived. After 2007, the PASF were often referred to as "the Dayton forces," in reference to US lt. gen. Keith Dayton, the chief architect of the United States Security Coordinators team (USSC) responsible for training the nine battalions that carried out the security campaigns in Balata and Jenin refugee camps. In a 2009 speech in Washington, Dayton saluted the "new Palestinian men" his team had created and quoted senior IDF commanders as asking him, "How many more of these new Palestinians can you generate, and how quickly?" The US general also referenced the words of a senior Palestinian official speaking to a graduating class of PASF troops in Jordan that were trained under USSC auspices. "You were not sent here to learn how to fight Israel," Dayton quoted the official as saying, "but you were rather sent here to learn how to keep law and order, respect the right of all of our citizens, and implement the rule of law so that we can live in peace and security with Israel" (Dayton 2009). Such statements, in addition to the revelations from the leaked Palestine Papers,[13] further fueled negative public perceptions about the security coordination doctrine and its consequences on and implications for ordinary Palestinians' lives (Perry 2011).

The vast majority of those interviewed in the camps expressed general dissatisfaction with security coordination. A community leader in Jenin camp told me: "I don't have a problem with [it] as long as it is reciprocal. However, this is not the case. It'll be an entirely different story when the PA can ask Israel to arrest a settler and protect Palestinian people's security. There is no sense of coordination, only of domination." A community leader from Balata camp put it more bluntly: "The security campaigns did one thing: they minimized daily and direct Israeli aggression and outsourced to PASF the role of the occupation forces—what they did was create a division of labor."

The revolving door (*al-bab al-dawar*) phenomenon was a particularly sore point for those who had suffered from it. A respondent from Jenin camp who had done time in both Israeli and PA jails told me: "I was detained for nine months in the PA's Preventive Security Forces prison because I belonged to Hamas. Three weeks after my release from the PA jail, Israel arrested me on the exact same charges. They literally used the same words." For his part, a thirty-three-year-old Fatah cadre from Balata camp recounted: "After six months' administrative detention [without charge or trial] in an Israeli prison and before I could enjoy the taste of freedom, PA forces raided our house after midnight and detained me for eight months. They did not ask me any questions in jail. They simply showed me a document and said "*beseder*" [alright, in Hebrew]; *beseder*, your file is ready, and now all you have to do is wait for God's mercy!" Even those who thought that the security campaigns and reforms had achieved positive results were cautious in voicing muted satisfaction.[14]

"We Are Doing Our Job"

The PA's security personnel held altogether different views than the ones conveyed by the broader public. They understood their job in technical terms and expressed a keenness to play by the rules as these were explained to them by their commanders. "Business is business, and I am doing my job," a PASF member in Nablus told me. "Go and ask people and you will realize that we are doings things right and all the rest are wrong," he added. "You can't have two roosters in the same coop," another local security official asserted confidently. "It's either the PA security forces or militias and armed factions. There is no justification for the PA's existence if its numberone task isn't security enforcement." An officer of the above-mentioned Preventive Security forces put it like this: "There is no such thing as resistance (let alone armed resistance) and this is why security conditions are better. Unfortunately, security campaigns also mean that the PA must devour their own (*al-Sulta lazim ta'kul wladha*). I mean everyone talks about prisoners and torture, even though there is no such thing, but no one talks about the problems facing interrogators. This is their job and they need to interrogate prisoners, but no one protects them if the prisoners later decide to seek retribution."

When asked about the PASF's aggressiveness and its excessive use of force both during the campaigns and inside PA prisons, a security official in the liaison office for the Nablus Police told me: "Well, excessive use of force may be a problem, but in certain instances there's no choice but to resort to it. International law allows to the use of force according to what European and local experts taught us. But those laws are very biased [toward humanitarianism] and they need to be amended because we need more leeway to use physical force with detainees." When I relayed these words to a senior Ministry of Interior official in the PA, his initial response was to ask, "Why are you surprised? That's our job." Then he added, "At the end of the day, the fact that Palestinian security forces are operating under [the auspices of the] occupation is embarrassing for everyone because people wish that these security forces would protect them from the Israelis, but that will never happen."

Conclusion

Security sector reform under the PA's post-2007 state-building agenda did not only aim to enhance the PASF's functionality and effectiveness and to ensure stability and security for Israel but it also sought to tame resistance to Israel's occupation and colonial domination by criminalizing militancy and stripping it of its basic infrastructure. The PA and its security forces used harassment, marginalization, arrest, detention, and torture against those engaged in resisting Israel, and they dismantled the structures supporting such resistance through the conduct of aggressive security campaigns within the occupied West Bank's most militant spaces.

As suggested by the ethnographic evidence gathered from ordinary people, what I have called the voices from below, in Balata and Jenin refugee camps, the security campaigns were widely perceived as both illegitimate and ineffective. The voices from below fundamentally challenged the claim that the PASF were doing their job to maintain law and order and argued that rather than feeling a greater sense of security, they had witnessed the transformation of the PA into an authoritarian regime whose security forces conduct themselves in ways approaching a police state in the making. In sum, while the benchmark of security reform was to build a professional security establishment, ordinary people wanted protection from their major source of insecurity, namely the Israeli military occupation. As one respondent put it, "It means nothing to me if we have the best security forces and army in the world if they are not able to protect me."

Capturing the narrative of ordinary people is a particularly challenging task. It is especially difficult in the case at hand not only because security issues are sensitive per se, but also because of the high level of frustration and despair among Palestinians resulting from the last two decades of Israeli occupation and increasingly authoritarian PA rule. On the way out of Jenin camp on the last day of my fieldwork, a number of people were gathered around a man. "When my child wishes to die, it is so painful to hear such a wish," he screamed at passers-by. "When I don't have one shekel to give her, then I better go kill myself. When the Palestinian leadership is hanging us upside-down in the air, then what is left of this life?" Holding a bottle filled with gasoline and matches in one hand, and his daughter in the other, he was only dissuaded from starting the fire by the child's terrorized cries. Such incidents are not particularly exceptional when misery, anger, and injustice are the defining features of daily life.

Notes

1. A version of this chapter was first published in the *Journal of Palestine Studies* XLVI (2) (Winter 2017).
2. The entire governorates of Nablus and Jenin (including other refugee camps, neighborhoods, and villages) were subjected to security operations and campaigns but Jenin and Balata refugee camps were the yardsticks by which the success of other security campaigns was measured. Balata and Jenin were two of the most rebellious locales against Israeli incursion during the second intifada, and political factions (whether Fatah, Hamas, or others) have a long history of entrenchment in those camps.
3. In July 2004, Zakaria Zubeidi, a leader of al-Aqsa Martyrs Brigades in Jenin, told a journalist, "I am the highest authority." A week later, he told another journalist "I'm in charge. The police? They just disrupt the traffic. If there's a problem, people come to me." He added, "I don't take orders from anyone. I'm not good at following." In early 2005, when PA president Mahmoud Abbas and Zubeidi were touring Jenin together during a presidential election campaign, crowds chanted Zubeidi's name and not Abbas's, see Marten (2014).
4. For more information on the role of the two camps during the second intifada, see Leech (2016) and Tabar (2007).

5. The PA's post-2007 state-building project aimed at establishing a Weberian monopoly of violence in the security sphere. This meant that the PA's statutory security forces were the only bodies with the right and exclusivity to control the security realm. In accordance with the Weberian model, other nonstate actors, nonstatutory bodies, and armed resistance groups had to be marginalized, dismantled, co-opted, integrated, disarmed, or punished. Within the overall context of Israeli occupation and colonization, however, the Weberian model is fraught with tensions and contradictions.
6. As a result of these security campaigns, the Arab Organization for Human Rights reported "the data collected from June 2007 to the end of 2011 indicates that PA security forces detained 13,271 Palestinian citizens, 96% of whom were subjected to various methods of torture resulting in the killing of six detainees and causing chronic illness in others." The Euro-Med Observer for Human Rights reported that in 2013 the Palestinian security forces in the West Bank arbitrarily arrested 723 persons and interrogated 1137 without any clear charge or a court decision or arrest warrant. In 2012, the Independent Commission on Human Rights (ICHR) received 3185 complaints, compared to 2876 complaints in 2011, and 3828 in 2010.
7. Unless otherwise stated, all quotations are taken from interviews conducted by the author in Balata and Jenin camps between August and December 2012.
8. Mohammad Dahlan is a former member of Fatah's Central Committee and former head of the Preventive Security Force in Gaza and the Palestinian National Security Council. He was dismissed from Fatah in 2011 and exiled (and currently lives in Abu Dhabi) in the aftermath of the growing rift between him and the PA president and Fatah leader Abbas. Dahlan was accused of corruption, of poisoning Arafat, and of preparing a coup against Abbas. In November 2016, Fatah held their Seventh General Congress to elect a new leadership and eliminate Dahlan and his followers from the organization's leadership. The PA conducts security offensives in Balata and Jenin camps to this day, on the grounds that they are Dahlan strongholds.
9. *Shabeh* is a "combination of methods, used for prolonged periods, entailing sensory isolation, sleep deprivation, and infliction of pain. Regular *shabeh* entails shackling the detainee's hands and legs to a small chair, angled to slant forward so that the detainee cannot sit in a stable position," see B'Tselem (1998).
10. I am indebted to Jan Selby for the conceptual framework of this section, see Selby (2003, 2013).

11. For a contextual analysis of the PASF's evolution in the last two decades, see Tartir (2015a).
12. For the Israeli perspective, see former President Shimon Peres's speech to the European Parliament in 2013. Expressing Israel's satisfaction with the state of Palestinian security, Peres stated: "A Palestinian security force was formed. You [Europeans] and the Americans trained it. And now we work together to prevent terror and crime" (Peres 2013).
13. The Palestine Papers is a collection of confidential documents relating to the Israeli–Palestinian conflict that were leaked by Al Jazeera in January 2011. The news outlet released nearly 1700 files and thousands of pages of diplomatic correspondence on the so-called peace process. Further information can be found on Al Jazeera's Palestine Papers page at http://www.aljazeera.com/palestinepapers/.
14. In both camps, the predominant feeling expressed by ordinary people and local leaders alike was that "the PA and its security forces hate us." In an attempt to provide an explanation for this, the head of Jenin's camp services committee stated: "The PA has been isolated, marginalized, and absent over the last eight years when the intifada committees were leading Palestinian society. Now the PA is back, and it is stronger, and because of that, they want to make up for all the years that eluded them and also to exact retribution."

References

Abbas, Mahmoud. 2014. "President Mahmoud Abbas: Security Coordination Is Sacred" [speech in Arabic]. Mahmoud Abbas Speech to an Israeli Audience in Ramallah Broadcast by Al Quds, posted by Talha M. A'abed, May 29. https://www.youtube.com/watch?v=UG5NcdkthQ0.

Abbas, Mahmoud, and Walid Al-Amri. 2006. "Mahmoud Abbas: Security Chaos and Palestinian Elections" [interview in Arabic]. *Al Jazeera*, January 17. https://goo.gl/1vgaFr.

Amnesty International. 2002. "Shielded from Scrutiny: IDF Violations in Jenin and Nablus," November 4. https://www.amnesty.org/download/Documents/120000/mde151432002en.pdf.

Amnesty International. 2013. "'Shut Up We Are the Police': Use of Excessive Force by Palestinian Authority in the Occupied West Bank." Amnesty International Briefing, September 23. https://www.amnesty.org/en/documents/MDE21/006/2013/en/.

Amrov, Sabrien, and Alaa Tartir. 2014a. "After Gaza, What Price Palestine's Security Sector?" *Al-Shabaka*, October 8. http://al-shabaka.org/wp-content/uploads/2015/01/AmrovTartir_PolicyBrief_En_Oct_2014.pdf.

Amrov, Sabrien, and Alaa Tartir. 2014b. "Subcontracting Repression in the West Bank and Gaza," *New York Times*, November 26. http://www.nytimes.com/2014/11/27/opinion/subcontractingrepression-in-the-west-bank-and-gaza.html?_r=0.

Arab Center for Research and Policy Studies. 2014. "Palestinian Public Opinion: Attitudes Towards Peace Negotiations and National Reconciliation." Arab Public Opinion Project—Arab Index 2014. www.jstor.org/stable/resrep12683.

Bronner, Ethan. 2008. "Palestinian Forces Dilute Hebron's Volatile Brew." *New York Times*, November 25. http://www.nytimes.com/2008/11/26/world/middleeast/26hebron.html.

B'Tselem. 1998. "Routine Torture: Interrogation Methods of the General Security Service." *Btselem.org*, February. http://www.btselem.org/publications/summaries/199802_routine_torture.

Calabresi, Massimo. 2009. "Can Obama's Model for Peace Survive Gaza?" *Time*, January 16. http://www.time.com/time/nation/article/0,8599,1872425,00.html.

Cambrezy, Mélanie. 2014. "Security Sector Reform in Palestine (1993–2013): Fragmenting the Political Scene While Building a 'Partner for Peace.'" Paper Presented at the 2014 International Studies Association annual convention, Toronto, April.

Chandler, David, and Timothy Sisk, eds. 2013. *The Routledge Handbook of International Statebuilding*. London: Routledge.

Dana, Tariq. 2014. "The Beginning of the End of Palestinian Security Coordination with Israel?" *Jadaliyya*, July 4. http://www.jadaliyya.com/pages/index/18379/the-beginning-of-the-end-of-p...c.

Dayton, Keith, Lt. Gen. 2009. "Peace Through Security." Michael Stein Address on U.S. Middle East Policy, Washington Institute for Near East Policy, May 7. http://www.washingtoninstitute.org/html/pdf/DaytonKeynote.pdf.

Ghani, Ashraf, and Clare Lockhart. 2008. *Fixing Failed States: A Framework for Rebuilding a Fractured World*. Oxford: Oxford University Press.

Giambi, Giorgia. 2009. *The "Jenin Pilot": A Monitoring Report*. Jerusalem: Center for Democracy and Community Development.

Human Rights Watch. 2002. "Jenin: IDF Military Operations." *Human Rights Watch* 14 (3). https://www.hrw.org/reports/2002/israel3/israel0502.pdf.

Human Rights Watch. 2014. "Palestine: No Action in Assault by Police." *HRW.org*, May 19. https://www.hrw.org/news/2014/05/19/palestine-no-actionassault-police.

International Crisis Group. 2008. "Ruling Palestine II: The West Bank Model?" International Crisis Group Middle East Report No. 79, July 17. https://www.crisisgroup.org/middle-east-north-africa/eastern-mediterranean/israelpalestine/ruling-palestine-ii-west-bank-model.

Israel Defense Forces. 2008. "Pilot 'Jenin': Details and Focal Points." Military Strategic Information Section, August 5. https://www.jewishvirtuallibrary.org/jsource/Peace/pilotjenin.ppt.

Leech, Philip. 2015. "Who Owns 'the Spring' in Palestine? Rethinking Popular Consent and Resistance in the Context of the 'Palestinian State' and the 'Arab Spring.'" *Democratization* 22 (6): 1011–1029.

Leech, Philip. 2016. *The State of Palestine: A Critical Analysis.* London: Routledge.

Marten, Kimberly. 2014. "Reformed or Deformed? Patronage Politics, International Influence, and the Palestinian Authority Security Forces." *International Peacekeeping* 21 (2): 181–197.

Mustafa, Tahani. 2015. "Damming the Palestinian Spring: Security Sector Reform and Entrenched Repression." *Journal of Intervention and Statebuilding* 9 (2): 212–230.

Peres, Shimon. 2013. "Full Text of Peres Speech to European Parliament." *Haaretz*, March 12. https://www.haaretz.com/full-text-of-peres-speech-to-european-parliament-1.5233679.

Perry, Mark. 2011. "Dayton's Mission: A Reader's Guide." *Al Jazeera*, January 25. http://www.aljazeera.com/palestinepapers/2011/01/2011125145732219555.html.

RRT. 2008. "Country: Palestinian Authority." Refugee Review Tribunal Research Response, No. PSE33593, August 5. http://www.ecoi.net/file_upload/1997_1300358528_pse33593.pdf.

Sayigh, Yezid. 2011. "Policing the People, Building the State: Authoritarian Transformation in the West Bank and Gaza." Carnegie Paper, Carnegie Middle East Center, Carnegie Endowment for International Peace, February. http://carnegieendowment.org/files/gaza_west_bank_security.pdf.

Schroeder, Ursula, Fairlie Chappuis, and Deniz Kocak. 2014. "Security Sector Reform and the Emergence of Hybrid Security Governance." *International Peacekeeping* 21 (2): 214–230.

Selby, Jan. 2003. "Dressing Up Domination as 'Cooperation': The Case of Israeli–Palestinian Water Relations." *Review of International Studies* 29 (1): 121–138.

Selby, Jan. 2013. "Cooperation, Domination and Colonisation: The Israeli–Palestinian Joint Water Committee." *Water Alternatives* 6 (1): 1–24. http://www.water-alternatives.org/index.php/volume6/v6issue1/196-a6-1-1/file.

Tabar, Linda. 2007. "Memory, Agency, Counter-Narrative: Testimonies from Jenin Refugee Camp." *Critical Arts* 21 (1): 6–31.

Tabar, Linda. 2012. "The 'Urban Redesign' of Jenin Refugee Camp: Humanitarian Intervention and Rational Violence." *Journal of Palestine Studies* 41 (2): 44–61.

Tartir, Alaa. 2015a. "The Evolution and Reform of Palestinian Security Forces, 1993–2013." *Stability: International Journal of Security & Development* 4 (1): 1–20.

Tartir, Alaa. 2015b. "Securitised Development and Palestinian Authoritarianism Under Fayyadism." *Conflict, Security & Development* 15 (5): 479–502.

Tartir, Alaa. 2016. "How U.S. Security Aid to PA Sustains Israel's Occupation." *Al Jazeera*, December 2. http://www.aljazeera.com/indepth/features/2016/11/security-aid-pa-sustai...161103120213593.html.

Turner, Mandy. 2015. "Peacebuilding as Counterinsurgency in the Occupied Palestinian Territory." *Review of International Studies* 41 (1): 73–98.

United Nations. 2013a. "Closing the Gap: Palestinian State-Building and Resumed Negotiations; Report to the Ad Hoc Liaison Committee." Office of the United Nations Special Coordinator for the Middle East Peace Process, New York, September 25. https://unispal.un.org/pdfs/AHLC-Sept2013_UNSCOrpt.pdf.

United Nations. 2013b. "Report to the Ad Hoc Liaison Committee." Office of the United Nations Special Coordinator for the Middle East Peace Process, Brussels, March 19. https://unsco.unmissions.org/sites/default/files/un_report_to_the_march_2013_ahlc.pdf.

UN OCHA. 2008a. "Balata Refugee Camp Profile." United Nations Office for the Coordination of Humanitarian Affairs, November. http://www.ochaopt.org/documents/opt_campprof_unrwa_balata_nov_2008.pdf.

UN OCHA. 2008b. "Jenin Refugee Camp Profile." United Nations Office for the Coordination of Humanitarian Affairs, October. http://www.ochaopt.org/documents/opt_campprof_unrwa_jenin_oct_2008.pdf.

UNRWA. 2014. "Camp Profiles." United Nations Relief and Works Agency for Palestine Refugees in the Near East. http://www.unrwa.org/where-we-work/west-bank/camp-profiles?field=12.

Zanotti, Jim. 2010. *U.S. Security Assistance to the Palestinian Authority*. Washington, DC: Congressional Research Service. https://fas.org/sgp/crs/mideast/R40664.pdf.

CHAPTER 10

Securitizing Peace: The EU's Aiding and Abetting Authoritarianism

Alaa Tartir

To speak of Israeli-Palestinian "cooperation" ... is to use no less than a misnomer. This is not, however, simply because "the outcome of cooperation between an elephant and a fly is not hard to predict," as Chomsky so pithily writes ... but because under Oslo, "cooperation" is often only minimally different from the occupation and domination that went before it. "Cooperation," in this context, is above all an internationally pleasing and acceptable signifier which obscures rather than elucidates the nature of Israeli-Palestinian relations. (Selby 2003, 138)

INTRODUCTION

The European Union (EU) and its member states have invested billions of dollars in aid over the past decades to induce peace and security in the Middle East, and it appears likely that they will continue to do so for the foreseeable future (Balfour et al. 2016; Lust 2016). The EU and its member states are now firmly established as the largest sponsors

A. Tartir (✉)
The Graduate Institute of International and Development Studies (IHEID), Geneva, Switzerland
e-mail: alaa.tartir@graduateinstitute.ch

© The Author(s) 2019
A. Tartir and T. Seidel (eds.),
Palestine and Rule of Power, Middle East Today,
https://doi.org/10.1007/978-3-030-05949-1_10

of the Palestinian state-building project. But in the absence of peace and security, they have instead prioritized political stability (Tartir and Challand 2016).[1]

Even as they continue, in theory at least, to promote the tenets and practices of "good governance" within the Middle East—including in the Palestinian West Bank-, the EU and its member states continue, in practice, to channel support and security assistance to authoritarian and repressive regimes throughout the Middle East (Cammett et al. 2015). This investment has created deep structural deficiencies in the recipient countries style of governance, most notably by elevating security establishments above other actors within the domestic political process. In addition, this funding and support has indirectly perpetuated conflicts and created new ones (Youngs and Gutman 2015). "Peace" therefore became a mere function of securitized processes and interventions, with "security first" paradigms and security-driven frameworks providing the engine of state-building intervention. The EU's ongoing state-building intervention in the occupied West Bank—and in the occupied Palestinian territory (oPt) more broadly—is an excellent case-in-point which provides considerable insight into this general development.

The oPt have provided the setting in which a substantial state-building experiment has developed over the course of more than two decades. Since the establishment of the Palestinian Authority (PA), international aid channeled to the PA has exceeded $30 billion (USD) (Tartir and Wildeman 2017, 16). The EU and its member states have accounted for almost half of this aid provision (Knudsen and Tartir 2017, 15), which has been channeled through both bilateral relations and multilateral institutions.[2] A large portion of the overall amount committed to good governance reforms has focused upon SSR. The Palestinian security sector employs around half of all civil servants, accounts for nearly $1 billion of the PA budget and receives around 30% of total international aid disbursed to the Palestinians (Tartir 2017b, 7).

The security sector consumes more of the PA's budget than the education, health, and agriculture sectors combined. The sector currently employs 83,276 individuals in the West Bank and the Gaza Strip (DCAF 2016). This figure includes 312 brigadier generals (232 report to the PA and 80 to Hamas)—here it should be noted that the entire US Army has 410 brigadier generals. The ratio of security personnel to the population is as high as 1:48, one of the highest ratios in the world (Tartir 2017a, 3). Despite the limited successes of this security-focused aid,

European aid continues to be invested in the expectation that it will help to build the institutions of a future independent and viable Palestinian state (Tartir 2014; Bouris 2014; Khalil 2017), and thus ultimately contribute to the establishment of a two-state solution. While it is focused upon internal security, this "investment in peace" is also invariably justified with reference to peacebuilding aims and objectives (Bicchi and Voltolini 2017; Bouris and Huber 2017; Persson 2017a, b). However, in the absence of the essential conditions for state-building and peacebuilding, European aid has produced a range of perverse effects which have negatively impacted the daily lives of Palestinians and their internationally recognized right of self-determination (Tartir and Edjus 2018). In apparent defiance of this pervasive reality, business-as-usual continues: EU funds continue to be spent on Palestine despite the fact that previous and existing provision has manifestly failed to produce positive outcomes in any of the priority areas: peacebuilding, security reform, democracy promotion and state-building.

There are numerous reasons why interventions in each of these areas have failed (Wildeman 2015; Paragi 2017). However, in seeking to identify the precise causes, international donors and political actors frequently overlook the *securitization* of peace and aid. There are two explanations which provide considerable insight into this oversight: firstly, the "domination of the powerful," secondly, the conceptual and theoretical supremacy of "security first" paradigms.

As a direct consequence, the PA's state-building dynamics, along with the contours and outlines of the wider peacebuilding project, continue to be driven and sustained by a security rationale and understanding (Tartir 2015b). Security, as opposed to the political priorities of the Palestinian people (specifically their interest in transparent, accountable and legitimate governance), therefore anticipated and underpinned the external engagement with the oPt from the outset.[3] Even the form of security that was envisioned quite clearly derived from the worldview and priorities of the powerful, as opposed to the powerless or colonized. Policy practice does not therefore render or reproduce the "bottom-up" human security approach that is so frequently evoked within the discursive representations and rationalizations of key European actors.

On the contrary, this practice instead more closely approximates to a top-down imposition that blurs a range of dichotomies (repression/security, violence/resistance and legitimacy/authoritarianism) and redefines them in the vernacular of powerful local and external actors. Jan

Selby's quote, which opened this chapter, quite clearly demonstrates that security is a power game that is conducted in the interests of the powerful. If external actors fail to acknowledge this fact, and specifically relate it to governance and security reforms, then external engagement will continue to be a deeply problematic enterprise that is underpinned by numerous contradictions.

Closer reflection suggests that it is the interest of the Palestinian people which is the missing variable in the equation of external intervention and general assessments of external "assistance" to the oPt's internal governance. The EU's Police Mission to the Palestinian Territories (EUPOL COPPS), which has operated over the past decade, quite clearly brings out this point and also reiterates that the organization's engagement with the PA security apparatus has produced a professionalization of authoritarianism. This occurred because this engagement has been evaluated within the framework of technical reform; as a consequence, the power relations which conjoin different actors have not been factored into the analysis.

The omission of Palestinians from the overall "cost-benefit analyses" (to adopt the EU's tortured vernacular for a moment) becomes even more problematic when the colonial attributes of the working context are acknowledged and considered in their full significance. When considered from this perspective, it is not merely the case that the basic meaning of security and peace has been insufficiently recognized or even subverted (Tartir 2016); rather it is instead the case that external intervention has perpetuated colonial relations by rendering a situation in which unrepresentative and illegitimate local authorities function as subcontractors to the colonial regime. Under these precise conditions, external "assistance" and "capacity building" becomes part of the problem.

This chapter's focus upon SSR is particularly concerned with the proposition that European actors, and in particular the EU, are part of the problem within the current existing dynamics, as opposed to the solution. The current chapter makes a distinctive contribution because it offers a Palestinian ("bottom-up") perspective which is diametrically opposed to the terms in which security, at least in the Palestinian context, is conceptualized and theorized. It offers an important innovation by suggesting that the perspective of the "locals" should be the starting point for an analysis and appraisal of ongoing interventions that are undertaken with a view to furthering SSR.

This, it suggests, is essential if observers are to fully "unpack" the wider implications which extend from "technical" initiatives that aspire towards improved capacities and capabilities. The ramifications of these interventions, it suggests, can only be fully appreciated within this wider context. This chapter develops in accordance with the following outline. It initially provides historical and political context by discussing reforms of the Palestinian security sector that were initiated through external intervention in the aftermath of the PA's establishment. After sketching these initial outlines, it then proposes to problematize the role of the EU by viewing it through the lens of the EUPOL COPPS intervention. The chapter then concludes with five key lessons and recommendations that could inform future EU interventions.

Palestinian SSR and External Intervention

The reform of the Palestinian Authority security apparatus can be broadly broken down into three separate phases: The Oslo Accords (1993–1999), the Second Intifada (2000–2006), and the post-2007 state-building project (Tartir 2015a).[4] Each phase was not particularly part of an intelligible process but instead reflected shifting donor priorities. These shifts in turn impacted SSR and had wider implications for European intervention in the Palestinian–Israeli conflict.

The first phase was characterized by a fundamental clash between the imperatives of state-building and national liberation. The former implied the construction of pre-state or state-like institutions (although in reality it resulted in an inflated bureaucracy); the latter instead implied the pursuit of the revolutionary program for self-determination that had been advanced by the Palestine Liberation Organization (PLO). Over time, the first imperative came to predominate, and Arafat used the PA security forces, in addition to nepotistic and patronage-based governing practices, to strengthen his authority and promote stability (Brynen 1995; Hilal and Khan 2004). Quantity, as opposed to quality, was Arafat's main priority. This resulted in the emergence of a bloated security establishment and forces with contradictory duties which nonetheless reported directly to Arafat. The 9000 recruits envisaged in the 1994 Cairo Agreement had grown, five years later, to more than five times this number (close to 50,000 security personnel) (Lia 2007).

This proliferation of the security forces, each of whom committed considerable time to spying on each other, had hugely negative consequences for Palestinians (Said 1995). The growth of the security apparatus enabled Arafat to establish security-based political structures, thus strengthening authoritarianism by blocking accountability mechanisms. This eroded legitimacy, contributed to heightened insecurity, and paved the way for future political fragmentation. However, rather than challenging endemic corruption and patronage (Dana 2015), the international community, and the EU was a foremost protagonist in this regard, chose to turn a blind eye. At the current point in time, the donor community is now grappling with governance-related challenges which can be traced back to this initial reluctance to disrupt the "peace process" (Tartir 2017a).

During the course of the Second Intifada, the PA's security infrastructure was destroyed by the Israeli army, in direct response to the fact that it directly participated in the uprising. This created a "security vacuum," which was filled by non-PA/non-statutory actors, with largely negative consequences for Palestinians. Exacerbated instability and political infighting meant that external donors, the PA and Israel became increasingly preoccupied with the question of how a strong and dominant security sector could be developed.

In June 2002, the PA announced its 100-Day Reform Plan (PA 2002). This was then followed by the 2003 Road Map. The latter explicitly called for a "rebuilt and refocused Palestinian Authority security apparatus" which would confront "all those engaged in terror" and dismantle "the terrorist capabilities and infrastructure" (United Nations 2003). The PA's security sector was therefore tasked with a relatively narrow range of tasks. In combating terrorism, it would apprehend suspects, outlaw incitement, collect illegal weapons. In addition, it would also provide Israel with a list of Palestinian police recruits and report "progress" in each of these respects to the US government (Agha and Khalidi 2005). In committing to these priorities, the PA was pitched into the "war against terror": as a direct consequence, resistance was reinvented as "insurgency" or "instability."

In each of these respects, Palestinian security reform continued to be "in essence, an externally-controlled process, driven by the national security interests of Israel and the United States, and characterized by very limited ownership on the part of Palestinian society" (Friedrich and Luethold 2007). The emergence of a new security doctrine (the "one gun, one law, one authority" strategy) (Abbas and Al-Amri 2006) was very much in the lineage of this initial characterization of SSR.[5]

The international donor community helped to implement this strategy starting from 2004, with both EUPOL COPPS and the United States Security Coordinator (USSC) playing a prominent role. These external actors were both sponsors and implementers.

The USSC and the EUPOL COPPS missions played a hugely important role in helping to shape the relationship between statutory and non-statutory security forces; in addition, they also made a significant contribution to the transformation of the PA's security sphere in the post-2007 state-building period. Their engagement had important implications for local ownership of security reform, and opened up a whole new section of the international aid industry, thus adding an additional layer of complexity to the process of SSR. EUPOL COPPS emerged in this context, being conceived as a response to ongoing security vacuums and a means through which an existing political opportunity could be fully exploited (El-Din 2017). A security vacuum gave rise to the agenda of securitization, the technical vacuum gave rise to various capacity-building initiatives and the political vacuum resulted in the EU assuming a more prominent role within the peace process.

The post-2007 state-building project was the third phase in the development of the PA's security forces. It aimed, primarily by working through EUPOL COPPS and USSC, to reinvent the PA security forces, both by reinventing them as "neutral" law enforcement bodies and enhancing their capacity to promote and uphold security. These interventions occurred under the broad heading of SSR and addressed issues relating to, inter alia, training and weapons procurement (PA 2008). It was envisaged that this training would enable PA security forces to confront Hamas militants, engage and co-opt Fatah-allied militants, and promote public order by cracking down on hotbeds of criminal activity (The West Bank cities of Nablus and Jenin were cited as key priorities in this regard) (International Crisis Group 2008).

However, these aspirations were substantially complicated when the "reformed" security forces were accused of human rights abuses and the suppression of fundamental freedoms (Marten 2014; Amnesty International 2013; Human Rights Watch 2014). Local and international human rights organizations openly voiced their concerns about emerging authoritarian trends (Hijazi and Lovatt 2017a, b). Some observers spoke of a PA which sought to rule with an "iron fist."[6] This was particularly uncomfortable for the US, as the PA's security forces had become popularly known as the "Dayton forces" (Perry 2011), in "honor" of the US Lieutenant-general who led the "professionalization and modernization" process.[7]

The EU'S practical interventions quite clearly undermined a number of its other, more high-minded commitments. In supporting the unelected Fatah leadership as it conducted security campaigns that were directed towards elected Hamas representatives, it quite clearly undermined its own commitment to democratic accountability and rule-of-law. A European aid official quite openly acknowledged this. He said:

> [On the] one hand, we demand democratic processes, transparency and accountability and constantly stress the importance of human rights. But on the other hand, we have for the most part been silent about the PA's extra-judicial campaign against Hamas. There is a huge contradiction in our message. (International Crisis Group 2010, 33)

While this statement was made at the apogee of the PA state-building project, other contradictions and tensions within the EU message (most notably the tension between its high-minded policy proclamations and the actual reality) continued to act to the detriment of its reputation and credibility. It would be no exaggeration to state that the tension between rhetoric and practice as emerged as a defining attribute of the EU's interventions in the SSR field. During this phase, Israeli security interests have consistently been prioritized and elevated over the interests and priorities of the oPt's inhabitants. Disarmament and criminalization have impaired popular resistance. In the contemporary West Bank, the PA's security forces are largely concerned with protecting the security of the occupier. The security rights of Palestinians have in turn been gravely imperiled by Israeli sub-contracting, in which repression has now become the PA's responsibility and priority (Amrov and Tartir 2014a, b; El Kurd 2017).

The security reform agenda can be seen, during this period, to have negatively impacted the national struggle, everyday security, the ongoing imperative of resistance to occupation and the coherence of the Palestinian political community. While blame for this state of affairs should be broadly dispersed and shared, it is nonetheless apparent that donors must shoulder a considerable amount of the blame.

In analyzing the process of SSR, it is first important to recognize a divide within the academic literature on the subject. The first set of contributions tend to function within a more technocratic framework of reference, and are predisposed to ask how external, elite interests can be more completely realized or embodied through a more effective implementation of the reform process. In contrast, a second set of contributions stress the need to consider this technical project within its wider social context.[8] The preceding discussion has consistently reiterated the importance of the second set of contributions in enabling a fuller, more holistic analysis of the EU's contribution to Palestinian SSR (Ejdus and Tartir 2017; Tartir and Ejdus 2018).

The Instrumental Purpose of the EU Intervention

For the EU, EUPOL COOPS had a clear instrumental purpose and utility. This "instrumental function" was reflected in the fact that this initiative enabled the organization to shift from being a "payer" to a "player" (El-Din 2017). When it was established, EUPOL COOPS was mandated to provide technical support to the Palestinian Civil Police (PCP). This support was provided in the expectation that it would enable local Palestinian security forces to align with internationally recognized "best practice." Over the past decade, EUPOL COPPS has gradually transitioned from capacity-building (training and equipment provision) to a more strategic role (Ejdus and Tartir 2017). By virtue of the fact that it is the EU's longest-running civilian crisis management mission, the institution has inevitably sought to present EUPOL COOPS as a success story. During an interview with an EUPOL COOPS staff member, I was enlightened about the EU's ongoing "achievements":

> EUPOL COPPS has made a significant progress in the past 10 years for both the Criminal Justice Institutions and the Palestinian Civil Police (PCP). The Mission has contributed in improving the safety and security of Palestinians, in line with the domestic agenda of the Palestinian Authority, reinforcing the rule of law. EUPOL COPPS has succeeded in promoting civil police primacy meaning that the civilian police should be the organization with responsibility for policing, and that it is under civilian control.[9]

The PA's political and security establishment have similarly expressed their satisfaction with the EUPOL COOPS intervention. One high-ranking PA security official even suggested that, as a result of this support, the PA now has "one of the best police and security forces in the region".[10] If it is no surprise to find a broad level of agreement between

Brussels and Ramallah on this point, it is perhaps surprising that the former evidences a slightly greater degree of caution. A European diplomat observed:

> Through the EUPOL COOPS, we developed the civil oversight, developed strategic planning in the ministry of interior, encouraged donors' mechanisms for better coordination, and we ensured the Palestinian ownership in all of this. Yet, the situation is not optimal or ideal, planning is something and implementing is another thing, and progress of reform is difficult and slow process because of politics.[11]

For its part, the Israeli government is also satisfied with existing arrangements: it views EUPOL COPPS as an integral component of the security coordination paradigm[12] which is explicitly concerned with the furtherance of Israel's security.[13] Ultimately it envisages that this support will enable the PA to effectively police the West Bank, crush dissent and counter insurgency (Ejdus and Tartir 2017, 2).

However, these positive appraisals are largely confined to a relatively small number of observers, who collectively function as the members of what is, to all intents and purposes, a tightly sealed political and technocratic élite. One well-informed analyst and observer, who has been closely engaged with EUPOL COOPS over the last decade, claimed that it was unrealistic to expect "complementarity" could be achieved within the projected timeframe given the level of staff turnover; other issues that were highlighted included staff secondment (level of operational and contextual knowledge and overall quality), resources and the length of EUPOL COOPS' mandate (which is renewed on a six-month or annual basis). Each of these defects, it was argued, acts to the detriment of the intervention's overall effectiveness, strategy, and sustainability.[14]

This broad appraisal is closely aligned with the critical literature, which is much more skeptical about the design (role) and application (impact, effectiveness) of the EUPOL COOPS initiative. EUPOL COPPS has been extensively criticized for failing to improve civil oversight and accountability. Its conventional train-and-equip approach can be argued to have enhanced the skill-sets of Palestinian security forces; however, any improvement in this respect should be considered against the clear failure to transfer training capabilities (design, planning, implementation) to the local level (Bouris 2012; Bouris and Reigeluth 2012; Kristoff 2012)—aside from anything else, this defect brings the sustainability of the claimed improvements into clear question. A more general critique can also be directed towards the way that EUPOL COPPS, along with the broader SSR apparatus of which it is part, has contributed to the spread and growth of authoritarian tendencies (Rose 2008; Sayigh 2011; Youngs and Michou 2011; Tartir 2015b).

Other critical readings also make an important contribution by bringing the narrow technical focus of the mission into clear question. İşleyen, for instance, has demonstrated how ostensibly benign demand-driven technical support has functioned to conceal a broad condition of power asymmetry, and has thus diverted attention away from the various ways in the EU problematizes, disciplines, and normalizes Palestinian security practices and strategies (İşleyen 2017). Other observers instead develop their critique from within a SSR framework to argue that the EU's prioritization of technical assistance neglects important political components of SSR, most notably the need for effective democratic governance (see Sayigh 2011; Bouris 2012, 2014; Mustafa 2015; Tartir 2017a, b). Mustafa develops this argument and maintains that the EUPOL COPPS mission has failed. In her view, "the separation of the teaching of technical skills from the political reality and the overall security system has created a police force that is highly skilled yet easily co-opted by political leaders" (Mustafa 2015, 225).

Finally, the inhabitants of the oPt are also broadly dissatisfied with the EU's contribution to SRR (Ejdus and Tartir 2017; Tartir and Ejdus 2018). Here it should be noted that the object of this dissatisfaction is not the narrow priority of service delivery but rather the broader contribution of Palestinian authoritarianism. "Voices from below," which have been strategically silenced by the technocratic discourse, offer a fundamentally different reading, in which the EU is, by virtue of its direct support for the PA and by extension Israeli strategic interests, viewed as being complicit in the perpetuation of occupation.

Conclusion: Five Key Lessons

European aid, policies, and interventions have, in attempting to work around the political realities of occupation, essentially become part of the problem. The EU's wider project of neoliberal state-building is similarly constructed upon an entirely artificial separation of "economics" and "politics" which is clearly open to critical challenge and contestation. Even at the level of basic logic, it seems inconceivable that a sectoral could ever address, or sufficiently engage, the structural forms of violence that are embedded within an occupation that has now persisted for 70 years. At a strategic level, SSR reform is just as open to criticism as the misplaced belief that economic development will provide renewed impetus to a peace process that has evidenced signs of stagnation and regression for the best part of two decades. In recognizing this point, and in seeking to move the terms of policy engagement forward, this chapter will now outline five specific proposals that have a clear practical significance and relevance.[15]

Firstly, the stated objective of the EUPOL COPPS mission is to professionalize the Palestinian police. This has been conceived as a prerequisite for peacebuilding—that is, as an "investment" in the wider peace process. European policymakers do not, however, appear to be registered that this aspiration is now further away than it was when the mission began. In addition to raising important questions about how "success" is identified and measured, this also suggests that European policymakers experience great difficulty in critically reflecting upon their ongoing interventions. In celebrating its own successes, the EU shows a quite striking detachment from material realities and Palestinian public opinion. This implies a far-reaching critical project which does not just question the end product but also the means through which policy practices and strategies are produced.[16]

The narrowness of the mission's "technical" mandate must also be questioned and challenged. SSR is not a technical project which can be conducted in isolation from wider historical or political context. Even if only for purposes of improved implementation, it should be acknowledged that this wider context will have a significant, and even determining impact, upon SSR implementation. For Palestinians, it is meaningless to speak of "security" when the main source of insecurity is not addressed or is treated as an inconvenient obstacle which can be worked around. A "human security" analysis helps to show up the inadequacies and shortfalls within the mission's applied definitions of "security" and "insecurity"; incidentally, it also serves to highlight the gulf between the EU's policy representations and the actual practice. In this instance, the pre-eminent question (*whose* security?) awaits a more sustained and satisfactory engagement.

Thirdly, the EU's engagement with SSR has done little to answer the question of which type of governance it would like to see emerge in the oPt. This is an inherently political question and the EU, whose foreign policy is grounded within a clear bias towards economic instruments (as evidenced by its abiding faith in trade and development) is poorly placed to answer this question. However, it would be both disingenuous and false for it to pretend that it has no interest or that this is ultimately for Palestinians to decide. The level of its financial investment has not been accompanied by a declaration of its clear political interest. Given that its interventions have contributed to the professionalization of authoritarianism (epitomized in the absence of a functioning parliament, human rights violations and the criminalization of resistance), it is clearly incumbent upon the EU to set out its political vision for the oPt. Upon assuming responsibility for the EUPOL COPPS mission, the EU sought to develop a unique role for itself. At the time of writing, this role is somewhat unclear and opaque.

Fourthly, any project of SSR must move beyond the limitations of a technical mandate to engage the structural forms of violence that are embedded within the oPt. One of the features of Palestinian life and society is that it is highly politicized in almost every aspect. Even the most prosaic and basic of everyday actions can easily become politicized.[17] Finally, the EU needs to seek to incorporate the views of those who are most directly impacted by its interventions—that is, Palestinians resident in the oPt. Local "ownership" and "participation" are buzzwords that are frequently invoked in the policy documents of EU officials; it scarcely needs to be noted that they are much less frequently reproduced in policy practice. In this regard, the EUPOL COPPS mission is no exception. There is clearly much to be done if the EU is to overcome the impression of one respondent from Jenin refugee camp. He said: "The US. security mission is the big and aggressive devil; the European security mission is the small and gentle devil. Both of them are devils, but packaged differently."[18]

The EU police mission has much to say about the limitations of the EU's contribution to and role in the Palestinian–Israeli conflict. It can, to this extent, be considered as a case-study of a specific instance of SSR. However, I would maintain that the implications of this chapter extend beyond this relatively constricted terrain. The EU mission, I would contend, clearly illustrates the limits of apolitical and technocratic approaches when they are applied in highly politicized spaces. In failing to offer a sufficiently critical appraisal of unbalanced power relations, they ultimately come to function as a means through which this power is reproduced. Far from shaping the world order with its normative power, the EU has, in the case of Palestine, become one of the conduits through which colonial rule is sustained. Its vision of a securitized peace promises little more than a stale repetition and perpetuation of the colonial dynamics that have disfigured Palestinian life and society for half-a-century. Sustained critical scrutiny is a clear precondition if the EU is to break this cycle and become part of the solution, as opposed to the problem.

Notes

1. A version of this chapter will be published in a forthcoming special issue (volume 27, no. 4) of the journal of *Middle East Critique* (The occupation at 50—EU-Israel/Palestine relations since 1967) edited by Anders Persson.
2. Anne Le More has previously observed that the World Bank, the Europeans, and the Americans and the Israelis each make a distinct contribution to the so-called peace process. The World Bank provides conceptual "capital," the Europeans provide extensive financial support, and the Americans and Israelis provide political impetus (Le More 2008).
3. While it is crucial to begin with a clear distinction of the "soft" and "hard" security approaches, which were enacted by EUPOL COPPS (EU) and USSC (US) respectively, it is similarly important to recognize that both actors have collectively contributed to two negative outcomes: firstly, their efforts contributed to a "better" collaboration with the occupying power, and thus helped to sustain the status quo; secondly, they contributed to the violation of Palestinian rights (and national security) by national security forces. Both "contributions" have been documented in extensive detail—see Human Rights Watch (2011, 2012) and Amnesty International (2017).
4. It could also be argued that a fourth phase began after Salam Fayyad, the PA Prime Minister, departed in 2013. This could be characterised as statehood with "less spark and momentum." In 2011, European sponsors broadly concurred with Fayyad's 2011 assertion that the "West Bank is already a state in all but name". However, in the aftermath of Fayyad's departure, the statebuilding project has clearly lost momentum: the international community, in the absence of any meaningful progress, appear content to support the reform of the PA security establishment and sustain the status quo.
5. This application of the Weberian concept of a "monopoly of force" clearly established that the PA's statutory security forces are the only actors with the right to exert force within the oPt. By implication, other non-state

actors, non-statutory bodies and armed resistance groups have to be marginalised, dismantled, co-opted, integrated, disarmed or punished.
6. Palestinians now often speak of a "double" or "triple" occupation, A youth from Balata refugee camp told me "I thought that having two occupations [Israel and the PA] is enough, but clearly that is not enough. Now we have a third one serving as an additional level of oppression thanks to all these external security missions, officers, complexes, academies, and vehicles".
7. While those who used this phrase were often referring to the Palestinian National Security Forces (NSF), it was often assumed to relate to other security forces, such as the Palestinian Civil Policy (PCP). Here it is important to note that a substantial proportion of the West Bank population do not distinguish between different security forces; on the contrary, it the PA's security forces are more often perceived and discussed as a single monolith. Dayton's notoriety extended beyond the West Bank however. He himself quotes senior IDF commanders who asked him: "How many more of these new Palestinians can you generate, and how quickly?" In 2013, Shimon Peres, the-then Israeli president Shimon Peres, implicitly acknowledged Dayton's efforts when he said: "A Palestinian security force was formed. You and the Americans trained it. And now we work together to prevent terror and crime."
8. It could however be argued that the interaction between the two has contributed to a third strand, which seeks to identify how more "holistic" perspectives and contributions can be assimilated into technical strategies and frameworks.
9. Interview, EUPOL COPPS, 18 September 2017. When I asked an EUPOL COOPS senior staff member about the ongoing needs of Palestinian stakeholders, I was informed: "For the PCP, they need a lot of equipment, vehicles and on top of which, they need funds to recruit more policemen and policewomen. For the criminal justice institutions, they need more training in the fields of prosecution, judges, lawyers and a functioning parliament." (Interview, EUPOL COPPS, 18 September 2017).
10. Interview with PA security official, Ramallah, Palestine, May 2017.
11. Interview 12, European diplomat, August 2017.
12. The 1993 Oslo Accords had a number of key objectives. It sought to establish the basis for a securitised peace process, doing so in the clear understanding that local-level security collaboration (between Israel and the Palestinian Authority) offered the best means through which this could be achieved. This securitisation remains a key part of the PA's security doctrine, a source of tension between the PA and the inhabitants of the oPt and an ongoing donor priority which is upheld through foreign aid conditionality.

13. Security coordination between the PA security forces and the Israeli military takes a number of different forms. These include: the arrest of Palestinian suspects at the request of the Israeli authorities; the suppression of Palestinian protests directed towards Israeli soldiers or settlers; intelligence sharing; and a "revolving door" prison policy, in which activists serve successive sentences in Israeli and Palestinian prisons, often for the same offence; Palestinian and Israeli security personnel also regularly participate in joint meetings, trainings and workshops (Tartir 2017b, 15). For further insight into security coordination, refer to Amrov and Tartir (2014a, b), Dana (2014), and Tartir (2017a).
14. Interview with a senior analyst and observer, Ramallah, Palestine, June 2017.
15. While these lessons have been conceived and developed within the context of the EUPOL COPPS mission, it is clear that they could potentially be applied to the EU's broader engagement with the Palestinian–Israeli conflict. For additional lessons and recommendations, refer to Lovatt and Toaldo (2014), Lovatt and Toaldo (2015), Lovatt (2016), and Dajani and Lovatt (2017).
16. When I enquired with an EU diplomat about the possibility that the EUPOL COPPS mandate might, after 11 years of being renewed, be terminated, I was informed that "[the EU is] not ready to close and terminate the EUPOL COPPS operations, it is a very political mission". (Interview 12, August 2017).
17. This was clearly indicated when EUPOL COPPS responded to a number of questions (pertaining to local ownership, democratic accountability and transparency) that I submitted in June 2017: "We cannot answer your questions because our mandate is purely technical, mainly mentoring and advising the Palestinian counterparts. Your questions are very political." (Interview 11, June 2017).
18. Interview, Jenin refugee camp, Jenin, Palestine, June 2015.

References

Abbas, Mahmoud, and Walid Al-Amri. 2006. "Mahmoud Abbas: Security Chaos and Palestinian Elections" [interview in Arabic]. *Al Jazeera*, January 17. https://goo.gl/1vgaFr.

Agha, Hussein, and Ahmad Khalidi. 2005. *A Framework for a Palestinian National Security Doctrine*. London: Chatham House.

Amnesty International. 2013. "'Shut Up We Are the Police': Use of Excessive Force by Palestinian Authority in the Occupied West Bank." Amnesty International Briefing, September 23. https://www.amnesty.org/en/documents/MDE21/006/2013/en/.

Amnesty International. 2017. "State of Palestine: Alarming attack on Freedom of Expression." Amnesty International Public Statement, August 23. https://www.amnesty.org/download/Documents/MDE1569832017ENGLISH.pdf.

Amrov, Sabrien, and Alaa Tartir. 2014a. "After Gaza, What Price Palestine's Security Sector?" *Al-Shabaka*, October 8. http://al-shabaka.org/wp-content/uploads/2015/01/AmrovTartir_PolicyBrief_En_Oct_2014.pdf.

Amrov, Sabrien, and Alaa Tartir. 2014b. "Subcontracting Repression in the West Bank and Gaza," *New York Times*, November 26. http://www.nytimes.com/2014/11/27/opinion/subcontractingrepression-in-the-west-bank-and-gaza.html?_r=0.

Balfour, Rosa, Francesca Fabbri, and Richard Youngs. 2016. "Report on Democracy Assistance from the European Union to the Middle East and North Africa." *EUSpring Report*. https://www.warwick.ac.uk/fac/soc/pais/research/researchcentres/irs/euspring/euspring_eu_demo_assistance_on_template.4.pdf.

Bicchi, Frederica, and Benedetta Voltolini. 2017. "Europe, the Green Line and the Issue of the Israeli-Palestinian Border: Closing the Gap Between Discourse and Practice?" *Geopolitics* 23 (1): 124–146.

Bouris, Dimitris. 2012. "The European Union's Role in the Palestinian Territories: State-Building Through Security Sector Reform?" *European Security* 21 (2): 257–271.

Bouris, Dimitris. 2014. *The European Union and Occupied Palestinian Territories: State-Building Without a State*. London: Routledge.

Bouris, Dimitris, and Daniela Huber. 2017. "Imposing Middle East Peace: Why EU Member States Should Recognise Palestine." Istituto Affari Internazionali (IAI) Commentaries 17, November 17. http://www.iai.it/it/pubblicazioni/imposing-middle-east-peace-why-eu-member-states-should-recognise-palestine.

Bouris, Dimitris, and Stuart Reigeluth. 2012. "Introducing the Rule of Law in Security Sector Reform: European Union Policies in the Palestinian Territories." *Hague Journal on the Rule of Law* 4 (1): 176–193.

Brynen, Rex. 1995. "The Neopatrimonial Dimension of Palestinian Politics." *Journal of Palestine Studies* 25 (1): 23–36.

Cammett, Melani, Ishac Diwan, Alan Richards, and John Waterbury, eds. 2015. *A Political Economy of the Middle East*. Boulder: Westview Press.

Dajani, Omar, and Hugh Lovatt. 2017. "Rethinking Oslo: How Europe Can Promote Peace in Israel-Palestine." *European Council on Foreign Relations Policy Brief*, July. http://www.ecfr.eu/publications/summary/rethinking_oslo_how_europe_can_promote_peace_in_israel_palestine_7219.

Dana, Tariq. 2014. "The Beginning of the End of Palestinian Security Coordination with Israel?" *Jadaliyya*, July 4. http://www.jadaliyya.com/pages/index/18379/the-beginning-of-the-end-of-p...c.

Dana, Tariq. 2015. "Corruption in Palestine: A Self-Enforcing System." *Al-Shabaka*, August 18. https://al-shabaka.org/briefs/corruption-in-palestine/.

DCAF. 2016. "Securing Gaza: Challenges to Reunifying the Palestinian Security and Justice Sectors." The Geneva Centre for the Democratic Control of Armed Forces (DCAF). Unpublished report, Geneva.

Ejdus, Filip, and Alaa Tartir. 2017. "Policing Palestine." *Sada Middle East Analysis*. Carnegie Endowment for International Peace, August 15. http://carnegieendowment.org/sada/72821.

El-Din, Amr Nasr. 2017. *EU Security Missions and the Israeli–Palestinian Conflict*. London: Routledge.

El Kurd, Dana. 2017. "Mechanisms of Co-optation in the Palestinian Territories: Neutralizing Independent Civil Society." Middle East Institute, February 28. http://www.mei.edu/content/map/mechanisms-co-optation-palestinian-territories-neutralizing-independent-civil-society.

Friedrich, Roland, and Arnold Luethold, eds. 2007. *Entry-Points to Palestinian Security Sector Reform*. Geneva: Geneva Centre for the Democratic Control of Armed Forces (DCAF).

Hijazi, Saleh, and Hugh Lovatt. 2017a. "Issa Amro and the EU's Palestinian Authority Problem." European Council on Foreign Relations Commentary, September 7. http://www.ecfr.eu/article/commentary_eu_palestinian_authority_problem.

Hijazi, Saleh, and Hugh Lovatt. 2017b. "Europe and the Palestinian Authority's Authoritarian Drift." European Council on Foreign Relations Commentary, April 20. http://www.ecfr.eu/article/commentary_europe_and_the_palestinian_authoritys_authoritarian_drift_7274.

Hilal, Jamil, and Mushtaq Husain Khan. 2004. "State Formation Under the PA: Potential Outcomes and Their Viability." In *State Formation in Palestine: Viability and Governance during a Social Transformation*, edited by M. Khan, G. Giacaman, and I. Amundsen, 64–119. London: Routledge.

Human Rights Watch. 2011. "No News Is Good News: Abuses Against Journalists by Palestinian Security Forces." *HRW.org*, April 6. https://www.hrw.org/report/2011/04/06/no-news-good-news/abuses-against-journalists-palestinian-security-forces.

Human Rights Watch. 2012. "Palestinian Authority: Hold Police Accountable for Ramallah Beatings: Donors Should Reevaluate Support for Palestinian Security Forces." *HRW.org*, August 27. https://www.hrw.org/news/2012/08/27/palestinian-authority-hold-police-accountable-ramallah-beatings.

Human Rights Watch. 2014. "Palestine: No Action in Assault by Police," *HRW.org*, May 19. https://www.hrw.org/news/2014/05/19/palestine-no-actionassault-police.

International Crisis Group. 2008. "Ruling Palestine II: The West Bank Model?" International Crisis Group Middle East Report No. 79, July 17. https://www.crisisgroup.org/middle-east-north-africa/eastern-mediterranean/israelpalestine/ruling-palestine-ii-west-bank-model.

International Crisis Group. 2010. "Squaring the Circle: Palestinian Security Reform Under Occupation." International Crisis Group Middle East Report No. 98, September 7. https://www.crisisgroup.org/middle-east-north-africa/eastern-mediterranean/israelpalestine/squaring-circle-palestinian-security-reform-under-occupation.

Işleyen, Beste. 2017. "Building Capacities, Exerting Power: The European Union Police Mission in the Palestinian Authority." *Mediterranean Politics* 23 (3): 321–339.

Khalil, Amir. 2017. "To What Extent Does the European Union Promote Democracy Effectively in the Occupied Palestinian Territories?" Arab Reform Initiative, Arab Research Support Programme II, October. http://www.arab-reform.net/ar/file/2005/download?token=G3wRtCr8.

Knudsen, Are John, and Alaa Tartir. 2017. "Country Evaluation Brief: Palestine." Chr. Michelsen Institute & Norad. https://www.norad.no/om-bistand/publikasjon/2017/country-evaluation-brief-palestine/.

Kristoff, Madeline. 2012. "Policing in Palestine: Analyzing the EU Police Reform Mission in the West Bank." The Centre for International Governance Innovation (CIGI), SSR Issue Papers No. 7. http://www.cigionline.org/sites/default/files/ssr_issue_no7.pdf.

Le More, Anne. 2008. *International Assistance to the Palestinians After Oslo: Political Guilt, Wasted Money*. London and New York: Routledge.

Lia, Brynjar. 2007. *Building Arafat's Police: The Politics of International Police Assistance in the Palestinian Territories After the Oslo Agreement*. London: Ithaca Press.

Lovatt, Hugh. 2016. "EU Differentiation and the Push for Peace in Israel-Palestine." European Council on Foreign Relations. http://www.ecfr.eu/publications/summary/eu_differentiation_and_the_push_for_peace_in_israel_palestine7163.

Lovatt, Hugh, and Mattia Toaldo. 2014. "Five Reasons to Recognise a Palestinian State." European Council on Foreign Relations. http://www.ecfr.eu/article/commentary_five_reasons_to_recognise_a_palestinian_state360.

Lovatt, Hugh, and Mattia Toaldo. 2015. "EU Differentiation and Israeli Settlements." European Council on Foreign Relations. http://www.ecfr.eu/publications/summary/eu_differentiation_and_israeli_settlements3076.

Lust, Ellen, ed. 2016. *The Middle East*, 14th ed. Thousand Oaks, CA: CQ/Sage.

Marten, Kimberly. 2014. "Reformed or Deformed? Patronage Politics, International Influence, and the Palestinian Authority Security Forces." *International Peacekeeping* 21 (2): 181–197.

Mustafa, Tahani. 2015. "Damming the Palestinian Spring: Security Sector Reform and Entrenched Repression." *Journal of International Intervention and Statebuilding* 9 (2): 212–230.

PA. 2002. "100 Days Plan of the Palestinian Government." Palestinian Authority, Ramallah, Palestine.

PA. 2008. "Palestinian Reform and Development Plan 2008–2010." Palestinian Authority, Ramallah, Palestine.

Paragi, Beata. 2017. "Contemporary Gifts: Solidarity, Compassion, Equality, Sacrifice and Reciprocity from NGO Perspective." *Current Anthropology* 58 (3): 317–339.

Perry, Mark. 2011. "Dayton's Mission: A Reader's Guide." *Al-Jazeera*, January 25. http://www.aljazeera.com/palestinepapers/2011/01/2011125145732219555.html.

Persson, Anders. 2017a. "Shaping Discourse and Setting Examples: Normative Power Europe Can Work in the Israeli–Palestinian Conflict." *Journal of Common Market Studies* 55 (6): 1415–1431.

Persson, Anders. 2017b. "Palestine at the End of the State-Building Process: Technical Achievements, Political Failures." *Mediterranean Politics*. Advance Online Publication.

Rose, David. 2008. "The Gaza Bombshell." *Vanity Fair*, April. http://www.vanityfair.com/politics/features/2008/04/gaza200804.

Said, Edward W. 1995. *Peace and Its Discontents: Essays on Palestine in the Middle East Peace Process*. London: Vintage.

Sayigh, Yezid. 2011. "Policing the People, Building the State: Authoritarian Transformation in the West Bank and Gaza." Carnegie Paper, Carnegie Middle East Center, Carnegie Endowment for International Peace, February. http://carnegieendowment.org/files/gaza_west_bank_security.pdf.

Selby, Jan. 2003. "Dressing Up Domination as 'Cooperation': The Case of Israeli–Palestinian Water Relations." *Review of International Studies* 29 (1): 121–138.

Tartir, Alaa. 2014. "Re-inventing European Aid to Palestine." European Council on Foreign Relations, June 4. http://www.ecfr.eu/blog/entry/re_inventing_european_aid_to_palestine.

Tartir, Alaa. 2015a. "The Evolution and Reform of Palestinian Security Forces, 1993–2013." *Stability: International Journal of Security & Development* 4 (1): 1–20.

Tartir, Alaa. 2015b. "Securitised Development and Palestinian Authoritarianism Under Fayyadism." *Conflict, Security & Development* 15 (5): 479–502.

Tartir, Alaa. 2016. "What Peace? State Disorders and Non-state Orders." *Open Democracy*, November 25. https://www.opendemocracy.net/north-africa-west-asia/alaa-tartir/what-peace-state-disorders-and-non-state-orders.

Tartir, Alaa. 2017a. "The Palestinian Authority Security Forces: Whose Security?" *Al-Shabaka*, May 16. https://al-shabaka.org/briefs/palestinian-authority-security-forces-whose-security/.

Tartir, Alaa. 2017b. "Criminalizing Resistance: The Cases of Balata and Jenin Refugee Camps in the Occupied West Bank." *Journal of Palestine Studies* 46 (2): 7–22.

Tartir, Alaa, and Benoit Challand. 2016. "Palestine." In *The Middle East*, 14th ed., edited by E. Lust, 707–736. Thousand Oaks, CA: CQ/Sage.

Tartir, Alaa, and Jeremy Wildeman. 2017. "Mapping of Donor Funding to the Occupied Palestinian Territories 2012–2014/15: Limited, Disorganized and Fragmented Aid Data Undermining Transparency, Accountability and Planning." AidWatch Palestine. https://alaatartirdotcom.files.wordpress.com/2017/11/aidwatch-study-published.pdf.

Tartir, Alaa, and Filip Ejdus. 2018. "Effective? Locally Owned? Beyond the Technocratic Perspective on the European Union Police Mission for the Palestinian Territories." *Contemporary Security Policy* 39 (1): 142–165.

United Nations. 2003. "A Performance-Based Roadmap to a Permanent Two-State Solution to the Israeli–Palestinian Conflict." http://www.un.org/news/dh/mideast/roadmap122002.pdf.

Wildeman, Jeremy. 2015. "'Either You're with Us or Against Us' Illiberal Canadian Foreign Aid in the Occupied Palestinian Territories, 2001–2012." PhD diss., University of Exeter.

Youngs, Richard, and Helene Michou. 2011. "Assessing Democracy Assistance: Palestine." FRIDE Foundation for the Future Project Report, May 11. http://www.fride.org/download/Assessing_Democracy_Assistance_Palestine.pdf.

Youngs, Richard, and Jake Gutman. 2015. "Is the EU Tackling the Root Causes of Middle Eastern Conflict?" *Carnegie Europe*, December 1. http://goo.gl/ScsmEj.

Index

A
accountability, 177, 178, 180–182, 189, 191, 192, 195, 197, 198, 232, 234, 236, 242
aid
 aid dependence, 176, 179
 foreign aid, 2, 4, 110, 175, 176, 178, 190, 241
annexation, 25, 26, 30–35, 39, 161
apartheid, vi, viii, x, 10, 14, 30, 32, 33, 36, 37, 39, 40, 111, 117, 166, 184, 185
apolitical, 157, 158, 167, 185, 239
authoritarianism, 13, 14, 66, 210, 229, 230, 232, 237, 239

C
civil society, 49, 54, 56, 59, 95, 110, 156, 161, 175, 176, 178, 180, 182, 183, 189, 198, 217
class, 11, 37, 88, 106–112, 114–116, 119, 122–124

colonialism, 2, 6, 12, 80, 164, 166, 184, 185
corruption, 192, 210, 214, 222, 232

D
decolonization, 39
de-development, 12, 29, 48, 164
democracy, x, 4, 9, 14, 16, 50, 107, 108, 154, 156, 161, 163, 164, 169, 175, 177, 229
depoliticize, 5, 6, 158, 169, 181
development, vi, 4, 6, 9, 12–15, 29, 48, 49, 55, 56, 60, 62, 63, 67, 80, 81, 95, 97, 124, 140, 153, 155, 158, 160–163, 166, 167, 169, 170, 175–178, 182, 187, 190, 192–198, 228, 233, 238, 239
domination, x, 8, 13, 53, 63, 64, 155, 164, 206, 218, 220, 227, 229
donors, 12, 13, 67, 154–166, 169, 170, 175–198, 209, 210, 229, 232, 234, 236

solidarity donors, 176–180, 182, 184, 190–193, 195–198

E
economic peace, ix, 154
European Union (EU), 12, 14, 27, 131–134, 137–140, 142, 143, 145–147, 187, 227–235, 237–240, 242
European Union Coordinating Office for Palestinian Police Support (EUPOL COPPS), 14, 143, 230, 231, 233, 235–242

F
Fatah, 117, 206, 208, 210–212, 214, 219, 221, 222, 234
fragmentation, 2, 14, 48, 53, 66, 178, 232

G
Gaza Strip, 23, 24, 29, 30, 33, 34, 48, 76, 101, 206, 218, 228
governance, 2, 4, 6, 8, 9, 161–164, 205, 228–230, 237, 238

H
Hamas, vi, 74, 142, 143, 206, 212, 221, 228, 233, 234
human rights, viii, 10, 30, 37, 67, 138, 143, 212, 213, 215, 216, 222, 233, 234, 239, 240

I
international relations (IR), 51, 54, 65, 137, 156, 180

intifada, 23, 26, 38, 75, 84, 105, 125, 138, 140–143, 159, 176, 178–180, 187, 197, 198, 206–209, 211, 215, 221, 223, 231, 232

L
leadership, v, vii, ix, 10, 24, 37–39, 79, 89, 99, 116–118, 169, 205, 212, 217, 218, 221, 222, 234
legitimacy, x, 67, 75, 76, 84, 87, 95, 161, 169, 177, 178, 180–182, 185, 190, 195, 206, 210, 212, 213, 217, 229, 232
liberalism, 12, 50, 52, 155–157, 164, 168, 170

M
Membership-based Organization (MBOs), 178–182, 184–191, 193, 195–200
Middle East, vi, 86, 96, 105, 133–136, 139, 140, 142, 145, 146, 153, 154, 158, 160, 168, 227, 228, 240
Middle East Peace Process, 29, 133
mobilization, 10, 11, 105–110, 112–114, 118, 119, 123–125, 159, 178, 179, 185, 187

N
Nakba, 23, 24, 71, 72, 75, 78, 79, 82, 85, 93, 95, 97, 100, 101, 207
neoliberalism, 2, 4, 6, 15, 16, 56, 155–157, 168
Nongovernmental Organization (NGOs), ix, 13, 59, 60, 95, 101, 110, 122, 157, 175–191, 193–199

INDEX 251

O

occupation, viii, 2, 10, 11, 13, 14, 23–25, 27, 29–32, 37–39, 47, 49, 52, 53, 55, 56, 58, 59, 61–63, 65, 67, 76, 88, 96, 106, 118–120, 122–124, 131, 134, 136, 141, 142, 155, 157–159, 166–170, 175–177, 179, 184–186, 188, 196, 198, 206, 207, 209–211, 213–215, 217, 219–222, 234, 237, 238, 240, 241
Oslo Accord, 4, 12, 31, 47, 48, 101, 112, 119, 138, 153, 161, 175, 183, 217, 231, 241

P

Palestine, vi, viii, ix, x, xi, xxvi, 2, 4, 6, 8–13, 15, 16, 23, 24, 30, 33, 37, 39, 48, 53–56, 59, 60, 62, 64–66, 68, 72, 79, 82, 90, 96, 97, 110–112, 125, 132, 141, 162, 183, 184, 190, 191, 196, 218, 223, 229, 240–242
Palestine Liberation Organization (PLO), 37–39, 73, 117, 123, 137–139, 145, 159, 231
Palestinian(s)
  activists, 11, 73, 74, 76, 80, 81, 83, 91, 95, 100, 217
  aid, 12, 157, 160
  in Israel, 11, 71, 72, 76, 79–82, 85, 87, 88, 90, 93, 97, 98, 100
  politics, 110
Paris Protocol, 48, 56, 165, 169
peace, v, vii, ix, xi, 4–6, 12, 13, 16, 31, 32, 35, 36, 40, 51, 52, 75, 84, 133–139, 142, 143, 145, 153, 154, 156, 158–162, 166–168, 170, 175, 198, 218, 223, 227–230, 233, 238, 240, 241
peacebuilding, 2, 4, 6, 9, 143, 158, 160, 165, 169, 175, 180, 229, 238
political economy, 1, 5, 6, 56–58, 61, 63
  critical, 180
political mobilization, 112, 124, 176
popular education, 12, 13, 176–180, 185–187, 197, 198
protest, 11, 72, 81, 84, 87–90, 102, 105, 106, 109, 112–119, 122–124, 207, 217, 218, 242

R

reform, 13–15, 159, 205, 209, 210, 219, 220, 228–236, 238, 240
repression, 10, 66, 109, 116, 123, 125, 159, 207, 229, 234
resistance, v, vii, viii, ix, xi, 2, 5, 6, 8–11, 13, 15, 16, 49–52, 54–64, 67, 68, 71–87, 89–91, 93, 96–101, 117, 125, 159, 176, 178–181, 186, 191, 198, 206–211, 213, 214, 216, 219, 220, 222, 229, 232, 234, 239, 241

S

securitization, 14, 229, 233
security coordination, 38, 77, 211, 217, 218, 236, 242
security sector reform (SSR), 13, 14, 205–207, 210, 220, 228, 230–235, 237–239
self-determination, viii, ix, 10, 66, 137, 138, 140, 145, 175, 181, 229, 231
settlements, v, x, 14, 24–26, 32–36, 38, 47, 48, 58, 66, 89, 111, 112,

119, 123, 125, 134, 136, 142, 145, 157, 158, 160, 161, 170
settler colonialism, vii, 2–4, 6, 8, 10, 24, 37, 39, 56, 62, 64, 155, 167–170
solidarity, vi, ix, x, 12, 37, 56, 57, 81, 87, 88, 116, 180, 191, 197
  donors, 176–180, 182, 184, 190–193, 195–198
sovereignty, 2–4, 10, 11, 14, 31, 34, 35, 39, 49–54, 61, 64, 65, 136, 164, 188
state-building, 4, 10, 13, 24, 38, 39, 48, 62, 63, 67, 68, 141, 143, 144, 162, 205, 209, 210, 217, 220, 222, 233, 234
status quo, ix, 10, 11, 14, 24, 26, 32, 33, 35, 106, 110, 158, 159, 166, 170, 176, 177, 240
steadfastness, 8, 10, 11, 49, 55–60, 62, 63, 71, 97, 208
Sumud
  active, 11, 72, 97–100
  transformative, 11, 100

T
two-state solution, 32, 35, 38, 47, 145, 187, 229

V
violence, 6, 11, 12, 15, 16, 36, 49–54, 62–64, 75, 76, 81, 112, 115, 142, 143, 153–155, 208, 209, 213, 222, 229, 238, 239

W
West Bank, vi, 7, 10–14, 23–36, 38, 47, 48, 53, 62, 63, 66, 76, 101, 105, 106, 112, 115, 118–120, 125, 142, 158, 176–179, 181, 184, 205–209, 215, 218, 220, 222, 228, 233, 234, 236, 240, 241
World Bank, 160–163, 165, 167, 198, 240

CPI Antony Rowe
Eastbourne, UK
June 12, 2019